SERVING GOD
GLOBALLY

SERVING GOD GLOBALLY

Finding Your Place in International Development

Roland Hoksbergen

Baker Academic

a division of Baker Publishing Group
Grand Rapids, Michigan

Published by Baker Academic
a division of Baker Publishing Group
P.O. Box 6287, Grand Rapids, MI 49516-6287
www.bakeracademic.com

Printed in the United States of America

Library of Congress Cataloging-in-Publication Data

Hoksbergen, Roland.
    Serving God globally : finding your place in international development / Roland
Hoksbergen.
        p. cm.
    Includes bibliographical references and index.
    ISBN 978-0-8010-3984-3 (pbk.)
    1. Social service—Religious aspects—Christianity. 2. Economic development projects—
Developing countries. 3. Voluntarism—Religious aspects—Christianity. 4. Humanitarianism—
Religious aspects—Christianity. 5. Faith-based human services—International cooperation.
I. Title.
HV530.H63 2012
261.8′5—dc23   2011050147

12   13   14   15   16   17   18   7   6   5   4   3   2   1

For young people everywhere who hear God's call
to care for others . . . and respond

In memory of Octavila Ipiña de Jordan
(September 3, 1931–June 13, 2011)

After a devastating earthquake in Guatemala, Doña Vila, who had lost her mother and grandmother in the tragedy, nevertheless accepted me, a young reconstruction volunteer, into her home. In addition to treating me as part of the family and teaching me Spanish, she and her husband Gustavo, more through example than through words, taught me more than I could ever take in about living a life of service. When I married one of their lovely daughters, they officially welcomed me into their family. I hope this book does its part in helping prepare young people for global service, but I also know firsthand that we need the Doña Vilas of the world to help us along and show us the way.

Contents

Preface

Servants at Work in International Development

> Working in the slums of Nairobi was the greatest thing I ever did and the best job I ever had. I loved every minute of it. It was not easy, but I consider it the greatest privilege of my life to have been there.
>
> Christine Bodewes, human rights lawyer, after eight years working in the slums

What kind of people work in international development? What is their overall mission? What do they do day to day? How do they get to where they are? What makes them effective? How does one prepare for service in the broad field of international development?

If you read the rest of this book, you will find answers to these questions and many others that might be on your mind if you have personally felt God tugging at your heart to join him in the mission of being an ambassador of global reconciliation.

As a professor, I have learned that most people listen to good stories better than they do to carefully crafted ten-point lectures. This book has some lectures, and I hope you will read them and learn from them, but the book is also filled with stories of Christian development workers who are "out there" trying to be faithful to God's call to care for people he loves. Maybe the stories, and even the lecture parts, of this book will inspire you and help you think more clearly about your own life of service.

Let's begin with a few stories. I would like to tell you more about Christine, a high-profile Chicago lawyer who heard the call to global service and shortly thereafter found herself in the slums of Nairobi. Right after that comes a story about Dirk Booy, who started as a college graduate with a global vision but no clear sense of how to put that into practice. He began his career living in a mud-and-stick home in a village in Sierra Leone and is now one of the global leaders of World Vision International. Who knows? Maybe your own vocational journey will look something like theirs.

Christine Bodewes: From Cook County to Kibera, a Lawyer's Journey

After receiving a law degree, Christine Bodewes was an up-and-coming lawyer in one of those high-rise buildings on the Chicago skyline. Combining the twin values of professionalism and service, Christine specialized in securities litigation for a prestigious Chicago firm. She also did pro bono work for worthy causes and people in need. Christine made partner after six years, but her path changed radically when she answered what she sees as an unmistakable spiritual call to overseas service.

It started with a surprise phone call from a college friend who was now a lay missioner with Maryknoll in Cambodia. Following a brief detention by the Khmer Rouge for participating in a peaceful march to plant trees, Christine's friend called and asked her to come. She flew to Cambodia and was introduced for the first time to mission work in a developing country. Christine became especially proud that her Roman Catholic tradition had birthed a group like Maryknoll, for even as most other humanitarian groups were abandoning the country in this time of serious need, the Maryknoll missionaries decided to stay. As Christine tells it, "This was probably my real baptism as a Catholic, because it was the first time I really understood what it meant to be a Catholic and to take an option for the poor."

The next four weeks in Cambodia were a time of intense spiritual encounter that set her on a completely different career track than the one she had originally envisioned. She came back to Chicago, but after a year of prayer, consultation, and spiritual discernment, Christine signed on with the Maryknoll lay mission program. One year later, Christine joined a team of Kenyan lawyers in a local legal-aid clinic for slum dwellers. Many of their clients' lives and livelihoods were seriously threatened during President Moi's campaigns of slum burning and landgrabbing. Her colleagues were arrested, but, as a foreigner, Christine never was. She found herself working to get innocent people released from prison and building legal cases to protect them and their homes.

After four years of this "intense grassroots human rights experience," Christine joined the pastoral team in Kibera, the largest and most densely populated slum in Nairobi. Her assignment was to coordinate their Office of Human Rights. Christine hoped that this ministry would thrive and that one day she could leave and hand it over to Kenyan lawyers. Everyone laughed at her. "Settle down, get married, and have children," they said, "because you're going to be here for a very long time." It would have been so easy to give up. Slums have that effect on people.

Christine kept at it, supported by a strong sense of calling, her abilities to love and serve, and a wonderful spiritual director. A few years later, two talented and committed women lawyers unexpectedly offered to work in the Office of Human Rights, and it was not long before the transition took place. Human rights work is extremely difficult where respect for rights is so low, but it is a central component of development work. Today the Office of Human Rights in Kibera still serves as a beacon of hope in a troubled part of the world as it provides free legal services, civic education, and advocacy for human rights.

With the human rights work in good hands, Christine studied for a PhD in African Christianity and researched how Catholic parishes can promote the rule of law, democracy, and human rights at a grassroots level in slum environments. She now works with a private foundation supporting faith-based work in Africa.

One might focus on Christine's tangible contributions, such as helping people keep their homes through her legal work or establishing a human rights office, but Christine is more inclined to talk about love: "I learned to put love first. It is the single most important thing and the single most difficult thing to learn. Putting love over your profession and desired goals, achievements, or assumptions is to me the heart of the mission experience."

You may not be called to East Africa or to the slums of Nairobi like Christine was, but wherever you serve, Christine stresses that it is not only "what you do but how you do it."

Christine has a professional degree, came to development work after starting another career, worked herself out of a job, and is now doing research and support work for Christian organizations in Africa. Read now the story of a man with a general college degree who began in community development and is now a leader in World Vision International.

Dirk Booy: Learning How to Really Help

At twenty-two, just graduated and newly married, Dirk Booy boarded a plane to West Africa and began a lifelong career in development. Possessed with an inherent wanderlust and a strong desire to serve, Dirk had been talking in his senior year with his church's development agency, the Christian Reformed World Relief Committee (CRWRC) about working overseas. Today Dirk expresses surprise that he and Joanne, his wife, were hired, but in those days it seemed easier to land an overseas position. CRWRC was beginning an innovative program in Sierra Leone and offered them a spot on the team.

Part of CRWRC's plan was that Dirk and Joanne would live directly in a rural village, building their own mud-and-stick home, gathering their own water, killing their own chickens, learning the local language, and generally doing everything they could to "bond" with the community. The Booys had two children while living in the village, and the family lived there for six years. When the children reached school age, Dirk and Joanne knew it was time to move out of the village, but they stayed in Africa for fourteen more years.

Looking back on his entry-level experiences, Dirk says that those six years in rural Sierra Leone were "some of the most important in my entire career. They are why I am able to do what I do now. We lived in the village, learning firsthand and face-to-face with people in the community what their problems were, what they faced on a daily basis, and what it was like to really live on a subsistence level."

The Booys learned many lessons in those years that have inspired and guided Dirk throughout his life and career. "To be right there, living day to day, and not knowing where your food will come from and what tomorrow will bring really teaches you what life is like for many of the world's people."

There were many other lessons too, like how skilled one must be to survive in a subsistence economy. Along with their community, they had to learn how to survive. They got sick. They were emotionally drained and psychologically burned out. One day a village elder came to talk with them. "Why do you want to be like us?" he asked. He continued, "We want you to be like who you really are so that you can help us." Dirk remembers this as an epiphany moment, "This was a great revelation to us, because we began at that moment to comprehend that we needed to respect the people and be part of their community but also to bring something new and helpful. We needed balance, and it was then that we gained the confidence to contribute more ideas in community meetings and let the community make their own decisions about them."

Another huge lesson was how important it is to listen to the advice of elders or, in Western terms, to find experienced mentors who can shine some light on our path.

Over the next fifteen years, Dirk received an MA in international development, moved to Tanzania, and joined World Vision Tanzania as the national director. A major accomplishment was that World Vision raised 35 percent of its funds, or $6 million, right in Tanzania through national campaigns and local fundraising. "We learned," says Dirk, "that nobody is too poor to give and that a big part of community development is providing people the opportunity to express their concern for others and to help each other out."

After two decades in Africa, the Booys moved back to Canada where Dirk took on more administrative roles for World Vision International and was then named to the position of partnership leader for global field operations. Throughout his career, Dirk has tried to serve, whether from a mud-and-stick house in Sierra Leone or from the pinnacle of the world's largest Christian development organization. He has discovered his vocation in God's world according to the gifts God gave him and the opportunities God put in his path. It is a path he is still walking.

Dirk now serves in a high-profile role, traveling frequently, talking with lots of people (mostly in offices); but as is true for many development workers, he longs to return to grassroots community development where he can once again bond with people and be "where the real action is, where my real heart is, and where I get the most satisfaction. Truly, there is nothing like being on the front line."

Throughout his career, Dirk has followed the call to be a part of the restoration of God's kingdom through development work. He also believes that God is calling each and every one of us to join him in this wonderful mission. Will you?

Dirk had a general college degree but was then fortunate enough to learn through experience and additional formal education. He served directly in the community, then in a national office, and now in an international office. He was mentored by others and is now a mentor himself. He and Joanne had to manage both family and vocational commitments. We will come back to all these points throughout the book.

Other Development Professionals You Will Meet in This Book

Christine and Dirk are just two of the many development workers you will meet in the pages ahead. As I contemplated writing a book on vocations in international development, I realized I needed to gather the experiences and the wisdom of people who are in the field because the field of development is broad and varied. Christine works with human rights and governance, and Dirk focuses especially on community development, but other development workers are involved with health, microenterprise, job creation, peacebuilding, forestry, urban planning, governance, economic policy, agriculture, access to clean water, gender relations, justice advocacy, and so much more. There

Who Was Interviewed

The fifty-seven people listed below were interviewed during the spring and summer of 2010.[1] Names are followed by professional affiliation at the time of the interview. Some had recently completed terms of service and were waiting to see what would come next. For those, I have identified the position they moved into. While not everyone listed here is individually referenced in the book, I can honestly say that every single interview was informative, fascinating, and influential to the overall message.

1. Milton Amayun, family health team leader for the United States Agency for International Development (USAID), Benin
2. Jillian Baker, project assistant for World Vision Uganda
3. Dana Bates, executive director of New Horizons Foundation Romania
4. Christine Bodewes, head of the Africa Desk for Porticus (a private foundation) in the Netherlands
5. Tim Bollinger, project comanager for Sal, Luz, Saude in Mozambique
6. Dirk Booy, partnership leader for global field operations for World Vision International in the United Kingdom
7. Duncan Boughton, associate professor for the Department of Agricultural, Food, and Resource Economics at Michigan State University
8. David Bronkema, director of development programs at Eastern University
9. Alisa Buma, program coordinator for Samaritan's Purse in Liberia
10. Alicia Clifton, director of Health and Family Services for Jericho Road Ministries in Buffalo, NY
11. Dana DeRuiter, senior policy advisor for Global Health at USAID, Washington, DC
12. Beth Doerr, intern manager for Educational Concerns for Hunger Organization (ECHO) in Fort Myers, FL
13. Dana Doll, field organizer for Micah Challenge
14. Nathan Dowling, deputy director at PRO-COM in Rwanda
15. Faith Wise, global mission director for Providence Church in Westchester, PA
16. Jason Fileta, national coordinator for Micah Challenge in Portland, OR
17. Belinda Forbes, commissioned missionary to Nicaragua for the United Methodist Church
18. Karen Genzink, on staff with Future Now Enterprises in Cambodia
19. Luke Hamstra, founder and supporter of Omwabini in Grand Rapids, MI, and Nairobi, Kenya
20. Bernard Haven, stabilization planner with Canadian International Development Agency (CIDA) in Afghanistan
21. Hayden Hill, director of community development initiatives for Westminster Reformed Presbyterian Church in Suffolk, VA
22. Vernon Jantzi, professor at the Center for Justice and Peacebuilding at Eastern Mennonite University
23. Mark Kaech, new media specialist for Food for the Hungry in Phoenix, AZ
24. Brenda Katerberg, disaster relief coordinator for East Africa at CRWRC in Niger
25. Charlotte Keniston, Peace Corps volunteer in Guatemala

26. Ndunge Kiiti, associate professor of intercultural studies at Houghton College
27. Jacqueline Klamer, writer/project coordinator for Partners Worldwide
28. Lora Kleinsasser, regional facilitator for Latin America for Partners Worldwide in Nicaragua
29. Eunice Lee, Peace Corps volunteer in Cambodia
30. Carly Miller, English teacher in Korea
31. Hannah Marsh, liaison specialist for USAID in Washington, DC
32. Greg Matney, regional facilitator for Partners Worldwide in Hyderabad, India
33. Ryan Musser, program associate for the International Foundation for Electoral Systems in Washington, DC
34. Jennie Missner, owner of Venture Imports LLC in Grand Rapids, MI
35. Kris Ozar, program quality manager for Catholic Relief Service in Ghana
36. Jonathan Persenaire, owner/manager of a computer services store in Kampala, Uganda
37. Julie Peterson, vice president of American World Services in Washington, DC
38. Rachel Reed, microfinance consultant with Mennonite Central Committee (MCC) in Honduras
39. Stephanie Reinitz, executive assistant for International Justice Mission in Washington, DC
40. Sarah Rohrer, field organizer for Bread for the World in Dayton, OH
41. Emily Romero, codirector of Jubilee Centers International in Honduras
42. Elizabeth Rudy, World Vision US
43. Andrew Ryskamp, director of CRWRC, USA
44. Doug Seebeck, executive director of Partners Worldwide, Grand Rapids, MI
45. Jordan Smith, Mekong student life coordinator for Go ED in Vietnam
46. Mike Soderling, medical missionary in Guatemala
47. Carl Stauffer, assistant professor of development and justice studies at Eastern Mennonite University
48. Carolyn Stauffer, assistant professor in applied social sciences at Eastern Mennonite University
49. Brit Steiner, management and program analyst in the Office of Civilian Response at USAID in Washington, DC
50. Roland Vanderburg, program director for Christian Aid for Under-Assisted Societies Everywhere (CAUSE) in Canada
51. Rebecca Vander Meulen, community development director and HIV and AIDS coordinator for the Diocese of Niassa in Lichinga, Mozambique
52. Matt Van Geest, country program manager for Mozambique and the Democratic Republic of Congo for World Vision
53. Nathaniel Veltman, mission coworker with the Presbyterian Church in Ethiopia
54. Kurt Ver Beek, director of Calvin College's Honduras Semester Program
55. Alisa Yingling, MBA student at Biola University
56. Mary Ann Weber, human resources coordinator for MCC—Great Lakes Office
57. Michael Woolcock, senior social scientist with the Development Research Group at the World Bank

would be no way to get a reasonably accurate picture of what it is like to work in those fields and how people get into those fields without listening to the folks who have the experience. In addition, some work in small church-related missions, some in big secular nongovernmental organizations (NGOs), and others in large national or international institutions like the World Bank. There are even some who work in private business and intentionally engage in development work from there. You will meet people from all these arenas. Many of the interviewees have been in development work for a long time. Others are only a few years out of college and still finding their way. The wisdom of the old-timers that comes from maturity and long experience is a great asset and has much to teach us. The lived experience of the younger development workers will no doubt resonate more directly with readers who plan to enter the field in the next few years.

What unites all these diverse people under one umbrella is their commitment to be faithful to the mission God has given us in this world, so succinctly and beautifully expressed by the prophet Micah: "to act justly and to love mercy and to walk humbly with your God" (6:8). As long as children die of hunger, girls and boys are trafficked, wars bring death and destruction, the poor are deprived of education and excluded or marginalized from society, and people cannot find work or earn enough to survive, there is much acting and loving and walking that need to be done. All the people you meet in these pages are committed to this mission.

Why I Wrote This Book and Who It Is For

To explain why I wrote this book, I must briefly tell you some of my own story. One of the values I grew up with and have always tried to live out is caring for others, especially those who seem downtrodden. Admittedly, I do not do this as well as I would wish. Someone recently asked me where I thought that value came from. My first thought was to mention my parents' nurturing and the experiences I had when growing up, but it occurred to me instead that this is a characteristic that God implanted in us when he knew us in the womb. We are supposed to be like this. I started to realize that this value does not need to be explained. So that was my answer. "I'm normal," I said, "nothing to explain." I often fail to live up to this value, but I do aspire to it. What really needs to be explained are the people who lack this value. They are the ones who must answer the question of what has gone wrong.

Another manifestation of my normality is that I had little idea what I should study when I went to college. To gain some clarity on that, I took a break after two years. In March 1976, right after a horrific earthquake in Guatemala, an elder in my church suggested I join a mission to Guatemala to help in the rebuilding. Experiencing another country, improving my beginning Spanish, and actually helping people in need were all powerful motivators, so I went. I lived in a rural town for one year and helped build one-room (plus porch) cinder-block houses. During that year I saw the desperate poverty but realized soon enough that there would be no easy answers to it. Still, I wanted to find some answers; most of all, I wanted to help. Like the young person you will meet in the introduction, I said, "Here I am, Lord. Send me." It was obvious that I had a lot to learn, however, so I came back to the United States to study economics. If I wanted to do something about poverty, knowing about economics seemed pretty basic. At graduation I went right on for a doctorate in economic development.

In the thirty years since then, as a professor of economics and international development at Calvin College, as the director of the Latin American Studies Program for three years, as a development worker in Nicaragua for several years, and as a citizen in Christ's kingdom the whole time, I have pondered the following two questions: What really works in helping people escape poverty and live rich and full lives? And how can (and should) wealthy people, like most of the people I live and worship with in North America, contribute to the well-being of every human being God created? These are the questions I have researched, written about, and acted upon my whole adult life.

A little over ten years ago I became the director of my college's international development studies program, and for the last six years, students at Calvin have organized an annual conference on "Faith and International Development" that usually attracts about three to four hundred students from all over North America. Among the biggest questions on their minds are the same two that I have asked: What works? And what can we do? These are followed by two additional questions, both extensions of the latter question: What should *I* do? And how do *I* actually do this and make a career out of it?

Together with the students and some of my professor colleagues in other Christian colleges, we looked in vain for written materials that really address these questions, especially in a Christian context. There are lots of good books about Christian missions, and there are good ones too, secular and Christian, about development work (some of these are listed in chap. 9). There are also secular reference books about how to find volunteer positions, intern positions, and jobs in international development. But we could find no vocational guides for Christians whose approach to mission is holistic.

So that's where this book came from. It is unabashedly Christian in its attempt to address the following themes:

what kind of development we are actually trying to accomplish

what the field of international development is like

what kind of people are most effective in development work

how to prepare oneself for this work in the college years

how to actually get into the field

If you have acknowledged God's gift to you of caring for others; if you have a love for the people of other countries; if you are wondering how we can really help, what your role might be, and how to get started, then this book is for you. Listen to the wisdom and advice of fifty-eight development professionals. That's the fifty-seven that we interviewed plus myself. In truth, there is a lot of wisdom in these pages from other fellow travelers as well. No one in this book knows it all. We are all on a journey of learning to live faithfully in God's whole world. We invite you to join us.

Acknowledgments

This book arises from the influence of two groups of young people. One is the college-age students I have talked with in my office, over coffee, and via emails about their educational paths, the field of international development, and the realistic possibilities of carving out careers in global service. The second group is the people—not quite so young anymore—who actually entered the field of international development, learned what serving God globally is like, and then shared their stories and wisdom so that I could pass them on to the next crop of college students. To both of these large groups I owe a debt of gratitude that is impossible to detail or quantify. They will remain nameless here, but if you sat with me and talked or exchanged emails with me at some point, either as a student or as a development professional, then I extend to you my heartfelt thanks.

The precise moment when the idea for this book took root was in a meeting in Washington, DC, when college professors and NGO representatives got together to think through the dilemma of how to bridge the gap between college and professional development work. At one point, someone, I think it was Ndunge Kiiti, said we needed a resource to help Christian young people know what development work is about, what the field is like—how to prepare for it and how to gain the experience necessary to get into it. Others agreed, and I started to plot how I might use my upcoming sabbatical leave to work on such a book. So thanks to all the participants in that meeting: Richard Gathro, Aleida Guzman, Chad Hayward, Mark Jorritsma, Ann Karl, Ndunge Kiiti, Ray Martin, Aaron Moore, Stephanie Saenger, Abe Scheaffer, Aaron Stuvland, and Evelyn Yang. You provided the initial push.

Many others are likewise to be heartily and cheerfully thanked, including:

All the wonderful development professionals, fifty-seven in all, who consented to be interviewed and whose names and affiliations are listed in the preface. Their willingness to spend time with me, often over the phone and sometimes over tenuous Skype connections, is truly appreciated. I fear only a small portion of the wisdom they shared made it into the book, but I hope they are happy with what is here.

Three senior seminar classes at Calvin College, the first of which, in the fall of 2009, brainstormed the questions they wanted the book to address. The other two classes, fall 2010 and spring 2011, read the entire manuscript and discussed what spoke to them and what did not. One impassioned debate revolved around whether references to the Star Wars movies are still relevant to today's young people. As you will see, I left them in.

Emily Daher, my student assistant in the summer of 2010. Emily transcribed almost all of the interviews, wrote first drafts of specific sections, did much of the research for chapter 9, interviewed thirteen recent Calvin College graduates who are now working in development, and provided a trustworthy sounding board for the ideas throughout the entire book. God go with you, Emily, as you embark on your own career path in global service.

My father, Alvin Hoksbergen, who read the chapters as they first escaped my computer. He gave me all sorts of solid advice about content, tone, depth, and wording. Thanks, Dad, for all you've done to shape this book, and also to both you and Mom for shaping me as a person.

Practitioners and academic colleagues David Bronkema, Rukshan Fernando, Jacqueline Klamer, Tracy Kuperus, Russell Mask, Mwenda Ntarangwi, and Amy Patterson, all of whom read through chapters and provided vital feedback. Thanks also for writing those letters of support needed at various junctures.

The staff and partners of the Christian Reformed World Relief Committee with whom I have been privileged to work over the years and who have taught me so much about effective international development work.

Calvin College, for its sabbatical program, and the good people at Baker Academic who helped push this project to completion.

Finally, my wife and friend, Lisseth, Gustavo's and Vila's second daughter, for being an encouraging presence and soulmate throughout the entire process.

Introduction

God, You, and the World Out There

"The poor you will always have with you." "Therefore . . ."

Mark 14:7; Deuteronomy 15:11

"And he looked for justice, but saw bloodshed; for righteousness, but heard cries of distress." "Then I heard the voice of the Lord saying, 'Whom shall I send? And who will go for us?' And I said, 'Here am I. Send me!'"

Isaiah 5:7; 6:8

An experienced missionary once told me "you can take all your kindheartedness and compassion and hope to change the world, but if you do not understand the world, then you can do a lot more damage than good."

Faith Wise, global mission director of Providence Church in Westchester, PA

Hearing the Call to Global Service

In 2003 well-known evangelical pastor Rick Warren traveled to Rwanda at his wife's urging and witnessed poverty and suffering unlike any he had ever seen before. At about the same time he was led to read the Bible with fresh eyes, noticing now the over two thousand verses that address poverty and justice for the poor. As with so many others who witness global pain and suffering up close and personal, Warren sensed God's call during his sojourn in this faraway land. He responded by helping to set up a new organization, the PEACE Plan, that would address multiple needs of the poor the world over.[1] He also started preaching much more on justice and our responsibilities to people in need.

Like Warren, Christians young and old have heard God's call, but unlike Warren, many do not have the international reputation, the wealth, or the self-confidence that allow them to think big and to set up a global organization that envisions involving a billion people. Most people are not gifted like he is either, and many are young people just getting started. Warren was already in midlife and fully established in a productive career when he happened to hear God's call to care for the poor and responded by getting involved. But how about the people who hear this call in their youth, when their career paths have hardly begun and when they are still wide open to what God wants them to do? How can they get involved?

Picture a group of young Christians as they attend a convention like Urbana and hear a compelling speaker like Rick Warren, Rob Bell, Tony Campolo, Shane Claiborne, Gary Haugen, Ruth Padilla-DeBorst, or Ronald Sider persuade them that the world is full of pain and that God wants them to be "ambassadors of global reconciliation,"[2] to carry God's message of love throughout the world to children with AIDS, to women oppressed and marginalized in their own cultures, to conflict or environmental refugees who have fled their own devastated lands, to Haitians suffering a death-dealing earthquake, to garbage pickers in Guatemala, and to people the world over who suffer the dull grind of crushing poverty every day of their lives. Imagine these same young people as they join a short-term mission trip to a developing country. Events and experiences such as these often weigh heavily on the hearts and minds of young people, as they should, and many emerge with an awakened spirit, a compassionate heart, and a firm conviction that they ought to do something.

Imagine further that their response to these experiences is to announce with great conviction that they are ready to go, ready to sacrifice, ready to serve, and ready to sign up to be witnesses and messengers of God's love to the world's broken and suffering peoples. They have heard a call similar to what Isaiah hears in Isaiah 6. "Whom shall I send?" says the voice of the Lord, and Isaiah responds, "Here am I. Send me." They too respond, "Here am I, Lord. Send me."

Striking While the Iron Is Hot

They are inspired, committed, and ready. Now what?

One thing that often happens is that this moment slips away. This could easily happen if during such days of strong commitment these willing servants do not receive helpful guidance and greater clarity about how to act on their commitment. It is much easier to get fired up about carrying out a great mission like this than it is to get equipped with requisite abilities and a set of particular skills. If new recruits find no practical guidance from the leaders of their faith communities, their energy may dissipate. There are many reasons for this, and it happens to all of us. Sometimes, because we are far away from the suffering, the passing of time dulls the sharpness of the call and the emotional attachment to the people we met on the mission trip. Sometimes the guidance we get from our elders does not really convince us or seem concrete or immediate enough to do much good. We might be encouraged to give to a certain Christian organization, live simply so that others may simply live, be a good citizen, and vote correctly (as if that's easy). Sometimes the problems just seem so big and complex that we lose heart and begin to question our own abilities. For those of us who are wealthy, another threat looms: every day we face the temptation to live a comfortable, self-centered life and just close our eyes to the world's pain.

One reason that reassurance and guidance are so important at this point is that it will not be long before our young friends hear the message that the sort of assistance and service they have in mind actually does more harm than good, or that people from rich countries should just stay away. For example, they hear that foreigners take jobs away from nationals, are too culturally insensitive to help, or are simply too expensive. Better to send money and pay locals to do the work, or not to send money at all and simply let the people solve their own problems. One message they might come across is articulated in a speech of Austrian philosopher Monsignor Ivan Illich, "To Hell with Good Intentions," which concludes with the following words: "I am here to entreat you to use your money, your status and your education to travel in Latin America. Come to look, come to climb our mountains, to enjoy our flowers. Come to study. But do not come to help."[3]

Messages like these could easily begin to lead well-motivated, compassionate, Christ-following people down a path of cynicism, despair, and withdrawal. Or their lives might simply take an inward turn, focusing on themselves and their families, careers, and local communities, but no longer on the needs of people around the world. As their lives unfold, they might periodically hear the messages and the calls, but they are no longer inspired. They may respond by giving a little money here and there, especially when a disaster strikes, and perhaps even periodically joining a short-term mission group building a school, a church, or a clinic in a developing country, but their hearts are not in it very deeply anymore, and sometimes their involvement seems more oriented to reducing their own guilt than to really helping other people.

Like the story of Scrooge in *A Christmas Carol*, this is how things might go. But they do not have to unfold like this. Let's return to the young Christians when they are still on fire. Here they are enthusiastically responding to the call with a firm and sincere, "Here am I, Lord. Send me." What do we tell them?

Two Words of Advice

I would like to offer two main words of advice, *affirmation* and *preparation*, both of which are vital. We all need to be affirmed in our sense of calling because it is part of how we nurture and cultivate our own identity as Christ followers, as people called to fulfill a purpose and to carry out a mission. Affirmation also gives us a sense of belonging and a place as members of a supportive community. The second, preparation, is vital because anyone wishing to embark on a mission must not only have clarity about what that mission is but also be well equipped to carry it out.

Affirmation

When you cheerfully respond to God's call to global service, it is the community's responsibility and joy to praise the Lord for your desire to be faithful and your willingness to explore how to live out a vocation of service in a global context. You should know that the desire to serve is a completely natural Christian response to God's love for us, but it is still something we should rejoice about. That is because our society tells us over and over again, in blunt and subtle ways but with numbing repetition, to take care of number one first, that it is dog-eat-dog out there, and that the one who dies with the most toys wins. Such messages thoroughly violate who God created us to be. As bearers of his image, we are created to love God and to love and care for our neighbors, especially those who are hurting. When the Pharisees ask Jesus what the greatest commandment is, he gives a two-part answer. The first, he says, is to love God. The Pharisees expect this, but Jesus surprises them with the corollary: "And the second is like it: 'Love your neighbor as yourself'" (Matt. 22:39).[4] Love of God and love of neighbor are tightly intertwined. You cannot do the first unless you do the second. Be assured that your desire to discover how you can help, a desire awakened by the messages and experiences that spoke to your mind and stirred your heart, is good and real and true. Read how Pope Benedict XVI puts this idea in his recent encyclical *Caritas in Veritate* (*Charity in Truth*): "All people feel the interior impulse to love authentically: love and truth never abandon them completely, because these are the vocation planted by God in the heart and mind of every human person."[5]

Caring about and for the broken and hurting people in this world is completely natural, because that love and care was planted there by God himself. As the pope says, it is our vocation, what we are called to do and meant to do. If and when you are sarcastically called a "do-gooder" or a "bleeding heart," your response should be, "Praise the Lord! Join me."

Be affirmed too that God expects this vocation of service born of love to be carried out in the world, in real time and space. God cares about every square inch of the world he created. Yes, the world has fallen into sin and is now a broken shell of what God wanted it to be, but God's vision for this world continues to be a grand one. Theologian N. T. Wright, in *Surprised by Hope*, sums it up by arguing that God's purpose in this world is nothing less than "rescue and re-creation for the whole world, the entire cosmos."[6] Such a grand vision doesn't leave much out, and it emphatically (remember those two thousand verses) puts before us the people around the world who are struggling to build better lives or even just to survive to the next day.

If you think that the combination of God's grand vision and the fact that he planted a spirit of love and care in your own heart means that he wants you involved, you are exactly right. And he wants you involved completely. You need to know up front that God isn't asking you to take a nine-to-five job with weekends off and vacations; this is a full-time assignment, 24–7, for your whole life. It is not something you do for a few years and then move on to something else.

Before we get ahead of ourselves, this does not mean that all of Christ's followers are expected to join a village co-op in Zambia, though it might mean that for some. The point is that no matter what specific life situation you find yourself in, whether in a direct role working with the poor in other lands or as a small-business owner in your home community, you are still expected to be on task with the grand mission. Not everyone is called to go and live in Zambia, but some of us are. If you sense that God may be asking you to be directly involved in serving people around the world, then you need to start narrowing down how it is that God wants you to serve. Much more on that later.

All well and good, you might say, but perhaps you are plagued by some nagging doubts about the extent to which Christians should be involved in social action. We will talk more about this in chapters 2 and 3, but for the moment I want to visit the Scripture passage that opens this chapter. It is the passage in which Jesus tells his disciples that the poor will always be with us. I have often heard this passage used to explain that we really cannot expect to do much about poverty. The argument is that we will never make much progress, so it would be better to stick with evangelism and traditional mission work, focusing on the soul rather than on the body. But a closer reading of the passage indicates that such a conclusion was not at all what Jesus had in mind. In fact, he was quoting from a passage in the law, Deuteronomy 15:11, which in its entirety reads as follows: "There will always be poor people in the land. Therefore I command you to be openhanded toward your fellow Israelites who are poor and needy in your land." The emphasis here is not on the fact of poverty but instead, as in so many other passages, on loving and helping—always helping. As we all know, there are plenty of poor and needy people in our land, and God expects us to be openhanded toward them.

If you are lucky enough to have the chance, one of the finest speechmakers you will ever hear is Gary Haugen, founder and director of the International Justice Mission. It is hard not to be moved to action when Gary gets to the part of his speech when, after telling a heart-wrenching story of young children who have been brutalized and trafficked, he wonders aloud why God lets bad things like this happen and why God does not do anything about it. "Doesn't God have a plan for dealing with such injustice?" Haugen implores. At that point, he looks his listeners straight in the eye and hits them with a striking challenge: "Well," he says, "I would like to tell you that God does have a plan. We are the plan!"[7]

God's vision is a big one, and his plan is to build a team of followers to live out that vision. There is a place for you on that team. In fact, there is a "no cut" rule, so you can rest assured that there is a role for you to play.

Preparation

What exactly might that role be? A perfectly reasonable question to ask at this point, which leads us to the second word of advice: preparation, something anyone going into global service will need in abundance. One of the tricky parts of this piece of advice is that no one can tell you precisely what preparation you need. Certainly there are some general guidelines, but you must yourself play a big part in finding exactly what position you will play on the team. That realization might lead to a number of fairly obvious questions, such as:

I want to help, but what do I have to offer?

Are short-term missions enough, or are we talking about a longer-term commitment?

Is there a career here? Will I be able to get a job?

Do I need to develop a particular skill? If so, which one?

If I go to school, what should I study?

Will I have to live in a developing country? Am I cut out to do that?

These are all excellent, practical questions. Once you get started thinking about these, you might be led to ask some bigger-picture questions, including:

Why are people poor, and what strategies to help actually work?

What is God's plan for people in this world, and what does development really mean?

Is there any hope for change when the problems seem so big and intractable?

Can foreigners, maybe someone like me, really help?

Note the doubts and concerns creeping in here. The first set of questions is more personal and the second more abstract and theoretical, but these are precisely the types of questions you should be asking. The very fact that you might ask such questions shows awareness of the significance of the mission and is a promising sign that you might actually make a positive contribution. Happily, there are good answers for all these questions, which we will get to as this book unfolds.

But now I must pause briefly to provide a rejoinder to messages that say it is not worth the bother and would be better if we did not get involved, such as the one from Ivan Illich above. First, though Illich is not ultimately right, we would make a serious mistake if we did not listen to him and ask what he is trying to tell us. In part, he wants us to know that people in other countries are not just sitting there waiting for us to come and fix all their problems. He wants us to know that people in other cultures have many good things about them that do not need fixing, and that we have many things in our own lives that do need fixing. He wants us to know that helping others is serious business and that helping people who speak other languages, live in other cultures, and have their own complex histories is not as easy as it might sound.

Joining in the struggle against global poverty is a high and noble calling, but there are many pitfalls. Signing up for this mission will require lots of study, lots of personal growth, and lots of practice. In the mid-1980s I wrote a short article on how North American young people could get started in their efforts to address global human suffering;[8] one of the people I interviewed offered this bit of wisdom: "study, study, study . . . listen, listen, listen." This is where we all need to begin. The road is long and hard, and the most important virtues to cultivate may be patience and humility. This is an especially important point because, for some reason, perhaps due to our wealth and education, we are often tempted to think that helping other people is easy . . . too easy. I am not trying to discourage anyone but to pump you up for the task ahead and to tell you that though the road is long, the destination is definitely worth it. As the saying goes, the view is worth the climb.

Maybe the following story will help clarify the issue. Suppose you were suffering from an acute pain in your lower abdomen and encountered at that moment a fine young Christian who deeply desires to be of service to God and to her community. Like you, she clearly loves God and her neighbor; it just happens at this moment that you are the neighbor in question. Suppose that your new acquaintance says she heard once that such pain is often associated with appendicitis and that her understanding is that you need an operation right away. Would you be surprised when she reaches into her pocket for her Swiss knife and offers to perform the operation herself, right there? Would you let her? I trust you did not have a hard time answering this question with a firm "no!" Why? For the simple reasons that this would-be helper is not a doctor, her diagnosis is not fully convincing, the conditions and equipment are clearly inadequate, and perhaps, most of all, you would almost certainly die should she operate on you. It would be much smarter to visit a doctor who had gone through medical school, been certified by the state board, done a residency under well-regarded internists and surgeons, and had access to a sterile and well-equipped clinic. As we know, training to become a physician takes time, and the road is long and hard.

Working in behalf of poor people in other countries is remarkably similar. The pain that poor people around the world suffer is very serious, often a matter of life and death. Like our knife-toting friend, there are many well-intentioned people who would like to help, which is a very good thing, but as Illich so bluntly lays out, good intentions are not enough and may cause more harm than good. In order to work on these serious problems, aspiring ambassadors of global reconciliation need to go to school, gain expertise in the discipline, develop skills in a specialized field, build cross-cultural capabilities, and practice as interns under the tutelage of experienced professionals. We expect this of our physicians; we should expect no less of development workers. People who see the problems in poor countries and rush in to help all too often do a great deal of harm, just as the young person would if she had been permitted to use her Swiss knife for an appendectomy.[9] Unfortunately, unlike you in the appendectomy story, poor people often do not have the ability or the will to say "no!" to a rich, educated foreigner who they have been led to believe knows what is best for them.

You might remember Luke Skywalker from the early Star Wars trilogy. As much as he wanted to rush in to fight Darth Vader and the dark side right away, it was Yoda and Obi-Wan who insisted that he was not ready, that he needed desperately to go through the training. It was a long process and one that frustrated Luke very much, but had he rushed into battle before being ready, he would have utterly failed to carry out his mission and done a great deal of harm. In the end, of course, he was successful, and it is my hope and prayer that you will be as well.

Finding Your Niche in International Development

The purpose of this book is to get you started on your way toward becoming a leader in the field that today is typically referred to as "international development." Another popular term is "human development." In Christian circles the terms "authentic human development" and "transformational development" have both gained increasing traction. As we will see, these terms do make a difference, but for now it is enough to say that development of people and their societies is about much more than fighting poverty. Yes, ending poverty is important, just as getting someone out of a burning house is important, but we must then face the more forward-looking issue of what kind of a world or community we want to live in. Development is thus a constructive idea, one that asks what we are to become, not one that just removes a problem. Thinking about development brings us to questions such as these: What kind of society does God want us to live in? What do we hope people will become, and what is it that we are hoping to become ourselves? How do we tell the difference between progress and regress? For example, on a national scale, is it good that everyone in Cuba has enough to eat and access to reasonably good health care? Of course it is. But is the lack of political freedom an acceptable price to pay for that? Perhaps not. Or consider another example: Does it help to teach a poor person how to fish or to farm more productively? Likely so, but what if the farmer uses his newly acquired knowledge to get rich and then starts exploiting his workers and cheating his business associates? Development is thus about a lot more than ending economic poverty. Obviously, what people have (and how much) matters, but it also matters what we do, who we are, and how we live together. *Having . . . doing . . . being . . . relating.* This can all get pretty complicated.

Right after World War II, which is more or less when people started getting serious about international development, the dominant view was that investments in infrastructure and business, along with specialization and trade, would kick-start the economies of poor countries. The poor would get jobs, living standards would improve, and we would all get on a path to a better world. On this view, development was mostly about *having.* Many people still think that.[10] Even Christians who ought to know better get sucked into that kind of thinking with entirely too much regularity. The basic idea is that if we all *have* enough, then we will use it well. We would all live long healthy lives, be at peace with each other, and generally be very happy. Well, it has not quite worked out that way, and for many years development scholars and practitioners have been studying why, rethinking their theories, and restructuring their practices. Much has been learned since then, though much remains to be learned.

One thing development professionals have learned over the past fifty years, even many of the economists, is that development is about a lot more than investment and markets. We have realized that we need the wisdom and involvement of people from many other fields of knowledge. Without going into all the interconnections inherent in what I am about to mention, we have learned that human development is about agriculture, culture, religion, identity, empowerment, gender, ethnicity, technology, health, business, politics, conflict, peacebuilding, urban planning, human rights, families, community, environmental sustainability, international relations, and much, much more. As you can see, there is a lot to learn about and many ways to serve.

We have also learned that development is about perspectives and worldviews, something patently evident (though quite overdone) in the blockbuster film *Avatar*. It is pretty obvious in this film that the human invaders and the local Navi have very different understandings of the meaning of life and of how to relate to the world around them. How we think of our world and how we act within it depend a lot on how we understand the purpose of the world and what our own goals are within that world. In other words, development is also about our beliefs and values. In fact, we cannot even talk intelligently about progress or development unless we refer to systems of beliefs and values, world and life views, or what some would simply call "faith."

This book, as I expect is abundantly evident, arises out of my own Christian beliefs and values and my own understanding of the Christian tradition of thought and practice. It is this faith that has long told me that we must all work with tenacious perseverance to alleviate the pain and suffering of this world, to help others along the way toward becoming what God would like them to become, and to contribute to the promotion of *international, transformational, authentic, human* development. I hope this book will help you assess what role you might play in God's grand mission, how to prepare for playing that role, and how to get started down the path. Our task here will be to learn about our broad vocation, understood as a grand, global, all-embracing mission, but it is also about careers in development. Many minds, hearts, and hands are needed in a lot of different fields, and I hope this book helps you think more clearly about what your own gifts and capabilities are, how those might be developed and employed to good effect in God's kingdom, and what actual career niche you might look forward to filling.

1

What to Do and Why

Four Contemporary Views on Development

One day Alice came to a fork in the road and saw a Cheshire cat in a tree. "Which road do I take?" she asked. "Where do you want to go?" was his response. "I don't know," Alice answered. "Then," said the cat, "it doesn't matter."

Lewis Carroll, *Alice in Wonderland*

Always be prepared to give an answer to everyone who asks you to give the reason for the hope that you have. But do this with gentleness and respect.

1 Peter 3:15

One thing I've learned is how important worldviews are. We must learn to evaluate worldviews, because they are so basic to what people do in life.

Hayden Hill, development worker in East Africa, 2007–9

An Illustrative Case

There are some things in development work that everyone agrees on. Children dying for lack of food is absolutely unacceptable. Young people being trafficked for sexual slavery is a terrible violation of human dignity that must be stopped. We cannot stand by when child soldiers, senses deadened by drugs and violence, are taught to torture and kill. Reckless and environmentally destructive deforestation cannot be tolerated. Christians, Muslims, liberals, and conservatives all agree on the above points. Agreement becomes much more difficult, however, when we try to identify the causes behind the world's pain and determine exactly what must be done to fight evil and promote the good.

Economist Jeffrey Sachs, one of today's most prominent development thinkers, argues in *The End of Poverty* that development is a lot like health and poverty a lot like sickness. He likens development workers to doctors who diagnose problems before treating them. Sachs points out that the symptoms of illness (fever, pain, listlessness) and the symptoms of unhealthy societies (hunger, infant mortality, violence) are indications of deeper maladies that must be diagnosed accurately before being treated. This is a helpful point, but there is another issue that Sachs does not address. He seems to assume that all doctors have the same understanding of health. He does not mention how significant which school of medicine the doctor attended is in determining the approach taken for treatment (e.g., medical, osteopathic, chiropractic, homeopathic). Just like in medicine, in development too there are distinct, prominent, and competing theoretical schools where today's development "doctors" go for training. Depending on which school development workers attend, they will understand human development in distinct ways and will treat recognized diseases quite differently. In deference to the famous Cheshire cat, if we want to know what road to take, we must know where we want to go and how we want to get there.

Consider the following story and ask yourself what the malady is, what the causes are, and what treatment would be most effective:

Chabekum Bibi was born in Bangladesh and grew up in a poor, landless, Muslim family. She did not go to school, and when she was twelve years old her parents arranged her marriage through a local matchmaker. When she discovered that her new husband already had a wife, Chabekum refused to stay with him. Her family rejected her, and for several years she lived with other relatives who then arranged her marriage to her present husband, Babul.

Babul's family used to have some land, but they lost it when a big landowner lent them money and took the land when they couldn't pay back the loan. Babul earned about one dollar per day as a worker on his family's old land. This left Chabekum with enough money to cook rice only once a day. Babul talked about starting a small business to improve the family's standard of living and to help their children attend school for at least a few years. Chabekum heard of some Hindu women who obtained loans from an NGO to start small businesses, but was afraid to join. She had no education and no access to credit. Besides, Babul would be humiliated if people learned that his wife needed to work in a shop to supplement his income.

Other families had left for the capital city of Dhaka to work in one of the new textile plants that were popping up there. Unfortunately, Chabekum had long since given up the idea of improving her life. She was used to the gnawing feeling of hunger, and her best hope was that something good might happen to one of her children.

You would probably need more information to have complete confidence in your diagnosis, but based on what you know, what do you see as the problems, and what treatment plan would you recommend? To spur your thinking, here are four ideas.

A The basic cause is poverty, which is in turn caused by the lack of access to functioning markets. Therefore, we should encourage Chabekum and/or Babul either to start a business by joining the loan group or to migrate to Dhaka to look for jobs.

B The basic cause is that Chabekum and Babul are oppressed and powerless, so we should help them organize protest movements that can fight against injustices like Babul's land being taken away.

C The basic cause is that foreigners come in with all their strange ideas and their NGOs and mess things up. It would be best to leave Babul and Chabekum to work things out in the context of their own culture, their own beliefs, and their own ways of life.

D The basic cause is that Babul and Chabekum are both so beaten down that they cannot participate in making choices about their own future. We should help provide education, food, and health services, as well as protect their rights, so that they can participate and decide for themselves what will make their lives better.

You probably noted right away that this question is like those on annoying college tests that seem to offer several good answers for each question, all of which you could reasonably mark down as being the best one. You might also notice that some possible good answers are missing. Why, for example, are gender issues left unmentioned when they seem to be a big part of Chabekum's distress? How about the role of faith? Maybe they are plagued by disempowering religious beliefs. But you are left to guess which answer your professor prefers. Personally, I hate when that happens. Those tests are supposed to be "objective," but so much depends on one's perspective.

In this case, the question and answer are not "objective" in the least, because the "best" answer would definitely depend on your professor's views on development. If your professor were a *modernizationist*, the answer would be A; if a *dependency theorist*, then B; if from the *postdevelopment* school, C; and if a proponent of the *capabilities approach*, then D would be the best answer.

Four Contemporary Perspectives on International Development

These are the four secular perspectives that dominate the world of development thought and practice today. Each is thoughtful and reasonable, and each
is associated with distinct ways of engaging in development work. To help us
understand these views and prepare the way for thinking about development
in a Christian context in chapters 2 and 3, I will summarize these four perspectives by highlighting key features of their particular ways of thinking. In each
case, I personify the perspective with a character whose name may help you
remember the big ideas. Get ready to meet Harvey Having, Libby Liberating,
Betty Being, and Charles Choosing. Each person/perspective we encounter
here is complex and multifaceted, with many surprising and subtle traits, but
I will resist doing a deep psychoanalysis of each one. As you are introduced,
ask yourself whether you like them and whether you would like to attend the
same development school where they are professors.[1]

Modernization—Meet Harvey Having

Harvey is an optimistic, cheerful, can-do sort of fellow from the modernization school. What really motivates him is a high standard of living and
the freedom to enjoy life. When you have access to goods and services, you
can do the things that bring joy to your life. If you have food, then you can
eat; a boat, and you can go sailing; a book, and you can read; a car, and you
can travel. Services are also important. Harvey can go to school to learn a
productive skill, thus giving him the potential of higher income in the future.
If his income allows it, Harvey can hire others to do things he would rather
not do himself, like mow his lawn or do his taxes, thus giving him more time
for leisure activities. Having goods and services raises the standard of living,
extends life expectancy, and generally makes life more enjoyable.

For modernizationists there is a synergistic relationship between economic
well-being and individual freedom, so much so that Harvey sometimes wonders which comes first and which is more important. Harvey will debate this
with his friends, but the happy conclusion is that they generally go together.

Harvey grew up in the West where he and others like him have a lot more stuff
than their ancestors did. *How much* more is measured by the Gross Domestic
Product (GDP) per capita. Harvey looks back and sees how far he and his nation
have come; he thinks that if poor countries want to change for the better, they
must follow in the tracks of the West. Just as Harvey and his forebears worked
their way to progress, poor countries can also overcome their poverty by expanding
individual freedom, becoming more productive, and generating economic growth.

If we want to help poor nations develop, we must learn the lessons of wealth creation in successful societies. Thankfully, Western democratic capitalist societies are blessed with a several-hundred-year history of discovering the secrets of wealth creation, so what the poor really need to do is learn these secrets and put them into action. If poor countries want to be rich, then they must build market economies and structure their politics, families, personal values, and ways of life around the characteristics of successful market economies. These are comprised of individual property rights; personal freedom; an entrepreneurial culture; limited government; private markets; reliance on science, technology, and industry; and openness to trade and finance on global markets.

If Harvey were to feel a call to development work, what could he do to help? There are any number of ways, but they can all be boiled down to helping poor nations become more like Western societies while also helping them integrate into the global market system. Here are a few typical strategies:

Teach Western ways of medicine.

Teach about and help structure private markets so they are well regulated but free from unhelpful government interference.

Promote Western business practices through teaching and mentoring.

Provide investment capital for major industrial investments as well as the microenterprise and small- and medium-business sectors.

Educate children to read and to love math and science and to adopt such Western values as punctuality, competitiveness, and a need for achievement.

Teach productive skills, such as agriculture or urban trades.

Influence political and justice systems to be more democratic and fair.

Teach Western values such as responsibility, saving, stewardship of property, and respect for private property through religious and cultural missions.

Were Harvey to advise Babul and Chabekum, he might encourage them to apply Western business practices in their local settings (financial lending, investment, production, sales), which could be achieved through a microfinance/microenterprise program like the one the NGO is offering. It would also be reasonable to suggest migrating to the city and working in a factory that is integrated into the global market. As developing economies industrialize, it is natural and important for poor rural people to migrate to the cities in search of work. Either of these two strategies takes advantage of markets to generate higher incomes that allow them to buy food and medicine and further their education in ways that make them ever more productive. Babul and Chabekum will thus take some first steps onto what Jeffrey Sachs calls the "ladder of development."[2] If they use their higher incomes to send their children to school, the children's productivity in the future will outstrip that of their parents, and they will climb still higher up the ladder.

To reach these conclusions, beliefs and values matter a great deal. Many of the modernizationist's foundational beliefs originate in Enlightenment philosophies that center on individual freedom, to the point that individuals decide on their own what their purposes in life are. Because science cannot tell us what the ultimate destination of life is or why we are here, and because religion is seen as a vestige from primitive, superstitious societies, persons decide for themselves what brings happiness. That is why freedom from government or religious imposition is so highly valued.

Some modernizationists, especially the economists, believe that humans are by nature highly self-interested and competitive. Other modernizationists, including Lawrence Harrison, believe people must (and can) be taught to be like this.[3] Ideally, through something like Adam Smith's famous "invisible hand," self-interested individuals in competition are necessary foundations of harmonious, democratic, peaceful, and wealthy societies in which standards of living are high for everyone and in which progressively higher standards of living are achieved by every new generation. In a memorable phrase, W. W. Rostow, one of the early modernizationists, identified the goal of development to be a "high mass consumption society."[4]

Lest you think modernizationists have everything figured out, they are fully aware that there is still much to be learned and that there are many life problems yet to be addressed. For example, they are still working on the best way for governments and markets to complement each other and how to resolve growing environmental issues, harmonize individual striving with social harmony, distribute foreign aid and development assistance, initiate business growth in developing countries, avoid financial crises, and ensure adequate and low-cost health care for everyone. None of this is easy, but the broad outlines of the good society and how to achieve it are nevertheless clear. Harvey is happy and optimistic in part because no other way of organizing society has come close to achieving the wealth of Western market societies but also because, as problems arise, he is confident that rational, scientifically and technologically inclined people will solve them.

I have drawn a sketch of Harvey (see fig. 1.1) that may help you remember some of his key characteristics. As with the other persons we will meet in the next few pages, beliefs are assigned to the head, values are located in the heart region, actions are associated with the hands, and issues are what Harvey walks through to get to the "promised land" of development. Notice that Harvey

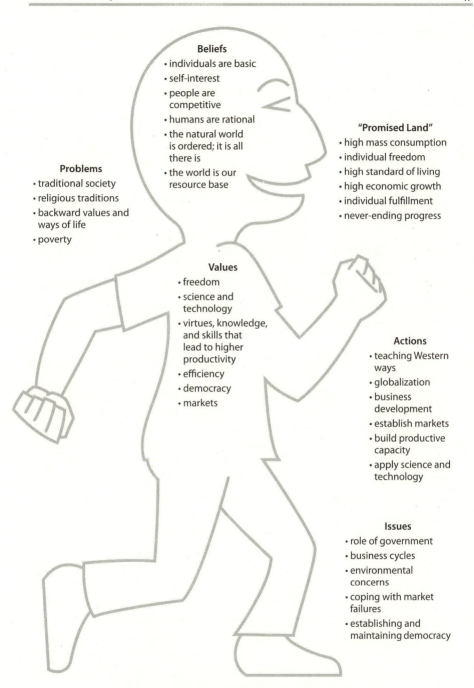

Beliefs
- individuals are basic
- self-interest
- people are competitive
- humans are rational
- the natural world is ordered; it is all there is
- the world is our resource base

"Promised Land"
- high mass consumption
- individual freedom
- high standard of living
- high economic growth
- individual fulfillment
- never-ending progress

Problems
- traditional society
- religious traditions
- backward values and ways of life
- poverty

Values
- freedom
- science and technology
- virtues, knowledge, and skills that lead to higher productivity
- efficiency
- democracy
- markets

Actions
- teaching Western ways
- globalization
- business development
- establish markets
- build productive capacity
- apply science and technology

Issues
- role of government
- business cycles
- environmental concerns
- coping with market failures
- establishing and maintaining democracy

Figure 1.1. Harvey Having—Harvey is a can-do sort of guy, an optimist who believes things will get better.

is walking away from what he understands to be life's major problems and toward what he sees as progress.

Dependency Theory—Meet Libby Liberating

For many years the strongest challenger to modernization came out of the intellectual tradition of Marxism, a philosophy of life and society that arose as a reaction to the failings of the economic system that Karl Marx called "capitalism." Marx, a German, witnessed the same horrible consequences of industrialization that his English contemporary Charles Dickens did (e.g., workhouses for the poor, people being forced into the cities and the mills through the enclosure movement, etc.). Instead of writing novels depicting the horror, however, Marx created a whole philosophy of social and economic progress. At the root of Marx's ideas, which were also rooted in Enlightenment thinking, is the notion of human beings as workers, as persons who can make things to improve their own lives. This quality is what distinguishes humans from other animals. As human history unfolds, it is our ability to work that leads to the oppression of some people by others, as those with power look for ways to take what weaker people make. Over time, however, it is this same aspect of human character that will one day lead to liberation for everyone from both material want and exploitation.

To see how this history proceeds, think of poor people in traditional societies. If hunting and gathering are no longer enough, they can build plows to farm. Having enough food allows the pursuit of other constructive projects such as making fishing equipment, writing books, and making medicines. Such pursuits allow humans to gradually beat back the material limitations of life in an ever-improving, ever-evolving process. For Marx, the expansion of production through the use of technology and science was a part of the process, but his goal was not just to have more stuff; it was for humans to use the products of their hands to become better people, to be liberated for what they might become.

Such progress would come through historical evolution, one that would pit powerful and contradictory forces against each other and result in progressive change for society as a whole. For while everyone is an individual, each person is also embedded in larger systems that evolve and change. For Marx, any one person's well-being, along with one's possibilities for liberation, is totally dependent on the movement of the whole system. Unfortunately for workers in the system, the underlying evolutionary forces fueling capitalism and industrialization function for a long time to keep workers in positions where they produce things for the rich and powerful in the upper classes of society.

People work, but elites force them into poor working classes. The poor remain poor in spite of their work and production. Marxists call this "exploitation."[5] Workers do not like this state of affairs. Sometimes they are resigned to their fate; at other times they get angry. Rich people know this anger could bring trouble, so they find ways to convince exploited workers to be appreciative of what they have and not to blame the rich for their troubles. One technique for diverting the anger of the exploited is to turn it against others, such as illegal immigrants, Muslims, or the Chinese. Present-day Marxists are not surprised that many of today's conservative media outlets encourage these types of attitudes, nor that they are heavily financed by the deep pockets of the wealthy. Another longstanding pacification strategy is to work through religion. Religions that promise a lovely afterlife and that also justify the current system are so effective in keeping workers both productive and docile that Marx called religion the "opiate of the masses." A final strategy, if these others fail, is violent suppression of troublemakers.

Social relations thus become a class struggle, with rich, exploitative classes pitted against productive but poor working classes. Like modernizationists, Marx acknowledges that the people in this struggle can be self-interested and competitive, but he believed it would not always be this way because it is poverty and the need for material things that make people greedy and acquisitive. In the future, when our abilities to make things expand and when poverty is no longer a normal condition of humankind, we will become new, virtuous people who cooperate with each other, care for each other, and aspire to more noble pursuits. The idea of development is thus about being liberated from a life of material need and from an oppressive class system in which the lower classes and poor nations are dependent on the wealthy and powerful: hence, the name "Libby Liberating" to represent Marxist dependency theory (see fig. 1.2).

Marx made some predictions as to how the current exploitative system would eventually give way to such liberation, and he had no doubt it would happen, because the forces of evolution are exceedingly powerful. One of his main expectations was that there would come a time when poor people would not be willing to take it anymore; at that time they would organize themselves and overthrow the rich capitalists and move toward establishing a society that would more fairly distribute all the goods being produced. Eventually, the monetary power of the rich would no longer be able to suppress the people power of the poor, who would triumph over the exploiters in a series of confrontations that would almost certainly be violent.

Marx himself was concerned with analyzing industrializing Europe in the nineteenth century, but his theories were compelling enough that in the twentieth century they became one of the main intellectual roots of dependency

Beliefs
- historical materialism
- evolution
- dialectical progress
- human perfectibility
- essential human quality is working and making
- economic determinism

Problems
- systemic exploitation
- alienation
- domination
- dependency
- underdevelopment

"Promised Land"
- liberation/ emancipation
- expansion of productive forces
- material progress
- gradual development of the "new person"

Values
- equality
- justice
- material well-being
- freedom from want and freedom for creative potential
- human ascent

Actions
- advocacy
- organizing
- social movements
- empowerment
- consciousness-raising

Issues
- class struggle
- world systems
- gender concerns
- moving beyond a market economy
- countervailing power

Figure 1.2. Libby Liberating—Though Libby believes that her future is ultimately a bright one, the current realities of oppression and exploitation give her an angry demeanor.

theory (DT), a theory that translates Marxist ideas into the international arena and shows how wealthy, industrialized nations take advantage of poor, agricultural nations of the third world. Embracing the themes of power and exploitation, DT sees rich and poor nations in a relationship that enriches the North and impoverishes the South. This is a story that has played out ever since rich Northern countries first encountered the South.

Consider some of the historical realities that seem well explained by DT. When Western industrializing countries needed more raw materials in the nineteenth century, they colonized the poor world. Supported by their military power, rich nations organized networks of collaborators and established compliant governments that allowed them to export what they needed back home and to pay very little or nothing for all that they took.[6] When colonialism officially ended in the years following World War II, Westerners continued their dominance through such institutions as multinational corporations, international bodies like the International Monetary Fund (IMF), Christian missionary organizations, and NGOs. Dictators propped up by Western powers borrowed money that they salted away in Swiss bank accounts, which led to a debt crisis and allowed the IMF to come and insist that poor nations go further down the road of establishing markets and integrating with the world economy. For DT, this was another example of rich countries using their power to control the global system to their economic advantage. Throughout this long period of time, the rich countries got richer and the countries of the South descended into poverty, corruption, vicious dictatorships, and, all too often, war. Many of these wars were proxy wars between the United States and the USSR, but it was the South that suffered the death and destruction.

Economic dependency is a serious enough problem by itself, but it gets worse as exploitation and corruption spread insidiously throughout the social and political fabric of dependent nations. For example, drug mafias and gang culture are incredibly powerful in many developing countries. Whether in producing countries such as Colombia or Afghanistan, or transshipment countries such as Mexico, Jamaica, or Sierra Leone, drug lords use their fabulous wealth to corrupt governments and security and judicial systems and to spread violence and fear throughout the land. They can do this because of the seemingly limitless demand for drugs in the United States and other rich countries. Alongside drug markets are the huge markets for small arms, which once again enrich the West, but which in dependent nations feed rebel movements, destabilize legitimate governments, and strengthen gangs and mafias that traffic drugs, immigrants, or children. The wealth of the North is the driver of all this, and the well-meaning people of the South suffer the wicked consequences.

It might be tempting these days to think that Marxism and DT are in decline, for as history has made clear, attempts by Southern nations to break away from Western influence and/or to establish socialist societies have not worked out very well. Yet this is not the case at all. In the context of global development, DT is very much alive and well, and to many people living in the developing world, it seems very compelling indeed. What happens to them and their countries depends on what rich people in the rich countries do. No surprise either that they see themselves as exploited victims. While the exact road ahead may not be clear in DT, one thing that is perfectly clear is that imitating Western ways and joining the global system on Western terms is a recipe for continued exploitation and ongoing suffering for the majority of people in the South. It is also clear that people in the South must find ways to gain power if they are to defend themselves against the exploitative practices of the North and mark out their own path to development.

What then can be done for people like Babul and Chabekum, who are among the waste products of a system in which the powerful take what they want? DT leads us to suggest strategies of empowerment so that these two exploited people can stand against the dominating forces that determine their lot in life. They need to be able to resist attempts by local landowners to steal their land, by loan sharks to get them indebted and then enslaved, and by business owners in the cities to pay them starvation wages.

And what is the job of the foreign development worker? If we agree that the system is unfair to the poor in Bangladesh and honestly want to bring about change, then our main task is to help Babul and Chabekum organize, develop a voice, and rise up to stand against the powers that oppress them. If they confront the powers as individuals, they are sure to lose. Chabekum is a bug to be squashed if she demands fair treatment and fights alone. But if she gets together with other women in similar circumstances and they can confront the powers together, their chances of success are much greater.

Here are some ideas for how outside development workers can help:

Educate the poor so that they come to understand their plight and how important it is to organize. The famous educator Paulo Freire had this in mind when he talked about consciousness-raising.[7]

Bring people together to share their stories and encourage them to imagine how they might organize to face the powers together.

Teach organizing strategies to the various oppressed groups, including small farmers, women, peasants, agricultural workers, ethnic groups, informal sector workers, and garment factory workers.

Engage in advocacy or support advocacy groups that fight against such maladies as debt, trafficking, low wages, land grabs, and ethnic or gender discrimination.

Develop networks of global organizations that support each other; for example, global women's movements or environmental activists. The movements will be more powerful if they are global and can support each other when local movements are under fire.

Form watchdog civic groups that hold governments and corporations accountable. United Students Against Sweatshops is one such organization that informs the public when certain companies mistreat workers in the garment industry.

Support or develop fair trade markets that skirt the markets managed by corporations.

As human beings, Babul and Chabekum are workers by nature. They want to exercise their humanity by liberating themselves from the daily difficulties of simple survival, getting out from under the oppressive thumb of the wealthy, enjoying the fruits of their own labors, and using those fruits to become better people in a better society. We can help them by strengthening their ability to stand up to the oppressive powers and ensuring that those who would take advantage of and exploit them are held in check.

Postdevelopment—Meet Betty Being

The third perspective is called "postdevelopment" because its proponents want to move past the era of "development." If this term brings to mind the more familiar term, "postmodernism," well and good, because postmodernism is the philosophical grounding that informs postdevelopment thought and practice. The main idea in postdevelopment theory (PDT) is that societies function best when they develop on their own terms. There is a marked tendency toward relativism in this view, but maybe the more operative concept would be nonjudgmentalism. For when judgment comes from the outside, followed by well-meaning development programs, the consequences are almost certainly destructive instead of helpful.

Along with Marxism, PDT agrees that global capitalism is harmful to most people in the world. Even when the North tries intentionally to share the good parts of its "development" with the rest of the world, especially when those from the North come to teach new ways of doing things, they bring nothing but trouble. What modernizationists imagine as "progress," PDT sees as a curse. That is about all PDT shares with Marxism, for its critique falls equally heavily on Marxist dependency theorists, who, just like modernizationists, take the knowledge and analyses gleaned from their own societies and use that to interpret and act upon societies that are structured quite differently. PDT's main criticism of both these perspectives on development is that they treat everyone and every culture as essentially the same and believe that everyone follows more or less similar paths to development. Modernization and DT thus impose universal theories and practices on the rest of the world, and in the process they deny or ignore the vastness and the wonder of human and ecological diversity. Both are equally ethnocentric, culture-centric, and geography-centric. Their understandings of and their solutions for the South are wrong and misguided because they hardly recognize, much less appreciate, any way of life other than their own. For these reasons, the very term "development" must be jettisoned; it too is a Western, or Northern,[8] concept that is imposed, top-down and coercively, on unsuspecting "beneficiaries" who learn too late that what "development" really means for them is destruction.

Before returning to the story of Babul and Chabekum to suggest what advice PDT might have for them, I would like to take a look at the lives of people in another country, Guatemala, where direct descendants of the Mayans live in cultures that are distinct and traditional but also under attack. Focusing on a people who still have a defined culture will help illustrate the power of this perspective. Think of Maria, a woman born into one of the Mayan communities in the Guatemalan highlands. As Maria grew up, she learned her local language, what to value and what to fear, how to grow traditional crops, how to eat chili peppers, how to prepare the foods that have kept their people alive and healthy for thousands of years, how land is distributed, how conflicts are resolved, how community decisions are made, how to respect authority, how the spiritual world interacts with the material world, how the Mayan people came to be, why they eat corn, which behaviors are good and which are not, how to choose a mate, how to raise her children, and so much more. When you realize how culturally embedded Maria is, you may also see that all these areas of life are systemically interrelated. For example, the games she and her friends played as children taught the values that would help them mature into good adults and community leaders. Religious beliefs help to justify planting and harvesting patterns. Behaviors contrary to community well-being bring sanctions from recognized authority structures. As Maria grows up, she finds her place in her family and community and becomes increasingly integrated into that community. Without her community, she is nothing. She has no identity and no sense of belonging. Within her community, she becomes a woman, a wife, a mother, a leader, a textile maker, a Mayan. Through it all she becomes a complex, integrated, whole person with a deeply embedded identity.

And then "development" comes. Missionaries arrive with new religions and new guidelines about proper ways of living. Naming practices change, which is why Maria bears a popular Roman Catholic name instead of a traditional Mayan name. Roads are built, bringing tourists and businesspeople looking for ways to make a buck. State-run schools bring modern teaching methods, and students learn about such things as the US Declaration of Independence. Maria's children become confused about whether to listen to their teachers or their parents. Agricultural extension agents bring expertise and incentives for producing new crops for export. Political representatives arrive to entice people to join their party and support them in the next election. After the election, a mayor from the capital is assigned to the town by the winners. Property rights are assigned and deeds written up, but community members have never managed their land this way and do not understand how it works. All too soon, opportunistic and well-connected business people from the city find devious ways to take most of the land for themselves. The community rebels, but military personnel show up to defend the property rights now assigned to the interlopers and to generally maintain order.

The new landowners consolidate the land and begin to farm with modern equipment, reducing the need for labor. Food production is already down because of the new emphasis on export crops such as coffee and cotton. Wages for landless day laborers fall and the community descends into poverty. The few local people who still farm their own land must use the rocky soils of the steep slopes that rise above the river valley. Then things really get bad. The nation's need for electricity means the river must be dammed, so the remaining lands and the community itself will soon be under water. Being increasingly poor and powerless, Maria's people become pawns in a bigger game. The government promises to give them better land elsewhere, but once removed from their land and out of the way of progress, they and the promises are forgotten. Even if new land were to be offered, how could it ever replace the sacred land on which their ancestors are buried and which they had seen as their god's gift to them? At some point their anger and their despair lead them to listen to Marxist students from the national university. They tentatively join in some acts of armed rebellion, but the army comes down strong, razing whole communities and indiscriminately killing males between the ages of fifteen and fifty. Their community and way of life gone, their connections to their heritage and to their god broken, husband and father murdered, Maria and her children migrate aimlessly into the city slums, into a world she does not know and whose language she is unable to speak.

Maria and her community never asked for "development," and this is what "development" has brought them: the destruction of people and communities, all with identities, traditions, and functioning cultures. It is the story Chinua Achebe tells in his famous novel *Things Fall Apart*, and it is repeated all across the world, in multiple languages and contexts.

PDT theorists are deeply troubled that massive violence, like the conflict that killed Maria's husband, seems inherent to "development." But even apart from the violence, they do not believe that Northern ways are so obviously better than the traditional ways of the Mayans or any other cultural group. Not only can they find no foundation on which to make such a judgment, but they have many reasons to question whether modernity itself is on its own road to destruction. Focusing as it does on economic growth and individual freedom, "development" has undermined human relationships and broken down communities. It has brought about world wars and countless small wars, making the twentieth century the most violent in history. Science has led people in supposedly developed countries to reject religion, but these detached individuals then search in vain for meaning in consumption, drugs, career achievements, or someplace else that ultimately leads to nowhere but despair. And all this leads them onto what some have called a hedonic treadmill that churns out more and more goods that generate less and less well-being, all the while destroying the planet in the process, not to mention generating weapons of mass destruction that threaten the existence of life itself. For all its bluster and arrogance, the "developed" North is on the road to its own destruction and yet has the audacity to believe it can help the poor by teaching them to live as it does.

The answer that PDT gives to all this is that we must return to a simpler, smaller, more diverse world, one in which communities live in their own geographical locations and learn on their own to live in ecological harmony with it. This is what societies have been doing for millennia, and unless we return to such a "small is beautiful" model, it is hard to see how we can avoid the cataclysm that awaits. To do this, we must all let go of our universal, technology-based, economic-growth– and consumption–oriented model of development. We need a new paradigm of understanding, one that allows for all sorts of diversity at the local level. PDT argues that we must engage in a process of reimagining who we are, how we live in this world, and how we live together cooperatively and in harmony. Instead of people from the rich North telling the poor around the world what to do, we should encourage them to relearn some of their longstanding traditions and ways of life that have been lost to the technological juggernaut of globalizing economic growth.

A common criticism of PDT is its weakness in offering solutions, yet Richard Peet and Elaine Hartwick distill three main ways forward based on the principles of PDT. The first is radical pluralism, which implies greater openness to alternative belief systems and ways of life. The second is simple living, an essential change for everyone if we wish to get back in line with ecological health and sustainability. And the third is a concerted effort to respect distinct cultures, to allow them to flourish, to learn from their wisdom, and to grow in our appreciation of other cultures rather than seeing them as problems to be overcome.[9] All three of these strategies are oriented toward respecting and building up a people's identity within their own cultural context and their geographical place. Because of this strong emphasis on cultural integrity and identity, or being, the representative name for this perspective is Betty Being (see fig. 1.3).

David Korten is one contemporary author who gives clear guidance on how this can be accomplished when the universalizing powers of the North, what he calls "Empire," are so very influential. The way to fight against these powers is to form what Korten calls "people's organizations" with affiliates in every community and every country. These organizations will help people at a local level to support and learn from each other as they recapture their own cultural heritage, thus reestablishing local control over their own lives. To prevent getting overwhelmed by the forces of globalizing empire, these organizations must form global alliances across borders so that similar organizations in Guatemala, Bangladesh, Zambia, and even communities from the North can form a global presence and thus provide alternative developmental paths. New development visions, locally generated but globally supported, will challenge the universalizing and globalizing forces that are part of the empire mentality. Korten calls this alternative "earth community."[10]

What would a postdevelopment perspective mean for Babul and Chabekum? What they would need to do is gather with others in their community, not so much to be a countervailing power against the landowners but to recover their own culture and ways of life and to regain a sense of their own individual and cultural identities. They would search for alternative ways to build lives of meaning and hope outside the structures of domination that modernity brings. As they grow in confidence in their own identity and culture, they would seek alliances with other like-minded people and organizations in nearby communities, in Bangladesh and other nations around the world, and perhaps even with groups that organize and give voice to Mayan women like Maria.[11]

It might appear that there are limited roles here for foreigners. Whatever roles there might be would definitely differ from what most of us have grown up hearing about, because most of what we hear comes out of the modernization perspective. Still, there are definitely some key roles that foreigners can play, especially because global realities have put them in positions of power. Here are some ideas:

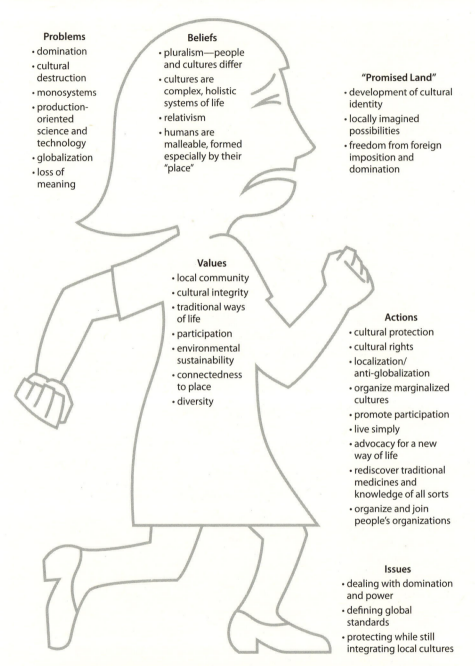

Problems
- domination
- cultural destruction
- monosystems
- production-oriented science and technology
- globalization
- loss of meaning

Beliefs
- pluralism—people and cultures differ
- cultures are complex, holistic systems of life
- relativism
- humans are malleable, formed especially by their "place"

"Promised Land"
- development of cultural identity
- locally imagined possibilities
- freedom from foreign imposition and domination

Values
- local community
- cultural integrity
- traditional ways of life
- participation
- environmental sustainability
- connectedness to place
- diversity

Actions
- cultural protection
- cultural rights
- localization/anti-globalization
- organize marginalized cultures
- promote participation
- live simply
- advocacy for a new way of life
- rediscover traditional medicines and knowledge of all sorts
- organize and join people's organizations

Issues
- dealing with domination and power
- defining global standards
- protecting while still integrating local cultures

Figure 1.3. Betty Being—Betty's overall demeanor is one of sadness for the loss of culture and ways of life. She has witnessed the destructive consequences of development imposed from the outside and sees how many people suffer because of it.

Start by living it yourself. Break away from the destructive patterns of modern life by living simply in your own community and encouraging others to do the same.

Support local, ecologically sound farmers. Buy and eat local foods, encouraging others to do the same. Support local food movements around the world.

Join a local people's organization that learns about living sustainably with your local ecological environment and then puts those ideas into practice locally.

Protest globalization through advocacy but also through your own consumption choices. Be a stewardly consumer.

Join people's groups that support indigenous cultures and indigenous development choices around the globe.

Link up with other such groups around the world to develop a global voice to advocate against multinational companies (e.g., the oil companies that are invading the Amazon region or national dam-building projects that destroy whole regions).

Resist genetically modified foods and support organic crops that have long ecological standing in the areas where they are grown.

Join environmental protection groups.

Support efforts to recover cultural traditions and languages of peoples the world over, including Native American tribes in the United States or cultural affinity groups in developing countries.

The Capabilities Approach—Meet Charles Choosing

When dependency theory, nourished by its Marxist roots, responded to modernization, these two perspectives were seen as polar opposites. But then PDT arose and argued that dependency and modernization are really quite a bit alike after all. Both are different versions of universally applicable economic-growth models based on science and technology. Both suffer delusions of global empire. Emphasizing pluralism and the local, PDT thus presents itself as the polar opposite of both. There was not much room for compromise among any of these three perspectives. Each sees itself as definitively right.

Then along comes the capabilities approach (CA), represented in figure 1.4 by Charles Choosing, with a perspective that actually does try to build on the best insights of all three of these perspectives. It respects economic growth and wealth creation, recognizes the importance of fighting against economically powerful class interests, and also acknowledges the centrality of human identity

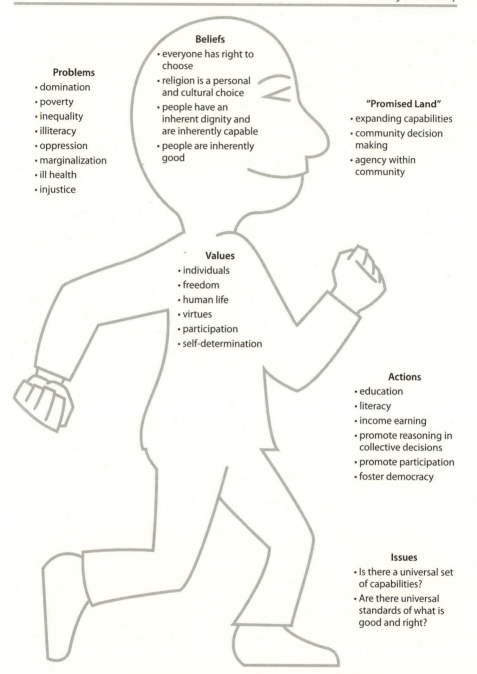

Beliefs
- everyone has right to choose
- religion is a personal and cultural choice
- people have an inherent dignity and are inherently capable
- people are inherently good

Problems
- domination
- poverty
- inequality
- illiteracy
- oppression
- marginalization
- ill health
- injustice

"Promised Land"
- expanding capabilities
- community decision making
- agency within community

Values
- individuals
- freedom
- human life
- virtues
- participation
- self-determination

Actions
- education
- literacy
- income earning
- promote reasoning in collective decisions
- promote participation
- foster democracy

Issues
- Is there a universal set of capabilities?
- Are there universal standards of what is good and right?

Figure 1.4. Charles Choosing—Charles has an overall hopeful outlook because he believes that humans are inherently good. Under the right conditions, they will make good and wise choices about life.

within the context of distinct cultures. This fourth perspective focuses not on economic growth (though economic growth might be necessary), not on the workings of the global system (though dealing with power is important), and not on the sanctity of local and diverse cultures (though life within cultures is part of who we are), but on the importance of allowing people to choose for themselves what kind of life they would like to live. Without imposing on people what their choices should be, the CA asks what conditions allow people to make such choices. If people are really going to choose, or to exercise their freedom, they must be "capable" of choosing. First, they must enjoy the health, education, and self-esteem to be capable of choosing as individuals. Second, the external conditions, such as sufficient income, security, respect of others, and social freedom, must be part of the community's general environment so that individual choices are actually honored and respected.

Consider Babul and Chabekum. They are poor, landless, uneducated, embedded in their own local cultures, and, to different degrees, marginalized and without power in their own society. This is especially true for Chabekum, who as a poor woman is on one of the lowest rungs of the social ladder. The CA asks what kind of life Babul and Chabekum would like to live and whether they are equipped to make the decisions and to take the steps necessary to lead such a life. In this way it focuses on their well-being, their agency, and their ultimate freedom, in the context of their community, to choose their own path in life and to live the way they themselves believe they should. Nobel Prize–winning economist Amartya Sen is among the most well-known proponents of the CA, and he is the author of one of the main CA texts, *Development as Freedom*.[12]

In order to make choices, what people need is basic: life, health, income, education, the respect of others around them, and a safe and secure community within which to exercise their choices. By focusing directly on what individual members of a society are able *to do* and *to be* (these are very important concepts in the CA), the CA avoids some big problems inherent in the other three perspectives.

Modernization emphasizes economic growth, or *having*, and thus finds itself constrained by a narrow view of what humans actually care about. In reality, however, the CA notes that humans really do care about much more than having stuff—relationships, beauty, and meaning, for example. Moreover, a nation may have a growing economy but then spend its income on building military might or monuments instead of health care or education. Economic growth does not directly translate into human well-being. The CA moves beyond a focus on having and asks whether the stuff people have is actually improving their lives.

Dependency theory sees people as embedded in oppressive systems with no obvious mechanism for changing those systems for the better. In the more orthodox forms of DT, human nature is determined by one's location in the system. The more predetermined our existence is, however, the lower the possibility of free choice. The CA, however, is not so pessimistic about our predetermined fates, believing instead that humans have a significant degree of control over their lives. Moreover, human nature is such that people do care about each other and about purposes larger than themselves. This view allows for the possibility that people from powerful countries can choose to exercise their freedom in support of others. It also expects that disempowered people will come to exercise their agency in reasonable ways. The CA has an abiding confidence in people and expects them, in general and over time, to make good and wise choices.

Postdevelopment theory embeds people in cultures and tends toward a relativism that forbids evaluation of customs that are, according to most standards, unacceptable. The suppression of women, political torture, female genital mutilation, and child slavery are among the ways of life that seem acceptable in some cultures, but PDT has little to say about such issues. The CA, on the other hand, allows that while people are clearly formed by their culture, they are themselves also shapers of culture and can exercise their agency as shapers only if they expand their ability to choose through the building up of their capabilities. For example, if Chabekum would like to exercise her voice by organizing for change within her own culture, the CA would definitely allow for this and even expect it.

In the case of Babul and Chabekum, their capabilities would be greatly enhanced if they had higher incomes, had enough nourishment for themselves and their children, received better education, were treated with respect, and were allowed to participate in the decisions of their community such that their voices were heard and respected. Under these conditions, they could start pursuing their own individual dreams of who they want to be and what they want to do, or, more generally, "to lead the kind of lives (they) have reason to value."[13] Their choices shape not only themselves but also their societies and cultures. They contribute to decisions about what kind of economy to have, land ownership patterns, who should go to school, what curriculum should be offered, and other matters of importance to themselves, their family, and their community.

One of the major tools that has arisen in tandem with the CA is the Human Development Index (HDI), assembled and published by the United Nations. Instead of measuring GDP per capita, which has long been a standard development measure of modernizationists, the HDI focuses more on capabilities by including three main items: income (especially for the poorer members of society), literacy, and life expectancy. This is a rough measure, but the idea is that people are more capable if they (1) are alive and healthy, (2) can read, and (3) have income to work with.

For the outsider, the CA once again has a particular set of guidelines regarding how to engage in development work, all of which are oriented toward building up people's capabilities and structuring an environment in which participation is expected and respected. Here are some of the strategies CA supporters might suggest:

Promote education that brings adults and children to a level of knowledge and skill that allows them to feel respected in their own communities.

Train everyone, but especially girls and women, in literacy and numeracy so they can read and understand laws, contracts, news, ideas, proposals, and so on.

Work with locals to ensure basic nourishment and health care.

Assist with income-earning and job-creation strategies, especially those in which the people themselves are brought in as primary decision makers.

Facilitate structures and practices for inclusive community decision making.

Support community groups that empower and educate those who are marginalized and excluded.

Help create secure environments through strategies that promote, for example, conflict resolution and peacebuilding, antitrafficking, and the rule of law and respect for human rights in general.

Beliefs and Values Matter!

All four of the perspectives reviewed here are highly influential in the world of international development. Supporters of each are found the world over, with concentrations in distinct locations and institutions. Modernizationists are especially prominent in international economic institutions such as the World Bank, the International Monetary Fund, and the World Trade Organization, as well as in the governments and intellectual institutions of wealthy countries in the North. They are also prominent in some political, economic, and academic communities in the South.

Dependency theorists have a few outposts here and there in the academic institutions of the North, but they are more prominent in academic institutions and governments of the South. Some global church institutions, like the World Council of Churches, contribute a fair amount of commentary on global affairs that draws on DT.

Postdevelopment theorists are scattered the world over, though I am not aware of an intense concentration anywhere. Anthropologists, ethicists, post-modern academics, and environmentalists are especially drawn to PDT.

One major home of the capabilities approach is the United Nations (its annual Human Development Report works from a CA foundation). Interest is growing among academics and practitioners, and the CA has been gaining in influence in recent years.

A major purpose of this chapter is to show that beliefs, values, and our overall perspective really do matter to the way we work. One's choice of which perspective to adopt has a huge impact on how development work is actually done. The way one addresses poverty—even thinks about poverty—differs greatly depending on which approach is chosen. Take something as simple and common as microenterprise, a development strategy that has spread across the world and that many Christian organizations have adopted as a major part of their programming.[14] In general terms, microenterprise, often associated with microfinance, finds ways to provide small loans to poor individuals so that they can engage in small but nevertheless important income-earning business activities. Depending on which perspective one adopts, microenterprise programs can be shaped accordingly:

Harvey Having would appreciate microenterprise for its income earning potential, for the training in business thinking, and for bringing the poor into the marketplace.

Libby Liberating might support microenterprise activities if they build a competing system to the capitalist marketplace and if they provide the means with which to fight against the oppressive powers.

Betty Being would want microenterprise activities to be locally owned and integrated into local systems of production, trade, and distribution. Locally generated ROSCAS (Rotating Savings and Credit Associations) are one example.

Charles Choosing might appreciate microenterprise for its income potential, but he would also want to use the program to build self-esteem and to improve group skills and capabilities for participating in group decision making. Microenterprise would be a means for capability building at a number of levels.

Finally, a few words of critique on how these perspectives view religion before moving on to a chapter that explicitly brings Christian beliefs and values into the discussion. All four of these views have arisen in contexts that made them hostile to Christianity and other world religions. Modernization and Marxism were products of the Enlightenment, a movement to discover the world's truths through objective science. They were (in some cases quite understandably) trying to overcome and undermine the authority of the church. Modernizationists, for example, in a manner explicitly stated by famed sociologist Max Weber, typically expect that development will result in the progressive secularization of society. As scientific explanations improved and spread, religious explanations relying on the magical and mystical would no longer be tempting to humans. Weber called this the "disenchantment of the world."[15] At best, modernizationists tolerate religion as a set of purely privatized, and essentially irrelevant, beliefs, but not as something that does or should have an impact on the way we live in society.

Marxism and DT have tended to see religion as relevant, but not as having anything to do with truth. Their biggest concern is that religion is used, as Marx himself famously said, as an opiate, a drug that dulls poor people's minds to their oppression and keeps them from understanding the extent to which the rich and powerful exploit them. Any religious beliefs that lead people to accept poverty and oppression in this world undermine motivations to demand systemic change. Every now and then there are times when religion proves useful, as when certain types of liberation theology are used to convince the poor that God cares about justice and wants them to join in the revolutionary cause.

PDT looks at religion differently again. Like modernization and DT, it has no appreciation for a single, universal deity, but it is more than willing to allow people in their own cultures to be spiritual and to develop their own religious stories and orientations and ethics. If religious stories and rituals provide meaning and purpose and functionality, great! Hence PDT honors all religions, but none in particular, and they are especially concerned when believers of any one religion try to push their beliefs and ways of life on others. PDT can be quite hostile to Christianity, but also to Islam and other global religions. Both Christianity and Islam, for example, see themselves as universally valid and encourage proselytizing people from other religions. For PDT, such universal claims are a major violation of the integrity of other cultures and religions.

Finally, similar to PDT, the CA sees religious beliefs as something totally up to the individual in the context of his or her culture. Religion is fine if it helps people cope with life, but the CA takes no explicit position on religion. Of the four perspectives discussed, this may be the least hostile to Christianity. All the others find Christianity to be quite troublesome, especially when it acts to motivate people to apply their Christian beliefs and values in their lives, and even more so when Christians try to convince others to think and behave like they do. For the CA, however, people should be free to choose whichever religion they prefer to follow.

To conclude this chapter, let's remember the Cheshire cat that famously asked Alice where she wanted to go. She did not know, and so the Cheshire cat told her it did not matter what road she took. I hope your awareness is increasing that not all roads lead to the same place and that we should be careful to choose well where we want to go and what road we should take to get there. To help us in this vital set of choices, we turn our attention in the next two chapters to contributions Christians have made to our understanding of international development.

Further Reflection and Action Steps

1. For each of the four perspectives presented in this chapter, identify and explain what you see as its major strength and its most serious weakness.

2. Review the beliefs and values of Harvey, Libby, Betty, and Charles. Explain which of their beliefs and values you agree with completely, reject completely, or find somewhat acceptable.

3. What do you think would be the best way to help Babul and Chabekum? How is your answer based on your own beliefs and values?

For God So Loved the World

Insights on International Development
from Four Christian Traditions

The Spirit of the Lord is on me, because he has anointed me to preach good news to the poor. He has sent me to proclaim freedom for the prisoners and recovery of sight for the blind, to set the oppressed free, to proclaim the year of the Lord's favor.

Jesus in Luke 4:18–19

Let my heart be broken with the things that break the heart of God.

Bob Pierce, raised in the evangelical tradition
and founder of World Vision[1]

Service is a Mennonite tradition. It is part of our DNA. It is not that we talk so much about service; instead, it is lived. Both our parents lived lives of service and they passed that on to us.

Carl and Carolyn Stauffer, with the Mennonite Central Committee in Southern Africa, 1994–2010, now professors at Eastern Mennonite University

Catholic Social Teaching was very much a part of my family when we were growing up. Every Christmas we would get up in the morning and spend the whole day retrieving people from a housing project, spending time with them, and making sure they had food and a good day. Then and only then would we celebrate our own family Christmas. I was always taught that service to the poor should be the primary motivation for what we do.

Christine Bodewes, human rights lawyer

The Reformed tradition taught me to bring calling and vocation together. Who I am before God and how God created me, which is my identity, gives me my purpose in life and tells me why I am here. My vocation has to do with how God gifted me and the talent and skills he has enabled me with. My identity and my vocation give me my calling, which is to be actively engaged in the field of development and actively serving the poor.

Dirk Booy, partnership leader of global field
operations for World Vision International

Jesus Is the Answer, but How?

Shortly after the January 12, 2010, Haiti earthquake, I participated in a panel discussion at a Christian seminary to address the question of what we should do to help. It was my assignment to provide a historical overview of Haiti and then discuss how we might help Haiti get onto a good path of development. Another panelist was a North American missionary who had herself lived through the earthquake. After briefly laying out what I viewed to be Haiti's tragic history and the terrible poverty many Haitians continue to suffer, I said that one major key to Haiti's future would be good governance and that developed nations, our churches, and civic organizations should do what they could to support better governance. As I finished, the obviously disturbed missionary asked for the microphone and denounced my remarks as negative and worldly. "Good governance is not the answer," she said. "Jesus is the answer." Taken aback by this unexpected intervention, and eventually making the point that I thought Jesus actually did care about Haiti's politics, I was nevertheless led once again to think hard about what role Jesus plays in Haiti's development. Most certainly Jesus is centrally involved in the answer, but how? What would Jesus's followers say to Babul and Chabekum if we encountered them in Bangladesh? How would we work with them? In what ways would it be any different than what the secular traditions would offer?

Throughout much of the past century, Christians have often addressed these questions in terms of a dualistic division between soul and body, heaven and earth, the afterlife and the present life. You encounter this division whenever you hear someone suggesting that the important part of any mission work is saving people for eternal life. You may have heard something like the following: "If the work being done and the dollars being spent result in the salvation of only one soul, then it is all worth it." If this view is correct, then Babul and Chabekum need, more than anything else, to come to a saving faith in Jesus Christ. Nothing else really matters in the long run. In addition, if material issues like food and shelter and jobs mattered at all, it would only be as a strategy for getting Babul and Chabekum to come to the Lord.

There is something unsettling about this approach to people in need, first because there is little sense of proportion. Are we really willing to invest all of our savings, all of our efforts, everything we have to save one soul? I have heard people talk this way, but I have not seen anyone really walk the talk. The second and deeper problem is that this approach suggests that the affairs of this world have no intrinsic value of their own. At best, they are hooks to win people for eternal life, or they make life more bearable for God's people as they anticipate an eternity in heaven. It is as if those two thousand verses Rick Warren found are essentially irrelevant. Could it be that God does not really love the world that he created, but only the souls who happen for the moment to be stuck in it? Such a view seems seriously flawed.

So how does all this fit together? First, let me say that there is enough complexity to this question that Christians have wrestled with it for centuries and continue to do so today. Second, I have noticed that all Christian traditions I am familiar with wrestle with this question in their own way and in their own contexts; they wrestled with it yesterday, they continue to think about it today, and it is my guess that it will not go away in the future. That is probably because it addresses such a basic question of life—about what the point of it all really is, why we are here, and what we are supposed to do. As author Steve Garber so poignantly asks young people, "Do you have a *telos* sufficient, personally and publicly, to orient your *praxis* over the course of life?" If his listeners are not sure what this means, he has a quick follow-up: "So what gets you out of bed in the morning?"[2]

There is a third thing I would like to say, which is that all the wrestling going on in these different traditions has yielded a clear winner. Today, Christians from many traditions are moving toward a consensus, which is that it all fits together, it is all important, and we must work on it all at the same time. God wants us to have good food; to live healthy lives; to build fair, just, and dynamic economic systems; to farm wisely; to love the world's environment; and to live together peacefully. This is all part of knowing, loving, trusting, and obeying God. There is no dualism. It is all part of one package.

This needs to be better explained, and to do that I am going to introduce you to four major Christian traditions of thought and practice, especially as they have thought about the part of mission work that since World War II has come to be called development work. Just as with the modernizationists, Marxists, and the other perspectives, the Second World War was a watershed because it was the moment when Christians in the North noticed the world's poverty and knew something had to be done. These four traditions—Roman Catholic, Reformed, Mennonite, and evangelical[3]—have all expanded their interest and their work in international development since the war. In fact, almost all of the most familiar major Christian development organizations— such as Catholic Relief Service, World Vision, World Relief, Church World Service, the Christian Reformed World Relief Committee, Food for the Hungry, Samaritan's Purse, and others—arose during or after World War II. Another well-known Christian organization, the Mennonite Central Committee, began in the 1920s to address the needs of fellow Mennonites around the world, but it did not turn its attention to global development work until 1952.

Each of these traditions has its own highly useful insights and practices, and each also has its own weaknesses. I should take a moment to share with you my own biases: I was born and bred in the Reformed tradition and started teaching at Calvin College, a Reformed institution, in 1983, but I also have great appreciation for the strengths of the other traditions. I married into a Roman Catholic family and did my graduate work in economics at Notre Dame, where I participated in lively discussions on Catholic Social Teaching. I have partnered with Mennonites over the years in development work and scholarly work, and my family attended a Mennonite church for several months in 1979. While living in Costa Rica and Nicaragua in the 1980s and 1990s, we joined evangelical fellowships and worked with students from evangelical colleges.

As I have come to know each of these traditions, I am fascinated by how, on the major questions of engagement in this world, all four traditions are converging toward consensus. While their respective denominational accents remain, and while their differences still make it hard for them to work together, there are nevertheless striking similarities in how they approach international development. As Christians struggle to find their voice in an increasingly secularizing world, it is encouraging to know that the broad Christian church has achieved a measure of unity.

It is impossible in a few pages to give a full, rich, and deep account of each of these four Christian traditions. But by the end of this chapter I hope you have an introductory awareness of the distinct journeys these traditions have followed and still follow, and how these journeys have led to some particular strengths for each. I also hope that whichever Christian tradition you embrace, you find the richness in that tradition while still appreciating and learning from the others.

Four Major Christian Traditions of Faith and International Engagement

Roman Catholicism and Catholic Social Teaching: Solidarity and the Common Good

In the aftermath of the sixteenth-century Reformation and then the more secular Enlightenment of the seventeenth and eighteenth centuries, the formidable political and cultural power of the Roman Catholic Church (RCC) declined precipitously. As a result, the RCC retreated from its involvement in science, politics, economics, and the affairs of this world in general, focusing instead on the Church's role as caretaker of spiritual concerns and the eternal well-being of the soul.

As the RCC withdrew from the world, the world moved on as the Industrial Revolution, new humanistic philosophies, and new political and economic systems all caused seismic shifts in virtually every area of life. With the RCC saying next to nothing about these events, parishioners drifted away from the Church and went looking elsewhere for answers to life's problems. In the latter half of the nineteenth century, capitalism and Marxist socialism, both of which grew out of non-Christian philosophical roots, were gaining many new adherents. In the midst of this roiling European milieu, the RCC decided it was time to reengage.

In 1891 Pope Leo XIII penned a Christian analysis of capitalism and socialism and their underpinning secular philosophies in a papal encyclical called *Rerum Novarum* (*New Things*). He thus initiated a period of reflection and rediscovery in the RCC that brought it back into the thick of world affairs. The Second Vatican Council, convened in 1962, was another watershed in the Church's reengagement with the world. What Leo XIII started in 1891 has come to be called "Catholic Social Teaching," the central message of which is that this is God's world, that God created humans to love and care for what he loves and cares about, and that humans cannot fully know what such love and care are unless they also know God. This means too that we care about the well-being of the whole person, all persons, and every dimension of life. Since 1891, thirteen encyclicals—teaching letters meant to be studied by Catholics everywhere—have called the faithful to a new way of thinking and a new way of life. Two of them, *Populorum Progressio* (*On the Development of Peoples*) in 1967 and *Caritas in Veritate* (*Charity in Truth*) in 2009, are completely dedicated to issues of global development.

Listen to some choice excerpts from these powerful statements:

The hungry nations of the world cry out to the peoples blessed with abundance. And the Church . . . asks each and every man to hear his brother's plea and answer it lovingly.[4]

The world situation requires the concerted effort of everyone, a thorough examination of every facet of the problem—social, economic, cultural and spiritual.[5]

To be authentic, [development] must be well rounded; it must foster the development of each man and of the whole man.[6]

Changes must be made; present conditions must be improved. And the transformations must be permeated with the spirit of the Gospel.[7]

Authentic human development concerns the whole of the person in every single dimension. Without the perspective of eternal life, human progress in this world is denied breathing-space. Enclosed within history, it runs the risk of being reduced to the mere accumulation of wealth.[8]

Testimony to Christ's charity, through works of justice, peace and development, is part and parcel of evangelization, because Jesus Christ, who loves us, is concerned with the whole person.[9]

Notice the emphasis on how the whole human family is a community in which we are all responsible for each other. Notice that every person and every aspect of that person and every facet of that person's life are important. Notice too how humans cannot be expected to understand fully how to live their lives in all this fullness without a connection to Jesus Christ. If we want to understand authentic international development, we must be broad by encompassing all of life, inclusive by engaging all people, and integral by holistically addressing all of this.

In addition to these broad points, Catholic Social Teaching has introduced some powerful concepts into our understanding of international development. Among these are the following:

Human dignity, which reminds us that every human bears God's image and is therefore worthy of great respect.

Solidarity, a way of saying that "we all belong to one human family."[10]

The common good, which is what God calls us all to care about—not just ourselves, but also the interests and good of others. It is our shared vocation, our job, to serve the common good.

Subsidiarity, a helpful idea to establish guidelines for who's responsible for what and for whom. It suggests that the people closest to the action are the ones most responsible for acting so as to bring about the common good. If the people closest to the action cannot or will not respond, then other members of the human family must step in to help.

Preferential option for the poor, meaning that when we evaluate how a particular society is doing developmentally, the people we look at first are the poor. When we evaluate actions, both personal and public, one of our first concerns will be their impact on the poor.

Authentic development, which is a way of thinking about development that goes beyond having stuff, being liberated, respect for cultures, and allowing people to choose. It reminds us of the depth and breadth of human development in its attempt to capture the full meaning of God's plans for us.

Returning now to the sixteenth century, religious and political leaders in Northern Europe were increasingly disenchanted with the power and influence of the RCC. There were many interrelated reasons for this, but among the big ones were the beliefs that (1) the RCC had amassed too much power for itself and was using that power to serve itself rather than God and the people; (2) the RCC had become deeply corrupted on a number of fronts, including the selling of forgiveness; and (3) the RCC had strayed far from Scripture, and its beliefs and behaviors were no longer faithful or biblical. Reformers such as Luther, Calvin, Zwingli, Simons, and many, many others tried first to work through the structures of the RCC to reform it. But RCC leaders resisted, often violently, all overtures toward reform. Because the reformers came to be protected by Northern Europe's political leaders, the die was cast for a long period of religious wars and the birth of what were called the "Protestant" churches.

Though unified in their sharp disagreement with the RCC, the reformers were not agreed on exactly what shape a more faithful church should take. Separated by geographical distance and different theological interpretation, they formed many new church movements instead of just one. Two of the main Reformation leaders, John Calvin and Menno Simons, led their followers in directions that resulted in longstanding, distinct Protestant traditions that spawned insights and practices that bear strongly on the arena of international development.

The Reformed Tradition: "All Things"

John Calvin was one of the main leaders of the French reform movement that ultimately came to be known as the Reformed tradition, while other Reformation traditions took on other names (e.g., Lutheran, Mennonite, and Anglican).[11] The fundamental idea of Reformed thought is that God is the center of everything or, as Calvinists say, God is sovereign. This contrasted with the prevailing practice of the RCC of the day, which seemed to take the position that the RCC itself was sovereign.

It might take a while for the significance of this to sink in, because at first glance this belief does not seem all that distinctive. But for Calvin it was the key to understanding God, the world, and ourselves. It also led to his famous, and highly controversial, views on divine election. For Calvin, there was no other way to see it. Whereas other traditions insist that people must take some action themselves to be "saved," Calvin put the emphasis entirely on God. As John Hesselink says, "It is not *my* conversion, *my* faith, or *my* good life that counts in the last analysis. *God's* goodness and grace and *God's* sovereign will are the bedrock of my salvation. This is why 'in a particularly profound sense Calvinism is theocentric theology. For the Calvinist the doctrine of God is the doctrine of doctrines, in a sense the only doctrine.'"[12]

While the debates over election and predestination have probably yielded enough heat to solve the energy crisis, I do not want to get waylaid by such debates here.[13] Instead, I would prefer to explore the implications of God's sovereignty for how we live in this world and how we work in international development.

One major implication of God's sovereignty is that it extends to absolutely everything. There is nothing that God does not own and does not ultimately control—nothing! Abraham Kuyper is famous for capturing this when he proclaimed that "there is not a square inch in the whole domain of our human existence over which Christ, who is Sovereign over all, does not cry: 'Mine!'"[14] When God sent his son to save the world, it was not just the souls of the Christians that were being saved; it was "the world" (John 3:16–17). Or, as Paul wrote to the Colossians, "He (Christ) is before *all things*, and in him *all things* hold together." And God works through Christ "to reconcile to himself *all things*" (see Col. 1:17, 20; italics added). Such broad, inclusive thinking led to the idea of *holistic development*: it is not just the souls of people, nor just spiritual lives, nor just the church that God cares about, but every part of the world. Embedded in the creation are all things God cares about, including the economy, the family, gender and ethnic relations, politics, religion, ecology, science, technology, medicine, psychology, sexual relations, sports, and everything else you can think of. "In him all things hold together." Everything is included in the word "holistic" because everything is part of the picture and everything is interrelated. Is one thing more important than the other? Not in any obvious way! Everything is important; that includes the spiritual side of life but also the economy, politics, business, family, education, and every other area of life.

A second major implication of God's sovereignty is the way Reformed Christians have come to view the creation-fall-redemption story. God created a good world, which fell into sin, and which God is at work redeeming. When Reformed Christians think about redemption, they have in mind its two sides. One side is to repair and/or heal what is broken, such as responding to pain and suffering of all sorts. The other side comes as a result of the "cultural mandate," by which God called on his image-bearing creatures to fill the earth, subdue it, rule over it, work it, and take care of it.[15] Development then becomes a major aspect of God's redemption, first to take away the pain of brokenness and second to restore the world to the plan God had when he created it. Development is not just about poverty alleviation but about inviting everyone on a journey toward creating an ever-better world, one pictured as a beautiful city in the new creation described in the book of Revelation.

Linking development with redemption has led to the idea of "transformational development," a term defined by Bryant Myers in his now classic treatment of Christian development work, *Walking with the Poor*. Myers uses the term "transformational development" to mean "positive change in the whole of human life, materially, socially, and spiritually," such that our goal in development is to "recover our true identity as human beings created in the image of God and to discover our true vocation as productive stewards, faithfully caring for the world and all the people in it."[16]

If everything is being transformed according to God's redemptive plan, it is worth asking what that plan looks like and how we will know when things are actually improving. That is a hard job and one that requires all of us, from many tribes and nations, to work at discerning. One idea advanced to characterize God's picture of a good society is the biblical one of *shalom*. This is a highly relational concept, one that embraces our relationships with God, with ourselves (our self-concept and identity), with each other, and with creation. The Bible talks of *shalom*, in passages such as Isaiah 65, as being the condition when all these relationships are healed. Discovering what *shalom* looks like and how we can contribute to it is a task that the Lord calls us all to take on.

A final implication of God's sovereignty is that the way we think is also part of God's world. Because all things are fallen, the way we think must also be redeemed. Reformed Christians often talk about "world and life views," and they are particularly sensitive to whether our theories and systems of thought are as good as they could be, and as good as God wants them to be. God gave us hands to work with but also minds to think with. This means we must critically evaluate such views as modernization, Marxism, postdevelopment, and the capabilities approach. Are they helpful? Redemptive? What insights do they have, and what can we learn from them? What aspects are flawed, and what must we ultimately reject?[17]

Mennonites: Service, Advocacy, and Peacebuilding

In my senior seminar class on development, we often read sections from the book *Development to a Different Drummer*, written by three veteran

Mennonite development workers who collect stories from other Mennonite development workers and then analyze them.[18] Even though Mennonites have been involved and influential in development work at the NGO level for a long time through the Mennonite Central Committee (MCC) and Mennonite Economic Development Associates (MEDA), their book is the first attempt to discover and then explain the Mennonite approach to development. That might seem odd, but it is because Mennonites are more engaged in practice than in theorizing, more interested in helping than in talking about it. About 40 percent of the book is stories and reflections of nine Mennonites who work in development. They tell about what motivates them, how they have been involved in development, and what they have learned along the way. Students in the class are quick to pick up on themes that come up again and again—people, relationships, service, discipleship, humility, simplicity. The reason these ideas jump out at students has much to do with who the Mennonites are, a story that begins in the Reformation.[19]

Like other reformers in the sixteenth century, the group that came to be known as Anabaptists ("rebaptizers," due to the fact that they baptized adults even though they had already been baptized as infants) was rereading Scripture too. They found no evidence for infant baptism, for a church body to mediate the relationships between individuals and God, for the seven sacraments as defined by the RCC, for downplaying the importance of Christian living, for state oversight of the church, and especially for any acceptance of violence. Anabaptists argue that these practices began filtering into the life of the church when Constantine's turn toward Christianity led to it becoming the official religion of the Roman Empire. In their efforts to restore the church to God's original intent, the Anabaptists came to believe that the church should baptize only believing adults, emphasize holy and obedient living, separate itself from the control of the state, and choose nonresistance over violence, come what may.

The restored church would be made up of baptized adults who would gather in a believers' community in which everyone would commit to Christ-like living. The Sermon on the Mount and the life of the early church in Acts were especially important guides. The community would provide a context of mutual support, but also one in which individuals would be held accountable to community norms. Adult baptism would bring people into a loving, nurturing, and sharing community, but also one that expected sacrificial giving, a life of service, obedience, and subjection of one's personal decisions to its scrutiny and evaluation. In those days, such a radical redefinition of community and its control threatened political and church leaders connected with the state, and these leaders persecuted the Anabaptists, torturing them mercilessly and martyring thousands.

To really follow Jesus, Anabaptists believed they must withdraw from the world and live in their own supportive communities, a belief and practice only strengthened by all the persecution. As these new communities formed throughout Europe, they emphasized the life practices of true discipleship and developed unique ways of life in their own contexts. Anabaptists see such diversity as normal and good, because each community is expected to discern for itself the plain meaning of Scripture as it applies to the community's own life and context.

One of the most well-known and largest Anabaptist groups is the Mennonites, who get their name from Menno Simons, a sixteenth-century pastor and teacher who shepherded the Dutch Anabaptist movement through some extremely difficult days. The Mennonites are of special interest because, relative to other Anabaptist groups like the Amish and the Hutterites, they have chosen to be more integrated into the rest of the world.

For several centuries the Mennonites worked mostly at maintaining the integrity, not to mention the existence, of their own communities. Then, in the early part of the twentieth century, their commitment to model their lives on Christ's example, on Scripture, and on the New Testament church led them into evangelistic mission and then to minister to a wide range of human suffering, including hunger, disasters, poverty, and conflict. For the Mennonites, it was their experience of serving the poor that led them into development work. As they encountered people in need the world over, they asked the simple question of how Christ would have them show love to the poor. They began preaching the gospel, but soon realized that love required them to address broader issues of human well-being. They were thus led through a historical journey of action and learning that has taken them from church-building missions to relief work in the face of disaster, to community development, to conflict mediation and peacebuilding, and even to advocacy work before governments. It has all evolved from their commitment to live Christlike lives.

There are at least five distinctive contributions that Mennonites have made to Christian involvement in development. First, the Mennonite emphasis on Christlike living has created a *culture of service* that is nurtured in local communities where people learn to care for each other, but that then extends to the whole world. Ann Graber Hershberger's story is representative when she says, "I was raised in a Mennonite farming community and [was] taught that service to others is an expression of faith in Christ."[20] A Mennonite young person once told me that the question for her when she was growing up was not whether she would serve but how and where she would serve.

A second contribution arises out of the Mennonite emphasis on finding joy in *community and simplicity*. Resisting the temptations of wealth and power that this world offers, they have focused more on finding true sources of human happiness, which, as even modern social science is now telling us, are found more in loving and caring relationships than in things. Hence the focus on people and the building of loving and trustful relationships. As our modern materialistic and technological age brings threats of nuclear holocaust and environmental destruction, the Mennonites have kept alive the message of what really matters in life.

These orientations have led the Mennonites, third, to focus more on the *process of development* than on results. It is often more important, for example, to be sure that good relationships are growing, that people are participating in decision making, and that community life is improving, instead of focusing on, say, agricultural yields, income growth, or specific health improvements. Not that these are unimportant, but they must not overrule respect for people, the building of trust, and the ability to work together and care for each other.

A fourth contribution arises out of the Mennonite resistance to being directly involved with governments, especially when governments use coercive power to get their way. Still, their work among the poor has brought Mennonite development workers to see how important government decisions are to people's well-being, so they have developed a practice of *advocacy to the powerful*, whether in government or in business. Mennonites have long been reluctant to embrace power, for they have seen over and over again how corrupting it can be. Instead of taking on positions of power themselves, Mennonites have developed a practice of "speaking truth to power," which is exactly how Christ himself and the early Christians responded to power.

Finally, in the last several decades, Mennonites have come to realize that one of the greatest contributions to development work is the practice of helping people in communities and nations resolve conflicts and establish processes that foster peaceful living. The terms they use to describe this work are "conflict," "transformation," and "peacebuilding." Training programs and graduate programs in these areas have become a major part of Mennonite development work and education programs at Mennonite colleges and universities.

Evangelicals: The Whole Church, the Whole Gospel, the Whole World

Like all Protestant traditions, evangelicals trace their roots back to the Reformation and especially to the revivals in England that led to the creation of Baptist and Methodist churches. What was distinctive about the evangelicals in England and then in other countries around the world was their emphasis on personal conversion, on accepting Jesus Christ as one's personal savior, and on being "born again." They still cared about the well-being of the world, but this would follow the salvation of the soul. Good people would bring about a good society. For example, evangelical churches were in the forefront of the abolition movement, the temperance movement, and many other initiatives to improve society. In evangelical missions, preaching the gospel and "civilizing" or "Christianizing" the whole of society went hand in hand. Today we look back and criticize those efforts, especially the condescending attitudes and practices, but there is no doubt that their focus was on the body as well as the soul. In the early part of the twentieth century, however, evangelical engagement with the world changed dramatically, and the story of the evangelical tradition most relevant to our interest in contemporary international development begins then.[21]

In the late 1800s there arose a tension in the evangelical community between "progressives," who wanted government programs to address social problems arising in new urban centers, and "conservatives," who were concentrated in more rural areas and did not support big social programs. This tension is alive and well in the present day! Back at the turn of the twentieth century, it became a full-blown split when a group of Christians touting the "fundamentals" of faith distanced themselves from the progressives, who were, the new fundamentalists thought, elevating science over traditional scriptural interpretations, questioning the historicity of Jesus and his divinity, subjecting the Bible to scientific criticism, focusing on structural sin instead of personal sin, and generally becoming more interested in the creation of a good society than in winning souls for Christ. The focus of the conservatives turned toward the spiritual well-being of individuals and to personal piety in behavior patterns. They moved even closer to a singular focus on the salvation of individual souls when dispensationalist theology and Pentecostalism rose in popularity. In dispensationalist theology, the world is headed for destruction, so the only thing worth doing is saving souls for eternity. Pentecostalism focuses intently on the spiritual side of life, such that spiritual well-being is considered much more important than physical or social well-being. The term "evangelical" came to be associated with those who focused on one's personal relationship with Jesus, on bringing people to Christ, and on one's assurance of eternal life with Christ.

In what has come to be called "the Great Reversal," the evangelical church lost interest in addressing the needs and problems of this world. All that mattered was preaching the gospel and bringing sinners into a saving faith in Jesus Christ. The post–World War II split of the world into the democratic capitalist West and the Marxist communist East only strengthened this trend. From the 1950s through the 1980s, and to some extent even up to the present, to be

overly interested in social programs, especially the sort that required government involvement, was to risk being called a socialist and to be linked with
what was thought of as godless communism. Evangelicals thus concentrated
on preaching the gospel, and people the world over responded. Evangelical
churches, often with a Pentecostal style, sprouted here, there, and everywhere,
and they grew and expanded with such spiritual vivacity that the face of global
Christianity is no longer the Caucasian Western face but the faces of people
from all across the developing world.[22]

As all this unfolded, many evangelicals—including such well-known leaders
from the North as Carl Henry, Billy Graham, and John Stott, and from the
South, Samuel Escobar, Melba Maggay, and René Padilla—found it troubling
that their tradition was turning a blind eye to the world's social problems. Over
time, what has gradually, if painstakingly, come about is a reversal of "the
Great Reversal." One of the major milestones on this journey has been the
Lausanne Movement, which began with a 1974 global conference in Switzerland that brought together 2,700 people from 150 nations to discuss the global
mission of the Christian church, especially in light of global poverty. Out of
this conference came the Lausanne Covenant, a statement that continues to
serve as a guiding star in the global evangelical sky.[23]

Here is one of the key passages (paragraph 6) from the Covenant: "In the
Church's mission of sacrificial service evangelism is primary. World evangelization requires the whole Church to take the whole gospel to the whole world.
The Church is at the very centre of God's cosmic purpose and is his appointed
means of spreading the gospel. But a church which preaches the cross must
itself be marked by the cross."

This message of the whole church taking the whole gospel to the whole
world has continued to resonate with the evangelical community, and there
is now no shortage of books and articles that make the point that the biblical story is not dualistic but a story of wholeness and completeness. One
recent example is a book by Richard Stearns, president of World Vision US,
tellingly titled *The Hole in Our Gospel*. After growing up in an evangelical
culture that taught him that preaching the gospel meant getting people to
say the sinner's prayer and thus be saved for life in the next world, Stearns
recounts how his encounters with the world's poor and a fresh reading of
the Bible brought him to see that he had ignored the Bible's emphasis on
life here and now. Thus the hole in his gospel. He shares with his readers
how he came to understand that being Christian "entails a public and transforming relationship with the world," which means that "God asks us for
everything . . . a total life commitment" and "to be His partners in changing
our world."[24]

As with the other traditions, there is so much more that could, and should, be said, but we'll end by stating the great contribution the evangelical tradition has made to the Christian efforts to promote global development—namely, keeping the *spiritual side of life* front and center. When confronted with a world situation in which all other aspects of life might seem more important, the evangelicals have stood firm in saying that the spiritual side of life, including the verbal and oral proclamation of the gospel message itself, can never be forgotten or ignored. We must not limit ourselves to working on physical health; we must also understand our inherent connectedness to the Father, the Son, and the Holy Spirit.

As an extension of their emphasis on the spiritual, evangelicals have insisted that local churches, meaning communities of believers who meet regularly to worship and pray, must be at the center of our development work, because it is the message of Christ and our response to his atoning death that is the heart of our human identity. If we are to fully understand and act upon our true identity as people saved by Christ's blood, then it is essential that the church and its myriad local church fellowships be centrally involved.

Four Traditions: Temptations and Weaknesses

In Brian McLaren's book *A Generous Orthodoxy*, he admonishes us time and again that we must beware of the arrogance that arises if and when we come to believe that we have achieved a reasonably complete and accurate understanding of the way things are. When that happens we become self-assured and judgmental. Throughout history, such certainty has combined with power to usher in dark periods of condemnation, imposition, and coercion. It is not pretty, and certainly not very Christlike. Rather than pointing out where others are wrong, McLaren looks for the strengths in different Christian traditions. That is what I have tried to do here by identifying the strengths of four major Christian traditions and how they engage in broad global mission. The apostle Paul asks us to do something like this in Philippians 4:8 when he tells us to think about what is true, noble, right, pure, and lovely.

That does not mean there are no dangers, challenges, or shortcomings in these traditions, but we will not be well served by focusing on them overmuch. Yes, the Roman Catholics have at times been corrupted by their power and hindered by their hierarchical church structure. Reformed Christians, for all their talk about transforming the whole world, all too often end up being transformed themselves by the world around them; it turns out that accommodation is a much easier path to take than transformation. Mennonites, because of their fear of power and their reluctance to work with governments, stay focused on small issues, and though they might "speak truth to power," they often leave it to others to get directly involved in politics. Evangelicals, with all their focus on the spiritual, continue to agonize and disagree over the proper place of social action in their lives and ministries. And all four traditions struggle periodically with arrogance and insularity, defending their own views and actions against critiques, and have difficulty learning from others and resisting the temptations inherent in their own traditions.

One final note about the traditions: Just because I highlighted evangelism and the spiritual side of life in the evangelical tradition, service in the Mennonite tradition, redemption in the Reformed tradition, and the global family in the Roman Catholic tradition does not mean that these features are absent from the other traditions. In fact, all four traditions have ethics of service, and all believe in God's redeeming purpose for this world, that evangelism is important, and that we are all God's children and hence in the same human family. Still, I find it helpful to know what each tradition has emphasized and what its particular strengths are. Without going into detail about it, the simple point is that there is crossover in the traditions and they do listen to each other and learn, even though there are times in their histories when they have trouble admitting that.

So Where Does This Leave Us?

We have reviewed four distinct Christian traditions as they address international development, and though they have different histories and have faced different challenges and temptations, it is striking that in the twenty-first century they are all converging to a similar perspective on what development is and how we should do development work. In the next chapter I will distill some of these main consensus views and lay out some of their implications for the work we do. This foundation will allow us to critique the secular development traditions reviewed in chapter 1, as well as lay some groundwork that I hope you can use to find your own vocational path in international development.

Further Reflection and Action Steps

1. Think of a Christian organization that addresses global poverty and then check its website to see when it was founded. If there is a history section, see if it discusses how the organization's sense of mission changed over the years.

2. What tradition of Christianity have you had the most contact with throughout your life? What did your church teach you about the proper role of Christians in global affairs? Make a list of the strengths and weaknesses of the training you received from your church and compare that with others in your group.

3. The overview of the four traditions in this chapter is much too brief. Still, is there something here that surprises, pleases, or disturbs you about one or some of these traditions?

4. Do a Google search for NGOs that come from a particular Christian tradition. For example, type "Catholic NGOs in the USA" in the search window. Find an organization, go to its website, and see if you can discern their motivating theology. Do the same with some secular NGOs. Are the differences obvious? Discuss what you find with others doing the same exercise and evaluate the organizations you have researched.

3

Common Ground

Basic Principles for Working in Development

Through their own distinct and unique histories, the four Christian traditions reviewed in chapter 2 arrived at the consensus view that God cares about souls, bodies, families, communities, the environment—basically the whole world, everything he created. Chapter 3 distills the contributions of these distinct traditions into a general Christian perspective on international development. This general Christian perspective is presented as ten foundational principles, each of which directly influences the way development work is done. The chapter culminates in the introduction of Tanya Transforming. Tanya is then pictured in a conversation with our four friends from chapter 1 to talk things over, to explain how she would view Babul's and Chabekum's situation, and to suggest what she would do about it.

Principle 1: Development Is about Transformation

> One of the joys in my work is when I see someone go through the transformation of developing convictions about addressing global poverty and then putting their new convictions into action.
>
> Jason Fileta, national coordinator for the Micah Challenge

The world today is not the way it is supposed to be. Sixteen thousand children die every day from hunger-related causes.[1] Over a million children are trafficked every year.[2] Millions have died over the last ten years in the conflict in the Democratic Republic of Congo.[3] This kind of list could go on for a long time: unemployment, immigration conflicts, stolen elections, racism, HIV/AIDS, crime, and on and on. In stark opposition to such horrors, Christians envision a different world, one referred to as "the common good," *shalom*, or the "whole gospel." In this world, brokenness is repaired and the beauty and glory of God's world is restored. Transitioning from the way the world is to the way it ought to be is sometimes known as "reconciliation," as in, God "reconciling the world to himself" (2 Cor. 5:19), but is also frequently referred to as "transformation." This vision of transformation is prominent in all major Christian traditions.

The idea of transformation is not all that special in and of itself, especially if we take it to mean something as basic as constructive change. What is distinctive about the Christian view of transformation is that the change envisioned is not one that we can imagine all by ourselves. Instead, we are trying to get on board with God and his vision for what the world should be like. Instead of asking what kind of world *we* want, we ask what kind of world *God* wants, and then we hope to work alongside him in realizing it.[4] In a general way, Scripture is reasonably clear about what kind of world that is: justice and peace will kiss (Ps. 85:10); the wolf will dwell with the lamb (Isa. 11:6); nations will no longer train for war (Isa. 2:4); good news is preached to the poor, prisoners are freed, the oppressed are released, the blind see, and the year of the Lord's favor is proclaimed (Luke 4:18–19).

It is one thing to claim this vision as an ideal, but to think we are supposed to help make it happen is incredibly daunting. First, as we learn in the opening verses of Romans 12, the vision does not conform to this world, so it is hard to get our minds around it. Second, beyond catching this ideal vision, we must wrestle with the fact that God's ways of achieving it, such as forgiving people who harm us and loving our enemy, are very hard for us to carry out and seemingly self-defeating. Like many of the Jews in Jesus's day, we do not want Jesus on the cross; we want action, power, and dominating force. Third, again from Romans 12, we must keep in mind our own need to be transformed and renewed, so that we can actually do what God wants us to do. This is the point Jason Fileta makes in his quotation at the beginning of this section.

We must admit, then, that our mission is essentially impossible. We are too finite, too weak, too shallow, too small, and too sinful even to really catch the vision, let alone actually live the way Jesus seems to want us to live. When we get down to specifics, we realize how hard it is. Just consider the arguments Christians have about these matters:

Jesus says we should help the poor, but doesn't helping poor people create dependency?

Jesus says we should turn the other cheek, but did he really mean that literally?

The environment seems to be imperiled, but what if global warming is a hoax?

Some say rich North Americans should give more foreign aid to poor countries, but what about those new books that say foreign aid actually hurts developing nations?

What role should the government play? Many argue for a major role, while others believe we must rely on the free market.

Most of us have been in such conversations, and they can easily lead to despair. Better to not talk about these things. It is too hard. In many churches today, we talk about how Jesus is the answer, but if someone says we ought really to do thus and so, it gets so controversial that it is just easier to let it go. We retreat into the comfort of platitudes.

We must find a way to get past this, to embrace the controversies, meet the challenges, and take up the mission. *The Hobbit* and the *Lord of the Rings* series by J. R. R. Tolkien tell a wonderful story of how the smallest and weakest beings in Middle-earth, the hobbits, also called halflings, actually do make a difference against insurmountable odds. In the movie version, as the hobbits Frodo and Samwise make their final push to Mount Doom, Gimli the dwarf responds to the call to battle with these memorable lines: "Certainty of death. Small chance of success. What are we waiting for?" The hobbits and Gimli have captured the idea that the task of transformation is not primarily about them. Still, they are in the story, and at this particular moment in history they have a role to play. The task of transformation is very hard, but it is the mission to which God calls us.

Here is another complicating factor: our talk of transformation often leads us to take an "I'm OK; you're not" perspective, meaning that someone other than ourselves needs to be transformed. We are very quick to blame others for what is wrong. Remember how neither Adam ("it's the woman") nor Eve ("it's the snake") took responsibility for their actions? How can we hope to remove the speck from the eyes of others if we do not even realize we have logs sticking out of our own eyes? If we are really going to work toward a transformed world, we will have to approach our task with a balance of conviction and humility. We will need to work with other finite, weak, small, and sinful people the world over to translate the vision of *shalom* into what it means here and now. We must then figure out how to work together, under God, in our efforts to make progress. As we join in the task, we must cope with cultural diversity, multiple languages, and power relations, let alone the forces of darkness that try to undermine our efforts at every turn. If transformation is the goal, and if we really want to be on God's side, then we must take care to negotiate these difficult issues with tenacity, charity, and humility. We might fail to see many fruits of our actions as quickly as we would like, and we might even die—but we have joined up with a loving and just God who will not fail.

What are we waiting for?

Principle 2: God Calls Everyone to the Task

> Development is not about doing the work yourself but about learning to value other people and other ways of doing things. We must allow other people to lead the process. We are there working with them, together, as partners.
>
> Carl and Carolyn Stauffer, who worked for many years with the Mennonite Central Committee, mostly in Southern Africa

Sometimes we joke about people who "want to change the world," as if they are naive or silly. Yet that is exactly what God calls all of us to do. Remember Gary Haugen's ringing challenge to us from the introduction, when he reminds us that we are God's plan to stop such terrible evils as the enslavement of girls and women in brothels? Here is how it works: at the same time that God reconciles us to himself through Christ, he also puts us to work by assigning to us "the ministry of reconciliation" (2 Cor. 5:18). This is a pretty big assignment.

That does not mean God ultimately depends on us, but he does want us to work alongside him. C. S. Lewis explains this well in *Prince Caspian*. At one point in the book, Lucy sees Aslan standing on a side path and believes he wants her and her companions to follow him. But she doubts herself, and the others doubt her. They argue, continue down the path of their own choosing, and get lost. Later on, Aslan tells Lucy that it would have been easier to win the victory had she followed him, and that it will now be harder and more costly, but the victory will be won nevertheless. God will not fail us or the world he created, even if we often fail him.

How about you? Have you "seen Aslan"? Do you know what path God would lead you down? To help you reflect on this, let's think further about the ideas of "calling" and "vocation." In their Latin origins, both words have essentially the same meaning, which often confuses us. Too often we think of our calling or vocation as our jobs, which is only a part of the meaning. Scholars who study this question say that the Bible speaks of vocation and calling in both a general way and a specific way. As Douglas Schuurman says, the general call is the one "to become a member of the people of God and to take up the duties that pertain to that membership. . . . The second meaning is God's diverse and particular callings . . . to places of responsibility within the covenant community or the broader society."[5]

Notice that God calls everyone to join with him in the overall mission. For Pope Benedict XVI this general idea of vocation links directly with global development: "Integral human development is primarily a vocation, and therefore it involves a free assumption of responsibility in solidarity on the part of everyone."[6] Like leaders from other Christian traditions, the pope emphasizes that no one is exempt from the call to promote human development across the globe.

Each of us also has a specific vocation or calling. Once we respond to the general call to join the team, we must then discern the specific position God would like us to take. To follow Haugen's language, if we are God's plan, what exactly will each of us do? Will we play frontline roles or supporting roles?

One major implication of the fact that everyone is called to this great task is that it is to be a community effort. None of us is a lone ranger, riding in on a white horse to save the town single-handedly. Instead, we take up a particular task consistent with our abilities, our passions, and the needs of the world, and we work on a team with others who have different roles. Also on the team are some who are easy to exclude or forget about—namely, those who are trafficked, marginalized, oppressed, sent away, or poor. We must take pains to include them.

If the mission is carried out by a team, and if everyone is called to be on that team, then participation and partnership necessarily become standard practices of our work. As the Stauffers remind us, if everyone is to live out their dignity in the exercise of their callings, we must all be given room to participate, everyone's voice and involvement must be respected, and we must work together as partners in mission.

Principle 3: Our General Calling Is Wide

Take a look at 2 Thessalonians 1:11. God gives us the boundaries of the playing field, but then we use our own gifts and experiences to fulfill our every good purpose, prompted by our faith. What God expects of us is not all that detailed.

We are called to exercise our agency, but the field is wide open. If we are faithful, God will bless what we do.

Dana Bates, founder of New Horizons Foundation Romania

Our calling extends across the whole horizon of God's world, as far as the East is from the West. Think of this as the horizontal principle. A few years ago at our church fellowship in Nicaragua, a guest pastor started off his sermon with a question: "How many of you are missionaries?" About a third of us raised our hands. He then asked us a very probing follow-up: "Why didn't all of you raise your hands?" As his message unfolded, he reminded the businesspeople, the teachers, the government workers, the medical professionals, the farmers, and everyone else that we are all missionaries. This mission is not limited to proclaiming the good news and bringing people into the church, though that is a part of it. The broad mission is about bringing the transforming light and love of God into every corner. God cares about every area of our life in society, and he wants life for everyone to be good. Every area of life needs to be transformed. He wants the blind to see, the lame to walk, the hungry to have enough to eat, the oppressed to be liberated, the homeless to have homes, the creation to be enjoyed and cared for, the nations to be discipled, the sick to get well, the conflict-ridden to find peace.

God's ambassadors of reconciliation are thus called to many and diverse tasks. God calls people to join the mission of transformation in agriculture, business, finance, creation care, church development, education, spiritual formation, information technology, human rights, law and justice systems, health, economic policy, diet and nutrition, housing, music and the arts, governance, transportation, urban planning, peacebuilding, family counseling, earth science, civil society, forestry, and water systems. Look more closely into any one of these fields and you find multiple specialties and needs within each one. Education, for example, would have specialties in school-based child education or adult education, basic literacy training or graduate education, and teaching or administration, to mention only a few. All of these enter into human development and all require people who are knowledgeable, capable, and committed to the mission of transformation.

For many of us, our stock image of a missionary is someone working overseas to bring people to Christ and/or to plant churches. This image itself needs to be transformed into something much bigger. We need to fuse our images of missionaries and development workers. To summarize, God calls us to work as missionaries in all of life's arenas. Some may be sent to the front lines, and most of this book is oriented toward helping young people called to frontline positions prepare themselves for the work. Still, as Pope Benedict XVI says, the general call is for everyone, so everyone needs to be in tune with the global ministry of reconciliation, being transformative influences in their own specific vocations and also supporting their brothers and sisters in direct global service.

Principle 4: Our General Calling Is Deep

In part, my mission is to care for widows and orphans, which is why I love working in Washington, DC, for USAID. Yes, working far away from where the projects are implemented can be hard, and finding your own impact is difficult. But in this job I am not only involved in helping others around the world; I can also live out my faith in this secular organizational context.

Hannah Marsh, liaison specialist at USAID

If principle 3 can be thought of as horizontal, then the idea of depth puts us into a vertical mode. Consider again the field of education. The primary recipient of education is the student. Yet any student's success in learning depends on so much else. For example, student performance depends on family support, teachers, the curriculum, the school building, the administration of the school, college programs that train teachers, and state and national government authorities that regulate and finance education. Quality education for students involves transformational work at all these levels.

Another example is food production in developing countries. Farmers are of course main players, but there are many others too. Farmers rely on businesses that produce and provide seeds, fertilizer, and equipment. They also need to know what land is theirs to farm, which requires governing authorities that define and defend rights to land and water. Turning crops into marketed food requires adequate roads and transportation systems, marketing systems, regulation of the marketplace, and quality and health standards. We are just getting started. National policies and laws often affect food markets. Agricultural policies, such as the ways the United States, Canada, and Europe support their own farmers, have major impacts on farmers in developing countries. Loans from the World Bank, global trade rules overseen by the World Trade Organization, and hunger programs sponsored by the United Nations are all relevant. When hunger strikes, the underlying cause might be at any one of these levels. At which level should we be working? By now you know that the answer is, "at every one."

Look back at Hannah Marsh's opening comment about her work at USAID. The fact that she is not in the field and close to the frontline activities does nothing to diminish the important role she plays.

Principle 5: Development Work Is Holistic

Professor of development Ndunge Kiiti was a development worker in Africa in the 1980s when the HIV/AIDS epidemic was just beginning. For Kiiti, the HIV/AIDS crisis provides ample evidence that development work must be holistic. Kiiti says that

> at first everyone was in denial. Then there were efforts to address the disease from a physical, medical perspective only. I soon realized that we needed to get the church involved, which increasingly led me to see that we have to address HIV/AIDS from a holistic perspective; otherwise we are in a losing battle. There were aspects of community, interpersonal relationships, and faith, in addition to national policies and social, political, and economic structures, all of which were of major importance in responding to HIV/AIDS. This crisis helped me see how holistic all of development really is.

We often hear these days that mission work, or development work done by Christian agencies, must be holistic. A simple formal definition of holistic is "emphasizing the organic or functional relation between parts and the whole."[7] The focal point is the "whole," but every whole is made up of individual parts, each of which plays a crucial role in making the whole what it is. For example, a car is useful for providing transportation, but cars are made up of many parts that do not on their own have much meaning or purpose, except that they are part of a car. Without the other parts, most car parts would be pretty useless, though some might serve acceptably well as boat anchors. There is a beautiful description of a holistic entity in 1 Corinthians 12:12–30, a passage that compares the body of Christ to a real human body. Just as the eyes and ears and hands of a human body are distinct, so too the healers and administrators and helpers and apostles of the body of Christ are all distinct. And yet all are parts of the body. It is the body that is important.

In Christian mission and development circles, the word "holistic" was initially used to help us recover from the dualistic tendency to separate the saving of souls from efforts to improve physical or social parts of our lives. For a long time, Christian mission was largely divided between soul-saving evangelism and what was typically called "social action." Some Christians talked about "word" versus "deed" ministries. Long a point of major contention in the Christian mission community, the major Christian traditions now increasingly accept that the spiritual side of life and the physical side of life make up an inseparable whole. Missions professors James Engel and William Dyrness make this point when they say "the reign of Christ demands biblical holism, which restores the unity . . . between evangelism and social transformation."[8]

The split between soul saving and social action was manifested not only in thought patterns and mission strategies; it also had an institutional character. Many church bodies developed "mission" agencies that focused almost completely on saving souls. Other Christians believed God wanted them to fight against poverty, which led to the creation of Christian social action agencies. There arose an uneasy division, with Christians in either type of agency having a hard time respecting those from the other, let alone working with each other. This unfortunate division is now healing, and as the Christian community as a whole becomes more accepting of the idea of holistic ministry, church bodies are finding ways to unify their ministries in holistically structured institutional bodies, perhaps with a name like "global ministries." Likewise, development organizations that initially focused on physical needs, such as Food for the Hungry and World Vision, increasingly integrate spiritual matters into their work.

This has been a welcome change (a transformation actually), but it does not go far enough. It is still too limiting to divide the human "whole" into only two parts, spiritual and other. Certainly we are spiritual beings, but we are also social, economic, artistic, emotional, political, intellectual, cultural, environmental, and biological beings. God made us all these things. The breadth of our holistic identities is important, because all these aspects of our lives work together in systemic, holistic ways.

In *Walking with the Poor*, Bryant Myers explains how to engage in holistic development. When discussing the place of the spiritual in our lives and as part of our developmental mission, Myers says the following: "For the Christian development worker . . . there can be no practice of transformational development that is Christian unless somewhere, in some form, people are hearing the good news of *the gospel* and being given a chance to respond."[9]

Part of the good news of the gospel is the story itself, which we would do well to come to know, believe, and follow. Myers is right that telling the story of the gospel is what we might call a *sine qua non* ("without which not") of development work, though knowing when and how to tell the story wisely and effectively are important issues. I would like to expand on Myers's statement to illustrate the holistic character of the gospel message. Telling the story is not the only *sine qua non* embedded in the whole gospel message. Read the sentence again, but this time replace "*the gospel*" with the terms and phrases that follow. "For the Christian development worker . . . there can be no practice of transformational development that is Christian unless somewhere, in some form, people are hearing the good news of *the gospel* and being given a chance to respond."

peacebuilding
economic well-being
political harmony
respectful gender relations
wise parenting
physical health
environmental stewardship
unity amidst ethnic and cultural diversity

Myers's sentence would be just as true with any of these alternatives, a point that Myers argues throughout his book. Even so, because our tendency toward dualistic thinking is so strong, it seems wise to spell it out. All of these aspects of life are part of a full life as God wants us to live it. We need to recognize that there are more than just two aspects of life that need to be holistically integrated with each other. Yes, spiritual aspects permeate the entire list above. But environmental stewardship permeates all other areas too. Every area of life is integrally and holistically united to all the others. The gospel message is not fully expressed unless all these elements are present.

There are several practical implications of such a holistic vision for working in development. One is that we need to think in terms of systems instead of single issues or causes. As Jeffrey Sachs says in his book *The End of Poverty*, many diseases manifest themselves in similar ways: fever, weakness, and pain, for example.[10] There can be many causes for these outward symptoms, and it takes the analysis of a trained physician to narrow down the list of possible causes and prescribe treatment. Poverty too is like a disease that can have many contributing and interrelated causes. If development workers assume that poverty always has the same single cause, whether lack of education, harmful cultural practices, poor government policies, or oppressive international structures, their abilities to diagnose and really help are seriously undermined. Going into any situation with just one idea or tool would be like a builder whose only tool is a hammer or a doctor who prescribes aspirin for every malady. A holistic understanding requires a broader mind and a variety of tools.

Another implication of this holistic vision is that development work requires some people who are trained to know how the whole system works, how such systems break down, what tools can be used to remedy the breakdowns, and how to use them. There is a thus a need for generalists who have a sense of the big picture and specialists trained in particular fields. This means that development work is best done in teams. A good example of this comes out of my experience in Nicaragua, where I worked for two years in partnership with a Nicaraguan organization called Acción Médica Cristiana (Christian Medical Action, or AMC for short). AMC was born in the 1980s with a primarily medical orientation for the simple reasons that its founders were medical professionals and there were serious health needs all around them. But experience quickly taught them that they also needed help from agriculturalists to advise how to grow more and better food, social workers to address community relational dynamics, pastors to address issues of spiritual growth, business people to help their communities produce and market better products, dieticians to work with the women learn to prepare nutritious food, and statisticians to help them evaluate their programs.

Finally, we must never forget that the people from the local community are among the most important members of the team. They may not have specialized technical knowledge, but they know their own communities in ways outsiders never will. Moreover, their energy, motivation, and involvement are vital to any successful development venture. A good place to start in working with a community is to discover what the people themselves want to work on, what resources (or assets) the community already has within it, and what they themselves believe needs to be addressed. If your training and wisdom lead you to think that the first priority in the community should be sanitation (e.g., latrines and clean water), but the community wants to put its energy into building a community center, you should almost certainly join in their efforts to build the center. At a later time their interests will undoubtedly turn to health and sanitation issues, perhaps a consequence of a community center where they can gather and talk about the health of their children. To think of development holistically requires a systemic approach that takes account of the wide variety of fields that make up our lives but that also brings in all the people who themselves are important parts of the system.

Principle 6: We Are All in Need of Development

When I started working with Bread for the World, I thought United States Christians would agree with our overall goals. I didn't think it would be an issue for Christians whether people should be able to eat or not. But I learned that this is an issue with church people, and I just find this astounding.

Sarah Rohrer, field organizer with Bread for the World

We cannot do good development work if we ourselves are not transformed. How can we help others be transformed if we are not being transformed ourselves? We have to look at ourselves and understand ourselves and recognize that transformation must begin with us. It is a very spiritual process.

Roland Vanderburg, program director for CAUSE Canada

A serious mistake we often make is to think that development is only about what happens "over there," in those other countries where people are poor and have all those other associated problems. Making this mistake leads us to believe that our mission is to teach "those people" how to live better. There may be a grain of truth to the idea that we have something to teach, but it is wrapped up in some harmful misconceptions, one being that other people do not really know much, and another being that North Americans and Western Europeans have it pretty much all figured out. When people from rich and poor countries actually spend time with each other, they soon learn that the others are capable, that their own knowledge and skills are not as advanced or as applicable as they thought they were, and that development work is more about working, sharing, learning, and implementing together than it is about teaching.

Doug Seebeck, executive director of Partners Worldwide, highlights this lesson in his recollections of an experience in Guatemala.

All the time I hear people say that we have to teach people how to fish instead of giving them fish. But this little mantra is false. People know how to fish. Poor people are talented and we must work with them the same way we think about ourselves. We ask how God has made us, how he has gifted us, and what he wants us to do. As for me, it is my dream to follow God in all this. But that is exactly the same dream that many poor people have. Here is a little example from Guatemala: We were in a slum and saw a big box, in a training center, filled with plastic pop bottles stuffed with paper. Young people were collecting them. Some Americans with us said: "Look at this. What is this about?" They said, "Oh, they probably do not know how to squash these bottles." One in our group said: "They do not know how to recycle because they do not know how to separate. We will teach them how to do that." Finally, someone else said, "No, you do not spend all this time pushing paper in these bottles without knowing what you are doing." So when we had the chance, we asked. We learned that they have this new block press that saves on cement by creating a big hollow space in the block. It is cheaper that way. Then you put the pop bottles in the hollow space as an insulation to keep the house warm. Furthermore, if there's an earthquake, the block wall acts like an airbag. Instead of heavy blocks falling, you have all these plastic bottles fall on you. That is what it was. Obviously, the people knew what they were doing. We did not need to teach them; we needed to learn how to work together.

Doug's group was wrestling with what Bryant Myers and others have called "god complexes," a condition that makes rich people from the North think they are the saviors, or the teachers, of the poor in the South. Not only are the poor more capable than we often give them credit for, but "developed nations" are not as advanced as many think they are. Consider some of the challenges rich countries face—homelessness, drug use, family breakdown, abortion, racism, rising inequality, failing schools, government debt, and polarized politics—and you realize things here are not as put together as we might imagine. In addition, as people from the North realize when they come into close contact with people from the South, we have a lot to learn about happiness, family, pacing in life, materialism, relationships, and our own pride. As we encounter others and get to know them in the context of their own cultures, we begin to comprehend Paul's advice to the Philippians: "in humility value others above yourselves" (Phil. 2:3).

Individuals, communities, and nations of the South are in need of transformation, as are individuals, communities, and nations in the North. We should also recognize that the way we all interact with each other, especially through the structures we set up to manage those interactions, is likewise in great need of transformation. Many of today's life challenges are not confined to local situations but are global in scope; what we do in one place affects people elsewhere. Such is the state of our global interdependence. Take, for example, the problem of illegal drugs. In the North, we struggle with drug use and its impacts on families and neighborhoods. For the countries supplying the drugs to North American markets, the problems involve drug cartels, government corruption, and horrific violence. Whole societies in the South, including their economies, politics, and social dynamics, are seriously distorted by the demand for drugs and the drug-related policies of the North. In this context it does not make much sense to act as if government corruption is a problem "they" must solve on their own. It would make more sense to collaborate on a global scale instead of addressing isolated symptoms in local communities.

There are plenty of other such issues, including legal and illegal immigration, ocean fishing, global warming, terrorism, international trade and finance, debt crises, population growth and environmental sustainability, small-arms sales, and human trafficking. To look at one more example, US markets in financial derivatives almost brought the global economy to its knees, endangering people the world over. The structures that we institute to manage such financial matters, as well as those that manage our relationships in other areas of our lives, are increasingly global. To address such issues honestly and transformationally, we must be willing to evaluate and transform such structures.

Consider now the more spiritual aspect of how we live as individuals in relationship to others, of our sense of being a global human family. Imagine being raised in a family where you personally get enough to eat every day, attend school, receive good health care, and generally feel loved and cared for. Imagine now that you have a brother or sister living in the same home, right beside you, who is offered none of the above. You live well, at least in a physical sense, while right beside you is your sister who is malnourished, poorly educated, unhealthy, and unloved. How would you feel about that? Could you accept this reality and do nothing to change it? I trust that you find this situation absolutely unacceptable, and you should. Clearly your deprived sister is in need of development, but if you closed your heart to her and did not do what you could to change things, wouldn't you be in need of some major transformation too, of a spiritual sort? Kind of like 1 John 3:17: "If anyone has material possessions and sees his brother or sister in need but has no pity on them, how can the love of God be in that person?"

Extend this thought experiment to a global level. If we are all God's children, and if he loves us all, then for the rich to accept the fact that others are poor and deprived but to do nothing about it is as wrong and distorted as doing nothing when impoverished siblings are seated right beside us in our own home. That is a pretty big spiritual problem, yet this is what Sarah Rohrer of Bread for World encountered in all too many North American churches. If we have closed our hearts to the poor, then we are seriously in need of development ourselves!

Development is thus about individuals, local communities, and nations and our ability to live together globally as family members and neighbors (both metaphors are used in Scripture). We must grow in our ability to love each other and to work together on interdependent issues of global scope. This is another reason for working in partnerships: they bring organizations from many countries into conversation with each other and from there to an ability to address issues in a global way. All voices need to be heard, and all the players need to commit to doing their part. Best practices can be shared across borders, and working plans can be built in complementary ways. Microenterprise and agricultural programs in a developing country may provide alternatives to growing cocaine. At the same time, partner organizations in North America can lobby the US government for more enlightened trade policies that encourage the production and export of healthy agricultural crops. All major Christian traditions are now global in their networks of church and parachurch organizations. These networks are already being employed in response to global issues, but in ways that could significantly expand and improve. In order to grow in our love for each other, we must come to know each other, understand each other, pray for each other, and live our lives in light of the well-being of our brothers and sisters who are part of our human family.

Principle 7: We Are Fallen Image Bearers

The economically rich often have "god complexes," a subtle and unconscious sense of superiority in which they believe that they have . . . been anointed to decide what is best for low-income people, whom they view as inferior to themselves.

Steve Corbett and Brian Fikkert, *When Helping Hurts*

Development workers don't have all the answers and we shouldn't feel like we need to in order to help others live better. We need to have a sense of humility about what we're capable of changing.

Brit Steiner, management and program analyst
in the Office of Civilian Response at USAID

For any building project, it is essential to know what the raw materials are like, both in terms of possibilities and potential weaknesses. In development, the raw material is people. To know what humans can do, we need to know what they are like. In contrast with the secular development perspectives presented in chapter 1, Christians believe that God paid special attention to the creation of man and woman, making them in his very own image and giving them responsibilities to rule, be fruitful, fill and subdue the earth, and work in the garden and take care of it. As Genesis tells us, this was not enough for Adam and Eve; they wanted to be even more like God. And so the world fell into sin, distancing the human race from God and ushering in an era of suffering, brokenness, and death. As descendants of Adam and Eve, we still bear God's image, which makes us capable of doing good things, but that image is so distorted by the fall that our capacity for self-delusion and for doing wrong and hurtful things is very great as well.

Image bearers are created to work, love, learn, choose, create, relate, serve, enjoy, and rest. Unfortunately, many of the poor around the world are so beaten down that they think themselves largely incapable of anything good. Some become passive and fatalistic. Others lash out with nihilistic violence. They may hope for better things in the next life but have given up on this one.

Following the ideas of Jayakumar Christian, Bryant Myers argues that how we live and what we do (our vocation) is tightly linked with our self-esteem and our understanding of our own identity. Distorted views of who we are spill over into distorted ways of behaving. If a group of people believe it is wrong for them to learn or make decisions, or believe they rightfully belong to a low class or caste in society, then they will not create or learn or choose or enjoy the way God intended them to. Myers calls this a "marred identity," and a big part of development work is to nurture an accurate sense of self, to build up self-esteem, to help people understand both who they are and how they should live.

The poor are not the only ones with distorted views of self. As Myers explains, the rich, and oftentimes development workers, also carry distorted views of who they are. They may have heard the call to care for and help the poor, but they see themselves as saviors of the poor rather than servants. For Myers, this understanding of self is just as marred as that of the poor, because the rich suffer from "god complexes." When rich people with god-complexes swoop in to save the poor, answers already in hand, they generally do more harm than good, because they reinforce the distorted self-esteem of the people they want to help. Development work thus requires transforming the self-images and the behavior patterns of people who are rich as well as people who are poor. Presenting the gospel message in context-appropriate ways is one essential tool in developing healthy self-images, ones that build the self-esteem of the marginalized and nurture humility among the rich and powerful. Myers calls this restoring our true identity and our true vocation.

Development work that is focused on physical or structural need must also take account of both sides of human nature. For our image-bearing side, we build structures and institutions that foster the freedom and conditions that allow us all to exercise our talents, gifts, and responsibilities. We become creators, workers, stewards, and choosers. In schools we build knowledge and strengthen abilities; in civic organizations we discuss problems, make plans, and carry them out; in businesses we foster entrepreneurship and stewardly production of goods and services; and in democratic governments we listen to each other and make wise collective decisions.

On the other hand, the fallen side of our nature means we must be wise in balancing the freedom to create, build, and serve with checks and balances that guard against corruption, violence, oppression, and other violations that arise when we use our freedom badly. Freedom and accountability must go together.

Yet another aspect of being image bearers is that, like our Triune God, we are made to live together in community, which means there are times when we choose to defer to others in the community, such as the leaders we agree to name and respect. We thus confer a degree of power to leaders in community institutions such as families, churches, NGOs, businesses, and governments. The power our leaders exercise to keep order and help us make collective decisions has great potential for good, but due to our sinfulness, we must check and balance that power with appropriate oversight and the ability to take power away when it is being abused. For example, churches must have ways to check and remove abusive leaders. NGOs must have adequate oversight of financial matters. Governing boards in all types of institutions need the authority to rein in wayward organizational directors and staff, and the board itself needs to be held accountable by members. Communities need police forces, even as those forces must themselves be guided and held in check by appropriate groups of citizens. These are just a few examples. Two highly respected global organizations, Transparency International and Amnesty International, though neither articulates its mission in Christian terms, are nevertheless acting on this general principle by overseeing and making public various types of corrupt practices and violations of human rights. Such organizations play a vital role in promoting development by holding leaders accountable at community, national, and global levels.[11]

Principle 8: Relationships Are More Important Than Stuff

Jesus told us about the two great commandments, and much of theology tries to avoid giving proper weight to the second one. We love and worship God through caring for our neighbor. Our neighbor is the highest expression of God as we may ever see it.

Dana Bates, founder of New Horizons Foundation Romania

We often talk about the MDGs [UN Millennium Development Goals], and those are good, but what people really want is dignity and respect. They need development workers who are humble and can engage in two-way learning. We often think that whoever has the funding, knowledge, and technology is in control, but that is not really true. We must learn to value people for who they are and build from there.

Ndunge Kiiti, professor of intercultural studies at Houghton College and consultant with MAP International

When short-term missionaries return from their trips, they frequently comment on the happiness and generosity of the poor, a discovery that causes them to reflect on their own lives and especially their own relationship with material things. If they happen to follow up their personal experiences with a little investigation, they discover that social science research confirms that happiness is linked less with income and wealth than with the character and quality of one's relationships.[12]

For Christians, this finding should be no surprise since the Bible conveys this same message. Yet for some reason we seem to have a hard time accepting it. This might be because the Bible is also pretty high on prosperity, especially in the Old Testament where God repeatedly promises prosperity to Israel. As Scripture unfolds, however, our ability to seek first the kingdom by maintaining proper relationships with God and each other comes into serious question. After centuries during which the Israelites failed to get this right, New Testament writers become much more circumspect about prosperity. Consider how Paul tells Timothy to beware of those "who think that godliness is a means to financial gain" and says that "those who want to get rich fall into temptation and a trap and into many foolish and harmful desires" (1 Tim. 6:5, 9). So here's the deal: in the Bible, the prosperity that God wants us to enjoy always results from having our relationships in proper order. Read through the books of the Law (the first five books of the Bible) and you realize that most laws address our relationships with God and with each other. In the New Testament, Jesus underscores this point when he is asked what the greatest commandment is. His answer is that loving God is number one, loving neighbor is number two, and the way we show our love for God is by loving our neighbor (Matt. 22:34–40).

Trying to make this point in today's world is like singing "Silent Night" at a rock concert. We get drowned out because we live in a world in which an unending barrage of messages repeats the story line that having more stuff is what life is really all about. Let's not kid ourselves; it is a very tempting message, all the more so because many of our own spiritual leaders seem to live and even preach the same message. As it was for Israel, so too for us today: it is exceedingly difficult to seek first the kingdom of God and to be patient as those other things are added on (Matt. 6:33).

For Christian development workers this message takes on added urgency. One reason we must be very intentional about seeking the kingdom first is that most of us in the North are quite rich, and it is of vital importance that we witness with integrity. Choosing a "What Would Jesus Do" lifestyle in housing, for example, is one of the most complicated and divisive issues foreign missionaries face. Should foreigners with salaries based on Northern standards live in nice homes in cities, perhaps even in exclusive communities of fellow expatriates? Many do. Or should they live incarnationally, among the poor themselves, more or less as the poor live? Some do this too. When these two groups get together to talk about where and how they live, the conversation is often poisoned with blame, guilt, accusation, envy, shame, and defensiveness. If you should happen to live overseas one day, you will certainly face this issue and find yourself in these conversations. The decisions you must make will not be easy. Pray for honesty, wisdom, and courage.

In our personal lives, emphasizing relationships over things witnesses to our personal integrity, which gives us credibility when our actual development work focuses on relationships too. To expand on the point in the previous section about marred identity, Bryant Myers builds his whole approach to development on restoring broken relationships with God, others, the environment, and self. This is one of the great takeaways from Myers's book.

What does it mean to emphasize relationships over things? One striking example is offered in a fascinating case study of two Mennonite Central Committee programs in Bolivia, where researchers found that the program emphasizing constructive relationships in the community and with MCC staff was more successful by all measures than the program that focused more on measuring material outputs.[13] Christian development organizations often focus on building community by strengthening relationships of love and care and responsibility within the community. Where conflict reigns, conflict resolution and peacebuilding strategies are common. Where businesses are needed to provide jobs and income, emphasis—in microenterprise programs, for example—is placed on cooperating with each other, serving the community, making ethical decisions, and ultimately being faithful to God. Oftentimes it simply means showing love, care, and respect for people you work with. Here is a story from agricultural economist Duncan Boughton, who learned about the importance of relationships early in his work in Africa:

> People matter. Development is about people and trying to improve their circumstances and relationships with other people. You must look past bureaucratic procedures, agendas, and wasteful organizations to the people on the other side. I had an experience early in my career that helped me keep it in focus. I was in The Gambia doing on-site [crop] trials. We went to a village and laid out these trials, but a very sick and malnourished child was there. This child would die if something was not done. My wife was working nearby at a public health clinic. We took the child and the mother to the local public health program and introduced them to my wife. She saw the severity of the situation and arranged for the child to be admitted to the nearby hospital. The nearby hospital was run by a team of Chinese doctors. For whatever reasons, they decided the child was a hopeless case and discharged her. My wife heard about it and immediately went back to the village, found the child and mother, and brought them back to the hospital and made sure this child was admitted.

We then had a fuel crisis and there was no fuel to go to the village and harvest the trial. When we finally had fuel again we hustled to the village and apologized for not keeping our word about returning to harvest the trial. When I arrived, the village greeted me and thanked me for the help the child had received. They took me to the trial. They had put a fence around it and a guard on it, and it was still there waiting to harvest. Where the birds had hacked at it they propped up the damaged stalks. They so valued what we had been able to do for one child that they were going to wait patiently until I showed up. They were not going to give up on me. This made me realize that one child matters. This lesson applies at the village level but also with government ministers. If you establish a personal relationship and gain trust and respect, then other changes will happen too.

Focusing on restoring and maintaining relationships of care is quite curiously one of the ways to assure better and lasting outcomes in areas like agricultural production or even income.

Emphasizing relationships in development work has three practical implications. First, a common truism we often hear is that "our goal is to work ourselves out of a job." There is something to be said for this, but it arises out of an understanding of development that is "things" focused. It assumes outsiders come in for a while and then leave because the need for things in the community is increasingly met. The relationships that form are of little lasting importance. If development is about holistic transformation that embraces all of us in community, maybe it would make more sense to grow the relationships so that we can take on even greater challenges in the future.

The second implication is similar, but more on an institutional level. There is a great and worthy effort these days to work in partnerships, meaning that organizations of all sorts and sizes should work together in respectful, mutually accountable relationships. And yet, just like the personal mantra of "working oneself out of a job," development organizations often talk about ending the partnerships after a certain period of time. A common term for this is "phasing out." But if relationships are at the heart of development, then, instead of phasing out, organizations might better look toward how to grow the relationship and move to the next level. When a child grows up and leaves home, the relationship changes, but the family remains intact as each member takes on new roles. It should be like this with our global partnerships too.

The third implication relates specifically to the practice of short-term mission trips. Many of these have tangible goals in mind, like constructing a building. But the deeper value of such mission trips is probably found in the relationships that form—within the community visited, among the group taking the trip, and between members of the two cultures. In his fine book on short-term missions, David Livermore suggests that these trips be planned with much more attention to their relational character and impact than to the more material goals that most trips focus on.[14]

In recent years Christian social scientist Michael Woolcock has been studying the role of social capital in development. Social capital is a technical term referring to how much we care for each other, trust each other, and work well together. The better we trust, collaborate, and work together, the higher our social capital. In an article written explicitly for a Christian audience, Woolcock notes a convergence in secular development theory and Christian theology. He says that that the "theory and practice of development are in essence about 'getting the social relations right.'"[15] Getting our relations right at all levels is a central purpose of development work. As shown in the study of the two MCC programs in Bolivia, the blessings of prosperity will likely follow.

Principle 9: Development Is a Journey

When I started studying development in the 1970s, it quickly became clear how hard it was to come up with words that honestly yet diplomatically describe what development is all about. What do we call those communities and countries where development workers go? Some terms, including "primitive," "backward," and "undeveloped," have been tried but are offensive, condescending, and inaccurate descriptions. We have also learned that it is self-serving and wrong to call the people in rich countries "developed."

Theologically, a term like "developed" is problematic. In a world suffering the effects of the fall, persons and nations are never finished with their development. No matter our current situation, we strive to do better, knowing that there are always improvements to be made. Development is not a destination, a place we get to, but more of a process, a journey that reaches landmarks but always has other good places to go. It is thus a mistake to talk about some people and countries as "developed." The biblical story itself starts in the garden and progresses toward the city in Revelation 21, but even that city will keep unfolding and developing.[16]

Calling a nation "developed" is wrong also because it indicates to other nations that they should aspire to become like these "developed" nations. But though there might be certain things that people in the South can learn from the North, Latin Americans do not generally want to become gringos. They enjoy being who they are. A good illustration of this is found in *Cool Runnings*, a movie about the Jamaican bobsled team. When they first arrive at the Olympic site, the Jamaicans try to emulate the Swiss team in their behavior patterns. It goes badly. Finally, one member of the team reminds them that they need to be proud of being Jamaican and need to be the best Jamaicans they can be. Things go better after that, and they have a lot more fun. They start by accepting who they are and where they have been placed, and then try to get better from that point. They are on a journey.

If developmental transformation is a never-ending journey or an ongoing process instead of a destination, one major implication for development work is that we must deemphasize the idea of getting to a certain end state.[17] The work is more focused on fostering the conditions in which participants can make wise decisions about how to organize themselves, define their mission, and carry it out. Our job is not to turn Jamaicans into Swiss but instead to facilitate processes in which Jamaicans make decisions and organize themselves to be better Jamaicans. As Paul says, to the Jews he became a Jew, to those not under the law (the gentiles) he became as a gentile, to the weak he became weak, all for the purpose of meeting people where they were and helping them get onto a better path (1 Cor. 9:19–23).

This is another of those points that is relatively easy to make but incredibly hard to live out in the real world of development practice, especially when donor demands for measurable results are so strong. All development manuals trumpet the importance of process, but when projects are funded and evaluated, all that really seems to matter is the tangible outputs. What happens is that processes and structures that may bear good and lasting fruit over the long term are often scuttled in favor of short-term gains that crumble as soon as the well of outside resources dries up.

For the development worker who wants to emphasize process and to help people cut their own developmental path, there are some excellent strategies to choose from. One is "asset-based community development" (ABCD), which works at getting a community to take stock of its own assets and to build from there. "Appreciative inquiry" is another such strategy that works to help people identify the strong points of their communities and culture, discover their best values, and then build on those to create constructive change.[18] Both of these strategies work well with communities or other organized groups in the process of constructive, transformational change.

Principle 10: Development Is about Worldviews

I suspect that when you met the four characters in chapter 1, you found some qualities attractive and others bothersome. As a teacher, I have found that students are fairly quick to either like or dislike these characters, but when asked why, they generally resort to citing one of the prominent features and let it go at that. One might say "I like Harvey Having because of the emphasis on freedom and markets," or "I don't like him because he is too materialistic and self-interested." Another might say, "I like postdevelopment because it respects other cultures," but her neighbor says, "It is not good that Betty Being accepts cultures that oppress women. She is too relativistic." The trouble with such responses is that they are presented without supporting rationale. The statements are too subjective, apparently based on little more than what the speaker happens to "like" or "dislike." Many young Christians today are also strongly disinclined to even attempt to persuade others that their view is the better one. To challenge others would be to violate some apparently sacred code of tolerance.

There is something increasingly normal about such responses in our post-modern era.[19] We have learned by now that the modern age was appropriately criticized because it fostered impositional, even conquering, attitudes and practices. But is the relativism that is often associated with postmodernism any better? If, as postmodernism has convincingly taught us, we have no ultimately objective proof of our own positions, how can it be right to impose our views on others or even think that we might have something to offer them? This is a question of monumental importance in development work because (1) development work, in its very nature, seeks to transform people, cultures, and ways of life; (2) as Christians inspired by distinct faith commitments, we encounter a world and other cultures with very different sets of beliefs and values;[20] and (3) we must decide how to interact with development perspectives and theories that are clearly at odds with Christian thought.

The question is whether we should evaluate other views and other cultures, as well as our own, on the basis of our faith. For me, the answer is a loud and clear "yes," but this raises the inescapable question of how we take our faith seriously, as an authentic rendering of what is true, while at the same time exercising Christian humility and respecting the viewpoints of other people, which may very well differ from what we see as the truth. This is an especially important question for those of us who feel called to work with people very different from ourselves, and not just work with them, but actually be involved with them in a transformational process that includes us both.

There is no doubt that our views on development should be shaped by our Christian worldview, which should also be a major resource for critiquing other viewpoints, perspectives, theories, and even cultures. But we need to be extremely wise about how we engage in such critique, because though we should not "impose" our views, we have nevertheless taken our stand and have good reason to explain why we are standing where we are and how things look from here. Far from leading us to accept or tolerate anything and everything, postmodernism actually invites us to enter the public arena with our ideas. In other words, we are fully in our right to put forth a distinct viewpoint and use that viewpoint to evaluate other ones, and then even to invite others to join us, to see how the world looks from where we stand, and to work out together what it means to live a faithful life.

This approach to navigating our pluralistic world is something I learned from some insightful and wise Christian leaders. One is Lesslie Newbigin, a long-term missionary to India who retired to England and then took on the task of responding to the postmodern challenge to Christianity. Newbigin made many insightful contributions to how Christians should think and act in this postmodern age. Like other leading Christian thinkers, he finds the main points of postmodern philosophy to be basically on target—for example, the point that there is no objective means by which to indubitably identify truth.[21] Far from seeing this as the final defeat of Christian truth, he argues instead that Christians must be much more aware of and much more confident in the legitimacy and relevance of our deepest beliefs and values. Just as the four secular perspectives already presented argue their positions, Christians also need to make their case in the public square. If our case is a good one and explains the world around us quite well, others may be persuaded. If we choose to withdraw from the public square into our own insular communities of belief, then our views and lives will grow stale and even our own children will leave the faith. Listen to Newbigin as he encourages us to stand firm in the faith while also respecting other people and their views: "We must affirm the gospel as truth, universal truth, truth for all peoples and for all times, the truth which creates the possibility of freedom; but we negate the gospel if we deny the freedom in which alone it can be truly believed."[22]

Another helpful Christian leader is Bruce Bradshaw, a scholar/pastor/development worker who has reflected on these issues for years.[23] For Bradshaw, we explain our lives with narratives, or stories. In North America we often explain our world with science-based stories, while other cultures explain their worlds in different ways. Bradshaw found that in the communities where he worked in Africa, magic and spiritual powers often played major roles in their stories. Bradshaw makes no judgment about which of these two sets of stories is better, but encourages all of us, in our own cultural contexts, to integrate the biblical story of redemption into all of our culturally situated stories. He calls the biblical story of redemption a "metanarrative," because it stands above all the local cultural stories. As finite, historically and culturally bound people, we must be willing to share our stories, to continually work to transform our stories in light of God's bigger story, to encourage people in other cultures to do the same, and to listen to others in order to learn whether elements of their stories should be integrated into ours. This is how we cross-fertilize, how we learn and grow, and how we are transformed bit by bit.

The huge implication of this principle for development work is that we must engage both our stories and the stories of others so that together we work to transform our stories, ideas, theories, and worldviews. Such a process will likely include the following:

> Knowing our own stories about who we are, what we are doing, and why. As Christians it is vital that we have a sense of what the biblical redemption story means for us and our work. We need to know how it affects the way we think about and do business, how it influences our practices of conflict mediation, and how it affects interpersonal relationships with coworkers.
>
> Listening intently to the stories of others, whether these stories emerge from local communities or secular development traditions like modernization. We can learn from their insights on business, conflict mediation, and relationships.
>
> Sharing our own stories with others, not in an insistent or imposing way but in an engaging, joyful way that invites others to see the reason, power, and delight of our own understandings and ways of life and work.
>
> Engaging in a mutual learning process of listening, sharing, and learning that allows everyone to improve their stories and the way we all live and work together. Some people think of this as an extended, ongoing conversation.

There is a lot of evangelism in these steps, though not evangelism as you might be used to thinking of it. Yes, the stories about Jesus—who he is, how he lived, how he died, how he rose from the dead and lives again, and what his death and resurrection mean for us—make up one set of important stories that need to be shared, but that is not the only story we tell. We are also telling stories about how, in light of the biblical story, we think of and treat women, care for our environment, organize ourselves to make collective decisions, produce and distribute goods and services, construct our diets, use technology, and resolve conflicts. We share these stories knowing that they are not perfect; some might even be quite wrong, but they are the best we have been able to do in our own context. Maybe there is something in our experience that will help others, and maybe there is something in their experience that will help us. In all these circumstances, we need to know what our own stories say, what the stories of others say, and how together we can improve our stories and the way we actually live together.

This is not a one-way street in which all the storytelling, or all the evangelism and teaching, goes from us to them. Rather, in a process Myers calls a "convergence of stories," our distinct stories get mixed up together— integrated and transformed—in light of the biblical story.[24] The process of transformation is like a multidirectional traffic interchange in which the traffic of ideas and life practices goes in all directions.

Transformational Development: Tanya Transforming Meets Babul and Chabekum and Sits at the Table with Harvey, Libby, Betty, and Charles

Even though our introductions to secular development perspectives in chapter 1 were brief, and our knowledge of Babul's and Chabekum's lives is only sketchy, we do have enough of a background to compare how and why Christian development workers will approach their situation differently. To help picture this comparison, please meet Tanya Transforming, a Christian development professional trained in the ten development principles of this chapter (see fig. 3.1).

Imagine that Harvey, Libby, Betty, Charles, and Tanya have all been introduced to Babul and Chabekum and have spent some time getting to know them and their community. They have also been introduced to each other and have now gathered under the village tree to share their viewpoints and ideas. The first four review their positions as stated in chapter 1, the outlines of which are repeated here:

> Harvey Having (modernization): The basic problem is poverty. Therefore, we should encourage Babul and/or Chabekum either to join the loan group associated with the NGO and start a business or to migrate to Dhaka and get a job there.
>
> Libby Liberating (Marxism/dependency): The basic problem is that Babul and Chabekum are oppressed and powerless, so we should work at organizing them and others like them so that they can fight against injustices like Babul's land being taken away.
>
> Betty Being (postdevelopment): The basic problem is that foreigners come in with their strange ideas and their NGOs and mess things up. It would be best to leave Babul and Chabekum to work things out in the context of their own culture, their own beliefs, and their own ways of life.
>
> Charles Choosing (capabilities approach): The basic problem is that Babul and Chabekum are both so beaten down that they cannot participate in

Problems
- suffering of people and the creation as a whole
- the fall—sin
- personal and structural sin
- brokenness in every area of life
- distance from God

Beliefs
- God created the world
- the world belongs to God
- the world fell into sin
- God is redeeming the world
- christ is Lord and Savior
- humans bear God's image
- Scripture is the word of God

"Promised Land"
- right relationships
- *shalom*
- new creation
- transformation/redemption
- eternal life
- convergence of stories

Actions
- redeem every area of life
- heal/ reconcile broken relationships
- share the good news
- service to those in need
- creation care
- share, partner, build community
- holistic responses
- telling, listening to and revising the stories

Values
- love
- human dignity
- servanthood
- justice
- a special heart for the poor
- work
- creativity
- humility
- discipleship
- stewardship
- community
- golden rule
- obedience

Issues
- this world—other world
- role/character of evangelism
- responsible freedom
- the problem of pain
- how to engage public life
- unity amidst diversity
- working transformationally across divides (language, ethnicity, gender, income, culture)

Figure 3.1. Tanya Transforming—There are plenty of reasons in this world for Tanya to be sad or angry, but knowing who she is and whom she serves, her attitude is one of abiding hope that gives her the resolve to be engaged in the work of transformation.

making choices about their own future. We should help provide education, food, and health, as well as protect their rights, so that they can participate and decide for themselves what will make their lives better.

And now it is Tanya Transforming's turn. I believe she would start by affirming some aspects of all four secular perspectives. "Harvey," she might say, "Babul and Chabekum are poor, so you are right that they need more material goods than they currently have—like food, for example. Business is a good way for people to become productive, so a loan group that encourages business development might indeed be a positive change." Turning to Libby, she might agree that "in this world, power is often abused and injustice is all too often the result, so organizing Babul and Chabekum into a support and advocacy group might give them some of their own power to check and balance the power of landlords." I envision Tanya saying to Betty that "Babul and Chabekum are indeed part of a tradition with a long history and a strong cultural and religious formation. Their cultural and religious heritage definitely needs to be respected and appreciated." Finally, she tells Charles, "It is certainly true that Babul and Chabekum need to be brought into the life of society as decision makers and choosers. Their basic dignity as human beings demands that we help include them as participating members of the community. Food, education, and health care are good places to start."

Tanya might then ask some questions, which are a gentle way of suggesting the limits and shortcomings of the other approaches. Would the business training Babul and Chabekum get include some attention to ethics? Would the loan groups be encouraged to develop their relationships to support each other in ways that go beyond the purely financial relationship? Would advocacy groups be self-oriented or community oriented, and what would be their underlying vision of justice? Are we really willing to accept the cultural tradition of families arranging their daughters' marriages when they are still children, or do we need to promote change? And what kind of education should Babul and Chabekum receive? Will it teach about self-esteem, relationships, how society is organized, and how choices can be wisely made? How will we work to heal the brokenness present in Babul's and Chabekum's self-image, and in their relationships with their families, with each other, with the landlords, and with other community leaders? And how will we address the religious mindset that supports what looks like the oppression of women, a social system based on caste, and the general sense of despair and loneliness that Babul and Chabekum seem to have shrunk to?

Finally, Tanya offers some suggestions. She knows that Babul and Chabekum are embedded in a large, complex, holistic system of life that will not be easy to break down into component parts and then rebuild. She also knows that the whole system cannot be tackled at once, partly because it is just too big and complex. Finally, she knows that lasting change usually comes slowly and incrementally, in accord with everyone's abilities to embrace change and adapt to it. This means that Babul and Chabekum must be included as central players, just like the landlords, bankers, governments, and NGO leaders. In fact, Tanya suggests starting at the lowest levels, right where they live.

The first thing we need to do is get to know Babul and Chabekum as people—real people with names and faces. Get to know them by talking with them, listening to them, showing care for them, and providing them with a space to reflect on their lives and their circumstances. It might be reasonable at some point to gather a group that includes Babul and Chabekum and their friends and have them do some self-analysis. Tanya would likely suggest a positive, asset-based approach like appreciative inquiry, which would get people participating and thus help them understand each other better, build some degree of trust, and think through how they would like to see their lives change. It may happen that a moment comes when individuals and the group as a whole are ready to commit to planning and carrying out a transforming act, generally a relatively small and achievable one. If so, that would be wonderful, and the successful completion of such a plan might lead to another round of analysis, planning, and action. Let your own imagination take you where this might go. My imagination has me dreaming that their involvement will lead them to start a business, organize themselves to defend their right to land use, advocate just policies before local governments, revise gender-based practices like child marriage, and eventually reflect on and reassess the worldviews that govern their lives. Maybe they will affiliate with similar groups in other regions and create a movement that has national and even international scope to address things as big as international trade rules. But that's my imagination. Your imagination, Tanya's, and mine are not irrelevant, but they must be secondary to Babul's and Chabekum's. Their freedom, their image-bearing qualities, and their dignity all require that we allow them to take the lead while we take on the role of facilitator and encourager.

As Babul and Chabekum begin to be respected by others and to respect themselves, there will be times when they need the support and collaboration and engagement of others—people in their own regions and nations and some from across the waters. There will be times when they ask for help in learning how to improve their farming practices, educational systems, community youth programs, organizational management, advocacy, communications, business knowledge, parenting, environmental care. When these requests arise, it would be good and helpful for people like Tanya and us to be there ready to help as we are able. It is not likely that one of their first requests will be to have their religious faith commitments questioned and changed, but that may come and should be welcomed when it does. More likely, they will request assistance with more practical matters. But as we help with those practical matters, three important things happen. One is that we build relationships of trust that gradually become a solid foundation from which to tackle bigger projects. The second is that we will tell and share stories all along the way. Conversations about business practice might lead naturally to discussions of business ethics grounded in stories of trust, community building, relationship formation, honesty, stewardship, and service. Third, we become a bridge across which information, ideas, requests, and stories can head back toward our own societies. With that sort of input, people in churches, mission agencies, development organizations, governments, and international institutions have a better sense of how to learn from Babul and Chabekum in ways that might lead us to change our own lives and the institutions in which we have a voice. What starts small can build into something much bigger.

All of this is illustrative, but I hope it provides some insight into how Christian development professionals with a transforming vision might go about responding to Babul and Chabekum and the situation they find themselves in. What you would actually suggest and do in a real, live situation might be quite different than this in its specifics. Making good and wise interventions in the lives of people like Babul and Chabekum is not something easy, nor is it to be taken lightly. There are no magic or scientific formulas. And yet there are people who are better at it than others. What makes them good is a mixture of raw talent or giftedness, passion for the mission, training in helpful knowledge and tools, virtues that make them effective, life experiences that contribute to wisdom, and many other intangibles.

It is time now to take our leave of Harvey, Libby, Betty, Charles, and Babul and Chabekum. We may refer to them again, but from here on our focus is on Tanya's colleagues, and on how you might get onto a vocational path to join them.

Further Reflection and Action Steps

1. Which two of the principles presented in this chapter do you find the most persuasive? Which two do you find least helpful? Can you think of some that are missing?

2. Think of a situation in which you personally were involved in some development work, either internationally or locally. Identify which principles

you and the overall project were following reasonably well and which ones you might have been able to incorporate better.

3. Development workers often struggle with the question of what their salary should be and how they should live among and interact with the people they work with and are trying to serve. What would your advice to them be, and how would you answer these questions for yourself?

4. What do you think about Tanya's approach to Babul and Chabekum? Is she on the right track, or is she missing something?

5. If Tanya were working in a developing country, and organizations with Harveys, Libbys, Bettys, and Charleses were there too, could Tanya partner with them, or would it be best for Tanya to set up a completely separate organization and try to get Babul and Chabekum to ignore the other organizations?

4
How Many Niches Are There?

An Overview of the International Development Field
. . . and Where North Americans Fit In

Trained in tropical agriculture, I often consult with organizations teaching drip irrigation and rooftop gardening. I recently went to Haiti after the earthquake to assess the agricultural situation.

> Beth Doerr, internship manager at Educational
> Concerns for Hunger Organization (ECHO)

I helped found and am now on the board of the Association for a More Just Society. We do human rights–oriented justice work from a Christian perspective. We work on land rights, labor rights, and victims' rights.

> Kurt Ver Beek, professor, development worker,
> twenty-year resident of Honduras

My natural calling is in populations of hungry and homeless people. I have come to believe that I have special gifts that allow me to work well in such environments.

> Sarah Rohrer, field organizer with Bread for the World

We have different gifts, according to the grace given to each of us. If your gift is prophesying, then prophesy in accordance with your faith; if it is serving, then serve; if it is teaching, then teach; if it is to encourage, then give encouragement; if it is giving, then give generously; if it is to lead, do it diligently; if it is to show mercy, do it cheerfully.

> Romans 12:6–8

What's Wrong with This Picture?

What image comes to mind when you hear the term "development worker"? For many of us, the image is of a person from a rich country living and working with poor people from a very different culture. The foreigner dresses differently than locals, and the scene takes place in the tropics. The development worker is probably teaching or giving something to smiling and grateful locals. I confess that this is the picture I had in mind when I went to Guatemala in 1976 to help with postearthquake housing reconstruction. I actually remember being on the plane and thinking how cool it would be to bring home a picture of the happy family that would move into the house I helped build. I am not sure whether to smile or cry today when I remember that. When I think of it now, I was like a hunter going into the wilds to bring home a trophy for display on my wall back in Michigan.

Maybe that is too harsh, because every now and then development work really does involve a foreigner doing something direct and tangible for someone in need, for which that person is indeed grateful. But even when it does happen like this, I wonder whether taking photos and showing them around is a good idea. In the real world, however, most development work that is genuinely helpful is not like that, and the picture suggested above is stereotyped, self-serving, condescending, mythical, troubling, and, for the most part, just plain wrong.

Here are a few things wrong with this picture. Most seriously, it feeds those god complexes that tend to plague us in the North. The picture shows us as saviors. Another conceptual flaw is that the teaching and/or giving is unidirectional, from us to them, instead of two-way or mutual, like it usually is in reality. In terms of the location, it is only on rare occasions that North Americans actually live in the poor communities depicted in such photos. More often they live in cities, sometimes even in North America, far away from the poor in other lands. For those who do live in developing countries, North Americans tend to work mostly with professionals who are as educated and professional as they are. Much of their time is spent in offices, sitting in meetings, talking on the phone, writing reports, and staring at the smiling faces of machines named Mac or Dell. Finally, the picture gives only a very limited idea of the myriad types of positions and work that North Americans might get involved with when they enter the vast, deep, and multifaceted field of international development.

Deep and Wide: Many Ways to Serve

If it is right to think of development as transformation of the whole world, then all our work in every area of life contributes to development. We are all missionaries, no matter where we work and what our specific vocation is. This is good and important to note, but it will be helpful to narrow our study of international development work to those whose professional lives are explicitly dedicated to helping people who are sometimes referred to as "the least of these." For purposes of establishing clarity on what international development work really is, I offer the following simple yet weighty definition: international development work is the set of intentional efforts and activities throughout the world that are designed to help people in need improve their lives by facilitating (1) *reconciliation* where there is brokenness and (2) *transforming growth* where there is potential for creative and constructive change.

Such a global focus puts us into international, multicultural, multinational, and multilingual environments that require particular types of work as well as particular types of virtues, knowledge, and skills necessary for becoming effective ambassadors of global reconciliation and agents of transformation. Coming to a realization of what type of work you might do and where you might fit requires careful consideration of your own capabilities, opportunities, and passions, as well as a sense of the overall scheme of things.

To illustrate the depth, breadth, and overall character of the development field, consider two images. The first image is that of a beehive. Like human beings, bees are both beautiful and useful. Each bee is a wonderfully made individual, but each single bee is nothing without its hive or home community. A beehive is a complex society that organizes itself to make honey, rear the brood, and do what it needs to do to thrive. In the process, bees pollinate fruits, vegetables, flowers, and trees the world over. Bees live in the wild, but they can also be domesticated, at least to some degree. I used to own a few hives until I had a bad day one fall, got stung too many times, had an allergic reaction, and was advised by an allergist to give it up. In my beekeeping days I discovered many interesting parallels to our own lives, including how they govern themselves, stay warm in the winter, and sacrifice themselves for the well-being of the hive.

One of the most fascinating aspects of bee life is that many different tasks must be done for the hive to thrive, such as tending to the queen, making the comb, feeding the young, and defending the hive. All the jobs are important, and the bees specialize to get them all done. If any one of the jobs is not done well, the hive dies. Like bees, people also specialize and work together for the well-being of the whole. So it is in international development work; there are many different jobs that must be done for the overall mission to succeed. Some workers are needed in the field, while others locate closer to home and work inside office buildings. If you feel called to work in international development, it might mean taking a position out in the field, but there are also many positions "inside the hive," or here at home, that need committed and competent people.

The second visual image is a diagram that attempts to capture the character and complexity of the development task and the work that needs to be done to make holistic progress. Think of the world as a wheel rolling forward in historical time (see fig. 4.1).[1] God set the wheel in motion when he completed his creative acts by forming human beings, bearers of his own image, whom he then placed in the center of the whole creation. The wheel thus puts the human person at the center, while the rest of the wheel, representing life in this world, is made up of all the different facets of life over which human beings are stewards. Here are a few things to notice:

> The wheel at creation is perfectly round, and all the parts make up a very good, strong, multifaceted wheel ("God saw all that he had made, and it was very good" [Gen. 1:31]).

> The wheel starts small but grows as image-bearing human beings work creatively and faithfully to improve their lives. This represents the unfolding of the cultural mandate, which is God's plan for us to be fruitful and to rule, fill, subdue, work, and take care of the earth (Gen. 1:26–28; 2:15). The created order was thus packed with potential for growth and improvement, which is definitely not the same thing as the economic growth that modern societies seem to idolize. Instead, authentic growth in all sectors of life will be consistent with *shalom*, such that relationships with God, self, others, and creation are increasingly right and good.

> Persons are individuals. As the smallest human unit, they are shown here at the center of the diagram, but these individuals are necessarily in relationships with other people, as members of families, communities, nations, and ultimately the whole global human family. These relationships are illustrated with the concentric circles that show larger groupings of people as the circles move away from the center.

> Our lives engage many different arenas, including economic, political, religious, cultural, artistic, technological, and others. These arenas extend through the whole wheel, somewhat like spokes. They relate to our individual lives, like when we make personal economic choices, but they are also relevant at a national or global level, like when big financial institutions create an economic recession. Each arena is a distinct shade, but there are no hard lines that can be drawn between them. At the borders, they blend together. For example, the government regulates the economy, our spirituality affects the environment, and so on.

Over historical time, the wheel rolls to the right. It becomes larger as humans exercise creative, productive, and artistic abilities, but the wheel becomes misshapen. Every part of the wheel is distorted due to the corruption that results from the fall. When some aspects of our lives are "out of round," then the wheel "clunks" as it rolls forward in time. Depending on the severity of the clunking, the whole wheel might diminish in size. If, for example, we fail to address global poverty in a reasonable way or fail to live sustainably within our environmental possibilities, then we are likely to see diminishment not just in the economic realm but also in such areas as health, political life, education, and environmental well-being. Every area of life has its own distinctiveness, but each is integrated with all the others. If one part of the body suffers, the whole body suffers.

The full wheel captures the whole of the global human family in all facets of its life. If nations within the globe are doing well, that contributes to the well-being of the whole. If a particular nation, such as Somalia or North Korea, is having serious trouble, the effects are felt not only within the country but also in the broader region and beyond. If, for example, Somalia's security situation is so bad that the well-being of Somalis is diminished, the country might also become a breeding ground for global terrorism and thus affect people throughout the world.

To capture the image of a particular nation, focus on the "nation" sphere and you can analyze the brokenness and the potential of the nation going "inward" toward the nation's communities and individuals. Or you can analyze the nation's situation going "outward" in terms of how it relates and intersects with all the relevant facets of life in the global sphere (like how its economy fits into the global pattern or how much influence proselytizers from other countries have had on it).

To see how transformational development work might be pictured in this diagram, imagine a North American named Sharla who lives in Tanzania and works with a Christian NGO to promote microenterprise. If the promotion of income-earning business activity is the primary orientation of her work, Sharla might live in a city and work together in a partnership relationship with a local NGO that actually carries out the microenterprise work in local communities. Individuals in these communities might join a solidarity group that would receive financial support and training from the staff of the local NGO.[2] Sharla's work and that of her sending organization would be channeled through the business/economics area of the wheel. As business practices and production improve, in both quality and quantity, the broken part of the

Figure 4.1. A dynamic development wheel

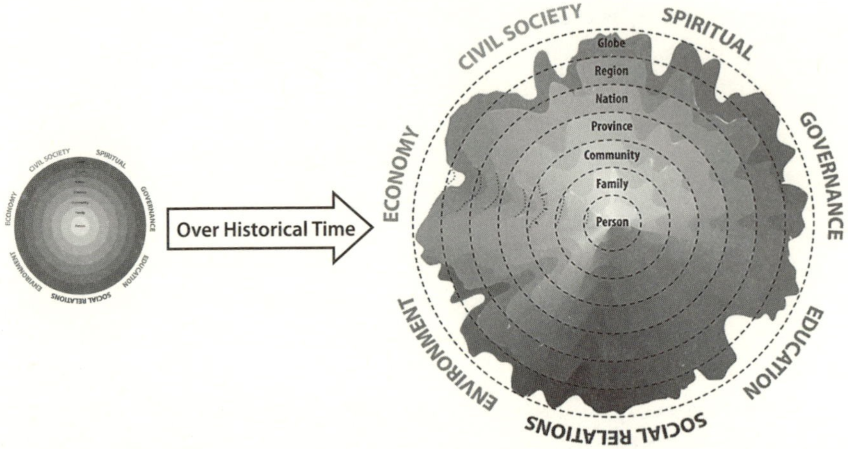

wheel is repaired and, as life improves, this section of the wheel grows and extends outward. As it does, it pulls up some of the distorted circles in the more inward sections of the wheel, while at the same time pushing, however subtly, the outward circles farther out, making the whole wheel rounder and pushing it toward its potential. This is all shown in figure 4.2.

The picture can become more complex. Even though Sharla's primary mission might be income generation through microenterprise work, there might also be secondary goals, such as reconciling ethnic groups, encouraging "green" businesses, or building a civic presence in the communities. If so, then the microenterprise work could be carried out in ways closely associated with ethnic, environmental, and civil society areas of the wheel.

Sharla plays several important roles here. For starters, she is instrumental in the transformation of community, family, and individual lives in Tanzania. Another important role she plays is as a human and informational bridge from the communities in Tanzania to the business/economics players and structures in her own country, and perhaps in the broader world. By living and working directly with Tanzanians, listening to them, interacting with them, and coming to understand the reality of their lives, Sharla carries knowledge and information back to her own organization in North America. Her experiences might lead her to point out how hard it is to do business in Tanzania when North American subsidies on farm products make these imported products cheaper for Tanzanian buyers than local products. With that information in hand, the North American NGO can inform its members, its donors, and its affiliated churches, who can then advocate for change with their political representatives. If such advocacy were to lead to constructive change, then the distortions and

Figure 4.2. Spread effects of development work

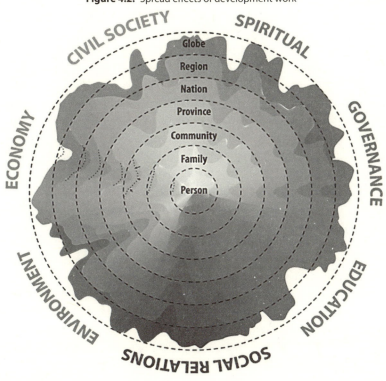

brokenness in the North American context might be healed, thus improving the local business climate for Tanzanian microenterprises. Repairing the wheel in North America would help solidify the business/economics section of the wheel in Tanzania.

Real Development Workers: Where They Work and What They Do

Sharla is fictional, introduced here simply to illustrate how the wheel can help us visualize the range and type of influence that individual workers might have. I would now like to introduce you to some real people working in development. The few people introduced here offer only a glimpse of the many ways to serve. In later chapters, you will meet health workers, agriculturalists, literacy specialists, community-development facilitators, peacebuilders, church organizers, academic researchers, youth leaders, teachers, and communications experts.

Jason Fileta graduated with a BA in sociology and international development. He became an organizer for Micah Challenge USA a few months later, and then became the national coordinator in 2008. Micah Challenge USA is a Christian advocacy organization that organizes churches, universities, and others for action, prayer, and holding government leaders accountable for meeting the Millennium Development Goals (MDGs) by 2015.[3] The United States office is linked with Micah offices in forty other countries. In terms of the development wheel, Jason is located in the civil society sector, which works especially through the church and educational spheres to encourage governments to enact policies that will affect economic, educational, social (especially gender-related), health, and environmental life around the world. If policies in the outer spheres improve, then the lives of persons, families, and communities also take a turn for the better.

Greg Matney graduated with a major in business and minors in economics and political science. Shortly thereafter he accepted a yearlong internship in Kenya with Partners Worldwide, a Christian NGO that is part of the Business as Mission (BAM) movement and works around the world to facilitate business growth that creates jobs and helps bring an end to poverty.[4] After the internship, Greg accepted a full-time position with Partners and now lives in Hyderabad, India, where he works as the regional partnership facilitator for Asia. His job is to promote partnerships among business leaders from North America and Asia, encouraging them in mentorship relationships and in other ways in order to promote business growth in countries where poverty is severe and jobs are sorely needed. Much of his work is with successful business leaders. Greg lives in India and works within both civil society and business/economic sectors. His influence is inward in these sectors as the business activities create jobs. Like Sharla, the fictional microenterprise professional that we encountered earlier, Greg's influence could also spread back through organizational channels to the United States and influence business practices and United States economic policies.

Stephanie Reinitz took a degree in youth ministry and biblical and theological studies and then worked for six years in urban youth ministry. During this time, Stephanie went on a mission trip to Malawi and felt increasingly called to address international human need. After studying for an MA in international development, she became executive assistant to the chief operating officer and chief of staff at International Justice Mission (IJM), "a human rights agency that secures justice for victims of slavery, sexual exploitation and other forms of violent oppression."[5] Stephanie does general administrative work as well as planning for events and projects, all in support of the executive department, which is responsible for carrying out IJM's vision, mission, and operating strategy. We might think of Stephanie as one of the worker bees inside the hive. She supports the work people do for IJM, which is a civil society organization working to help individual victims of injustice and to improve public justice systems. IJM works in partnership with local authorities to rescue individuals in the South and bring perpetrators to justice. IJM also advocates and works with local governments to improve broken public justice systems and strengthen rule of law in countries where their clients live. In terms of the wheel, IJM works inward in its efforts to help individuals in developing countries, and it works outward as it advocates for better rule of law at national and international levels.

Brit Steiner double majored in political science and history. During her college years she participated in two off-campus semesters that led her toward the work she does today. On a semester program in Cairo, Egypt, Brit took all the classes but also volunteered with Mother Teresa's Sisters of Charity Orphanage. Brit saw the overwhelming need all around her and sensed a call to global service. Upon her return to her home campus, she fit in some international studies courses. In her senior year Brit landed a competitive internship with the United States Agency for International Development (USAID). Placed in the Office of Conflict Management and Mitigation, Brit took the initiative to meet lots of people and build meaningful relationships that would later help her achieve the position at USAID that she now holds. Today, Brit is management and program analyst in the Office of Civilian Response, which oversees training, equipping, and deploying mission-ready civilian experts. Brit's primary responsibility is to coordinate deployments and support the civilian response team; she has provided logistical support to dozens of people around the world. Brit hopes to be out in the field one day but realizes that she may have to gain more seniority before that happens. For the moment, she feels connected to the field through her team of civilian response members and their various experiences.

Julie Peterson graduated with a degree in business, a desire to make a difference in this world, and a growing love of Africa. After spending some highly formative years working for the World Bank, USAID, NGOs, and private sector businesses, some of which took her to Kenya and South Africa, she became a partner at American World Service, a private consulting firm that helps develop job-creation and business strategies for governmental bodies and businesses the world over.[6] Julie spends a good portion of her time promoting business opportunities in countries like Rwanda, where business activities and jobs are desperately needed. She promotes business development by sharing best practices of successful companies and countries. She also reviews proposals and creates strategies for developing countries to integrate better into US markets. Much of this is currently pro bono work, but Julie envisions that her work in Africa will one day be profitable as well as helpful to the people there. Julie is located in the United States while working to influence the business/economic areas of life in other countries.

These five individuals provide merely a first idea of the range of possible work that can and needs to be done in development. Here are a few observations about these professionals and their work:

Only one is living in a foreign country, and he spends most of his time with business people, not with the poor.

All five fill particular niches in organizations. Each is a member of a larger team.

In terms of the wheel, some focus their direct work inward, Jason directs his work mostly outward, and Stephanie's work with IJM is oriented in both directions.

In a theme to be explored more fully in the next chapter, only two, Julie and Greg, both in business-related activities, have degrees specifically oriented toward the work they do. The other three are all "generalists."

We can also learn from these experiences what types of organizations employ development workers. One works in the private sector, one for the government, and three in the civil society sector. The civil society sector includes organizations and institutions that serve a public purpose but are not motivated by profit and are not controlled by the government. This sector is huge, diverse, and offers an amazing breadth of opportunities. Development NGOs are one example of a civil society institution, and they exist around the world. Some are explicitly Christian, others not.

One US-based consortium of Christian development organizations is Accord, formerly the Association of Evangelical Relief and Development Organizations. Accord has over seventy member organizations, including such diverse ones as ECHO (agriculture), MAP International (health), Opportunity International (microenterprise), and Samaritan's Purse (general relief and development).[7] Other Christian NGOs are not members of Accord, including the Mennonite Central Committee (MCC), Church World Service (CWS), the Adventist Development and Relief Agency (ADRA), Catholic Relief Services (CRS), and other Catholic organizations, such as the Maryknoll Sisters.

If you are especially interested in global health, check out Christian Connections for International Health (CCIH). CCIH has around 125 member organizations, most of which focus on global health issues.[8]

In the secular world, a well-known consortium organization is InterAction, which lists about two hundred member organizations working in global development,[9] some of which are Christian organizations that are also members of Accord or CCIH. At many of the websites of the member organizations, you can find internship or employment opportunities. Take a look at these and note the diverse array of skills and backgrounds they are looking for. See also the numerous opportunities for volunteer involvement and internships, some for a few months and others for a year or more. Many of the latter involve fundraising, but as we will see in chapter 7, fundraising is not as scary or impossible as it might first sound.

Where Do Foreigners Fit In?

We saw in chapters 1 through 3 that how one looks at the world makes a huge difference in the development strategies and interventions one chooses to work with, and I have tried to give some ideas of what taking our Christianity seriously would mean for the way we do development work. We need to dig a bit deeper into some practical questions that have not yet been fully addressed but that weigh heavy on the minds of those contemplating careers in international development. For many North Americans contemplating a career in international development, the first big question that arises is this:

> As a foreigner, what contribution can I make to the development of people in another country?

Behind this question are some lingering doubts:

> What right do I have to go into another society and try to change their lives?
> Do I know anything special, or have a special skill, that will be useful?
> Wouldn't it be better to hire someone local who knows the culture better and is a lot less expensive to send?

Thankfully, these questions have good answers, which take account of both the mission we embark on and the kind of people who are needed to carry it out. With the help of the people I interviewed for this book, I will try to answer this basic question in this chapter and address other questions in the chapters that follow.

Having observed young people embark on careers in international development for many years, I notice that they often progress through three stages in their thinking. Hopefully, they continue on to a fourth. Stage one often comes after an initial encounter with poverty or an inspiring presentation of the sort discussed in the first section of the introduction. There is a strong sense of the world's need and an enthusiastic desire to make a contribution. In stage two, after some initial study and overseas experiences, students of development grow in their understanding of the magnitude and complexity of the task. They learn that contributing to transformational change requires study, skill, and wisdom. It will be hard, but they embrace the task. At some point, however, visits to failed development projects and anti-aid books like *Dead Aid* by Dambisa Moyo begin to pile up, and any hope that may have survived the initial forays into development work now turns to despair; this is stage three. Making a contribution now seems so difficult, and mistakes that hurt people seem virtually unavoidable.

Each of the first three stages has its positives, but each is also fraught with temptations and dangers. The caring heart of stage one is a God-given motivation to love and is greatly to be praised, but if it is not followed up by serious learning, stage-one missionaries tend to rush in carelessly and do a lot of harm. These are the do-gooders that Paul Collier calls "headless hearts" in his popular book *The Bottom Billion*.[10] Many of the failures of aid result from such ventures. The danger of stage two is that we stay in the realm of interesting theories, talking them to death but never doing anything, much like the figure "Talkative" in John Bunyan's *Pilgrim's Progress*. On the positive side, the hope survives in stage two and the learning done here is an important step toward wisdom. This hope is lost in stage three, and though the world's pain and suffering are real, and though legitimate possibilities for change exist, the jaded foreigner becomes paralyzed and unresponsive, thus allowing evil to run free. In this stage foreigners wonder whether they have anything to offer at all, perhaps believing it is all so complicated that everything they do will turn out badly. The dangers of stages one and three are mirror images of each other. In stage one, the heart is willing, but the mind is weak. In stage three, the mind is strong, but the heart has lost its courage.

Fortunately, stage three is also full of redemptive possibilities. Aspiring servants have grown out of romanticized views of the world into more realistic assessments of themselves and the world around them. If they can make it through stage three, rookie development professionals have the potential for gaining the wisdom of knowing what needs to be changed, how to work in partnership with others to bring about that change, and the ways foreigners can actually contribute to bringing about constructive change. As Christian development workers transition into stage four, they also learn to rely less on themselves and their own abilities and more on God and others. Naive enthusiasm and paralyzing despair are conquered by a realistic hope. Stage four development professionals carry an awareness that change is hard and that mistakes are bound to be made, but they also see that change can come, if slowly, and that they themselves might be a part of that change. The good parts of stages one through three are now tempered with the wisdom necessary to avoid their inherent dangers.

Just knowing about these stages may help you anticipate and cope, but here is some advice that could help as well. Study a reasonable amount and gain a reasonable amount of experience through study programs, internships, and the like, but do not let the fear of making mistakes stop you from getting involved or lead you to despair. It may help to compare the job of the development worker to being a good spouse. Anyone going into marriage would do well to read some books, listen to mentors, and get some counseling on what to expect and how to make the marriage work before taking the plunge, but if everyone waited until they had it all cased, no one would ever get married. We must be willing to start out, accepting the fact that we will make mistakes and that there is still much to learn. When we actually take on that role, whether of a spouse or a development worker, we engage in it with love and care, with humility and patience, and with a willingness to respect the other, admit mistakes, ask forgiveness, listen, keep on learning, and work together. This will cover over a multitude of errors and establish a solid foundation for increasingly effective and transformative relationships.

The voices of experienced development practitioners agree that foreigners are needed and are able to make distinct contributions that no one else could. They also begin their reflections on the role of the foreigner by stressing how important attitude is, emphasizing that the best strategy is to take on the role of a servant, one who does not feel a need to lead, to make key administrative and technical decisions, or to have the status of what Greg Matney calls "the big man." Among the virtues of the successful development worker, cited with remarkable frequency, are patience, humility, and flexibility. Dispense with any of these three and problems are sure to follow.

When foreigners come with servant hearts, they can make a variety of distinct and valuable contributions, several of which are discussed in the sections that follow.

Solidarity and Sharing Traditions

Carl and Carolyn Stauffer worked with the Mennonite Central Committee in Southern Africa for fifteen years and came to see that development work had a lot to do with the mutual learning that comes when people from one tradition (or culture) come into close contact with people from other traditions. Sometimes foreigners have the idea they should totally assimilate, denying their own identity and tradition. The Stauffers say no to that. Learn to respect your own cultural heritage and ways of life, but learn how to respect other traditions and their ways of life too. As we learn from the people we encounter, they also come into contact with different and new ways of being and can then choose to what extent they want to integrate those ways into their own lives.

New and Fresh Ideas

Sometimes people get so caught up in problems, and so stuck in the same old failed patterns of trying to address them, that they benefit from having a new pair of eyes take a look at the problems, offer fresh perspectives on them, and possibly suggest some new and innovative ways of dealing with them.

There are times when bringing in new ideas involves teaching, but the foreigner should be careful not to teach in a top-down, this-is-the-way-it-is style. Instead, teaching will be less about instruction than it is about introducing ideas and possibilities that the community can receive and process, ultimately deciding themselves what to do. This is as true for agricultural and health practices as it is for evangelism. As Dr. Milton Amayun, family health team leader with USAID in Benin, says, "The foreigner can incite development, helping people dream of a better life, and he can also help people embrace new solutions to development problems. Still, true development will be sustained by the people themselves."

Modeling

When the Stauffers speak of intermingling traditions, there is an exchange of ideas that occurs, yet much of the exchange happens more from the way people actually live and behave than from what they say. The way development workers live and conduct themselves in their daily lives may be much more revealing and helpful (or harmful) than anything they might happen to say. Peace Corps volunteer Charlotte Keniston discovered that the women she worked with in Guatemala were seeing her as a model of self-esteem, dignity, and confidence in dealing with male authority figures. Seeing Charlotte behave in ways that were natural for her helped build the confidence of the Mayan women she was working and living with.

For the Christian development worker, the question of how we live is incredibly important. Where we choose to live, how we spend our money, how we relate to others, what kind of language we use, and so on, must be consistent with the messages we want to send. This is a responsibility not to be taken lightly, one that requires some soul-searching before entering another culture as an ambassador of Christ for global reconciliation.

Dana Bates, founder of the New Horizons Foundation in Romania, reflects on the importance of this type of modeling:

> You need to work humbly, but you have something to contribute, too. In Romania there is much apathy. In this context the existence of role models who are really engaged and energetic opens up new possibilities for the young people and actually changes them. In a post-Communist society where people have learned not to care, if you come and model caring and love in your whole being, that can be transformative. I have seen it a lot—but you have to be willing and wanting to see positive things already there in the culture too.

Particular Skills and Expertise

There are situations when particular skills are needed and local resources cannot provide them. These might be technical skills, such as how to set up a microfinance/microenterprise system (see Roland Vanderburg's story in chap. 5 about his work with this in Nicaragua) or how to build a sand dam (some of which were needed in Mozambique where the Stauffers were working). Or they might be human relationship skills, such as leadership formation or conflict transformation and peacebuilding.

Networks, Financial Support, and Other Resources

Being in the field allows the foreigner to act as a liaison between local communities and outside networks that might be able to support community programs. One especially important role here is linking donors back home with transformative programs in the field. The development worker can play a vital intermediary role here, helping communities find reliable donors for well-thought-out development programs but also instructing donors about how to support truly transformational work.

I must add a cautionary note here, because the financial relationship is surely the most difficult to manage in development work. This is one of the paradoxes of development work. We often think development assistance is a matter of money and funding levels, and yet the inflow of financial resources can overwhelm and scuttle local initiative. If not managed wisely, financial flows can be incredibly corrupting.

Among the temptations young development workers must resist is to rush in with resources in an attempt to correct problems they believe finances can correct (e.g., finding outside resources to pay for children's school fees). This is a particularly strong temptation when development workers are not fully convinced they have anything else to offer, so they rely on their connections to funding. Unfortunately, there is no end to stories of how money and finances have brought trouble instead of progress, failed projects instead of sustainable ones. As Ryan Musser, who has been on short-term assignments in several African countries, discovered, "foreigners can provide connections and resources, which can definitely be helpful, but you have to be careful with that because the solution is never just dumping resources into a community."

Speaking about his organization's overall working strategy, CRWRC's US director, Andrew Ryskamp, says that, "CRWRC doesn't do a lot of funding, but enough to get some programs going. I judge success to be when our partners say CRWRC doesn't offer much in the way of financial resources but [that they] do value the time we spend with them. The dilemma here is that you often think development will go faster if you put some resources in, but you have to ensure too that ownership is local and that the local organization is moving toward sustainability."

Channeling the Voices

One of the most important contributions foreigners make is to bring news of joys, challenges, and needs from one community to another. In development work, foreigners with an understanding of local affairs are well positioned to report accurately to their home community and country what is happening and what needs to be done. So it is with famines and conflicts and earthquakes, but so it is too with all sorts of other news that serves to bring our human family closer together and make us more able to care for each other as neighbors. For example, when local communities are suffering under a brutal dictatorship that North American governments support, foreigners can channel local voices so that their fears and concerns can be heard around the world in ways that may motivate their global neighbors to action. Such work might include direct support, prayer, or perhaps advocacy before the government.

After years of working in the field, Roland Vanderburg, program director for CAUSE Canada, is ready with an answer when members of North American churches ask him how they can help. He tells them what he has heard and learned from the people he works with around the world.

> Because we are from the powerful North, we need to tell our leaders that social justice is important to us. Our church communities often ask me what is to be done. We need to tell them that we should let our government leaders know that we care about social justice.
>
> We also need to instruct our home churches about development in general. Far too often Christian development work has not been done well and has not

really supported transformation of identity and vocation. We need to help the church at home engage in effective development-oriented mission work.

Building Kingdom Community

Finally, global development is about more than solving local problems and tackling global issues; it is also about forming global community. Development is about measurable results in such areas as agricultural output and disease prevention, but the relationships that form and the community that develops also have intrinsic value. It is difficult to build community unless you get to know each other, work side by side, worship and pray together, and share in each other's joys and sorrows. Some of this can be done at a distance, but not all of it. There is thus no getting around what some might call a "ministry of presence." A longtime colleague, Tom Post, caught my attention once when he said that "yes, we must pursue measurable results with tenacity, but we must also develop relationships of mutual respect, build each other up, and enrich each other, and so give us a sense of life in the kingdom of God." Relationships that build global community are thus one form of the Pentecost vision of people from every tribe and nation joining together in work, worship, and in the whole of life.[11]

And Now . . . A Word from Developing-Country Nationals

Up to now, most of the wisdom regarding the role of foreigners comes from the foreigners themselves. But what do development professionals from developing countries say about the role that North Americans can and should play? What qualities in North Americans are particularly appreciated and which are more problematic or even harmful? I asked these questions of eight developing country nationals from different parts of the world, all of whom have years of experience working with development workers from the North. In all eight responses there was a striking degree of consistency, almost approaching unanimity.[12]

They affirmed many of the roles already mentioned, using nouns such as "advocate," "role model," "mentor," "partner," and "facilitator," and verbs such as "sharing," "networking," "bridging," "financing," "empowering," and even "inspiring." One striking comment came from Chinyere Nwachukwu of Nigeria, who says that "the role of the North American is to be a listener. Expect to learn with the people and to work with the people. Do not focus on 'helping' the people." Helping is of course a good thing, but Chinyere is referring to a common tendency among foreigners to condescend and to behave with a superior air.

The most frequently cited qualities valued by developing country nationals in foreigners are their appreciation and love for the local culture, the people, and the language. These qualities are manifested in a spirit of joyful learning about local ways of life and the ability to develop relationships in the local setting. As I read over their comments, I was struck by the almost complete absence of such qualities as knowledge and skills. Yes, knowledge and skills are valued, but the fact that the general question elicits a nearly exclusive focus on attitudes and behavior patterns should not be lost on the foreigner entering a new cultural context. It is almost as if knowledge and skills do not matter if these deeper relational qualities are missing.

Finally, a few words about problematic qualities of foreigners. To some degree, one could simply cite the obverse of the qualities mentioned above. Pamela Mumbi of Zambia would like to avoid foreigners who "portray the American way of life, thought, and culture as the best." She notes that this is a prevalent tendency in young North Americans. Other negative qualities include arrogance, a know-it-all attitude, a judgmental or blaming spirit, and a tendency to throw money at problems. Of special interest are the comments by Davis Omanyo of Kenya, who says that some foreigners only want to give but are not able to receive, and by Kelia Garcia of Honduras, who would like to warn us away from "trying to solve the problems without giving locals the opportunity to identify their own solutions."

Once again, the importance of relational qualities comes through quite clearly. For the Christian development worker, this should come as no surprise when improving relationships and building community are such key components of our perspective on development.

The Virtues of Balance and Discernment

Remember the often-cited phrase in development circles that "our job is to work ourselves out of a job"? There are situations when this saying makes sense, particularly when the costs of a specific skill will go way down if a local person can be found to do it; but it is not always true. As shown above, there are some jobs that only foreigners can do, and sometimes, all things considered, foreigners are simply the best option for a particular job at a particular time. We should not enter these assignments with a sense of shame that we are doing them instead of someone else. Nor should we claim permanent ownership of a particular assignment or position. There may come a time when foreigners are no longer the right or best persons for a particular job, at which point the foreigner needs to step aside with grace and find another place to serve.

David Bronkema, director of Eastern University's master's program in development, offers some wise advice on this point—namely, that we all need to be listening to God's leading in discerning our special vocation. That includes an awareness of God's overall plan of redemptive transformation, but especially a sensitivity to whether any particular person—male or female, old or young, foreign or local—is the best person for a particular task. Such awareness is the responsibility of both the organization looking to fill a certain position and any person thinking of taking on this particular task. Bronkema says it makes no sense to make a rule along the lines of "foreigners can do these jobs, but locals must always be assigned these other jobs." He elaborates on this point by saying that, "there are many places where North Americans can contribute. God may call you to work in local communities. As communities grow and change, your role may change as you come alongside and find out what the needs are and how you might contribute. The possibilities will span the gamut. Development efforts are so huge that you do not know exactly where you will end up and what you will be doing. So much depends on being attentive to God's leading every step of the way."

Bronkema highlights the reality that people, communities, and the whole world are always in flux, ever changing. Today it might be your calling to work directly in a local community. Tomorrow it might be too; or maybe not. Maybe tomorrow it will be better, and more in keeping with God's overall plan, to assign that particular task to someone local, and for you to do something else in this ever-changing world. Be attentive to God's leading and do not be misled by categorical sayings. Ndunge Kiiti, professor of intercultural studies at Houghton College, suggests that North Americans—due perhaps to our wealth, education, and our problem-solving culture—are tempted to go in and fix things, or at least try to. In the context of international development, where local participation and ownership are so important, Kiiti reminds North Americans that "it is good for us to ask the hard question of whether we are the right persons for the job." If indeed you are the right person, then you should proceed, embracing the tension that exists between humility and confidence.

Finally, Greg Matney reminds us that the world is increasingly "flat," meaning that people with special skills are crossing borders more and more, and that many parts of our lives are increasingly globalized. If a program needs someone skilled in business development, or in HIV/AIDS work, or in building rooftop vegetable gardens, what does it matter if this skilled person happens to be Ukrainian, Zambian, Haitian, or North American? As Matney says, "I have heard it said that foreigners should stay no longer than a few years in a particular country, but as the world gets flatter, the role of the foreigner is just that of any conscientious person. In an increasingly flat world, I live in Hyderabad pretty much the way I would live in Chicago, and I need to always be thinking about what particular role I play on the overall team."

Rebecca's Vocational Path

Many possible roles await you if you feel called to full-time service on behalf of those in need around the world. Some of those roles will be in other countries, some right in the midst of local communities there, and others in your home country. Some will be in leadership roles, some in support roles. Those roles will likely change as the world changes and as you change. You may start working in a foreign country and switch later to your home country, or vice versa. When you end up at a certain place and in a certain position, you will likely look back and be amazed at how God led you there. For many development workers, their vocational paths are an adventure in and of themselves.

Consider Rebecca Vander Meulen's story and see how she and the service she provides have evolved. In middle and high school Rebecca went with her church on mission trips to economically depressed regions in the United States and to several developing countries. Through these experiences she came to realize that her Christian faith required her to pay attention to these issues.

As she headed off to college, Rebecca was blessed with a roommate who grew up in Central America as the child of development workers. She began to consider the possibility of doing development work herself one day and gradually came to see this prospect as entirely realistic. Studying biology with the idea of becoming a physician and serving in the developing world, she further explored career options in development by taking some courses in development studies, including a semester program in Honduras. In Honduras she learned much about the complexity of development work but also witnessed ordinary people following God's call and doing extraordinary things.

As part of a January-term class, Rebecca traveled to Washington, DC, and happened to visit the Christian advocacy organization Bread for the World (BFW). Upon graduation, she applied for an internship position at BFW, was accepted, and for two years analyzed development issues, becoming especially intrigued by the links between poverty and such health issues as nutrition and HIV/AIDS.

Her experience at BFW led her to a graduate program in global public health. Through a university contact, she traveled to Mozambique to do summer research for her master's thesis. Once in Mozambique, Rebecca met new people and grew familiar with the country, its history, and its culture. She returned to Mozambique after graduation for a two-year volunteer stint with Concern America, a community-development organization.

During this two-year period, Rebecca met the local Anglican bishop, who asked her to help launch a formal response to HIV/AIDS within the church. She accepted this assignment of helping to strengthen the abilities of local congregations to address the scourge of HIV/AIDS, and it soon became a full-time job, a job she still does today. Over the last five years, Rebecca has helped in the formation of "Equipas de Vida" (Life Teams) in 170 congregations, which are now taking responsibility to define their own strategies for responding to needs in their local communities.

Rebecca lives in Lichinga, a medium-sized city in the north, but travels frequently for training activities in churches throughout the region. Rebecca is a foreigner in Mozambique, but she now works for a Mozambican institution, receives a Mozambican salary, and works with Mozambican colleagues. As she evaluates her role there, she realizes that sometimes external skills are necessary, which is the situation that keeps her there, but she also knows that Mozambicans from the region may one day be better suited to do the job she now does. For the moment, however, she is where she belongs and where she feels called. Listen to Rebecca as she sums up her thoughts about her current role in international development: "Had I more actively dreamed long ago of an ideal job, it would have been pretty close to what I do now with the Anglican Church—strengthening the church and taking action on social development. God uses experiences, skills, and opportunities in so many different ways. I like very much the way things have come together to bring me to where I am today, though I did not plan it!"

Further Reflection and Action Steps

1. Come up with your own metaphor. Metaphors are a great help to our thinking, but they always get strained or break down at some point. Where does the beehive metaphor break down? Where does the wheel metaphor break down? What is another metaphor that describes the human condition and the character of development?

2. This chapter showed how Sharla, Jason, and Greg fit into the wheel model and what kind of impact they hope to have. Do the same type of analysis with Stephanie, Brit, Julie, and Rebecca. Where do they fit in the wheel, and what is their impact?

3. What is your niche? Imagine what contribution you would like to make to international development. Place yourself in the wheel; then show the channels through which you would work and what impacts you would hope to have.

4. Using the consortium sites listed in footnotes 7, 8, and 9, find one development organization where you would consider applying for an internship or a position. Write a brief statement about why this organization appeals to you and what its approach to development is.

5. Consider Rebecca's story. Rebecca feels called to be where she is now, working directly for the Anglican Church of Mozambique. Is this the sort of position to which you might aspire? Why or why not?

5
Becoming an Effective Foreigner

What Kinds of People Are Needed in Development Work?

Love without disciplined intelligence is inefficient, naive, and, in its bungling good intentions, catastrophic. And intelligence without love breeds a brutalizing technocracy that crushes people.

Denis Goulet, development ethicist[1]

Christian development workers cannot compromise on excellence. As someone on our team said, "Christian sloppy is still sloppy and not God honoring." Being in a cross-cultural context does not mean we can compromise on our ethics or standards.

Mike Soderling, medical missionary in Guatemala

For most people going overseas, you need a balance between generalist abilities, skills that carry you [in] any place and time, and particular skill sets that actually make you useful in a way that other people would not be.

Carl and Carolyn Stauffer, development workers with MCC in Southern Africa

Eighty percent of being successful in life is showing up.

Woody Allen in *Play It Again, Sam*

Introduction: Want Ads versus Formation

Have you ever looked at employment listings and found something like this?

Wanted: Astrophysicist. Must be Nobel Prize winner, speak ten languages fluently, and have thirty years of experience.

Maybe this is a slight exaggeration, but if you do a Google search for "careers in international development," you will find a lot of postings for which you are utterly unqualified. On the one hand, it could be a depressing exercise, because it may seem that you will never qualify for any of the positions listed. You will also see names of organizations you never knew existed, and you may wonder about them. Are they reputable? Are they the sort of organization you would like to work for? Do their ideas about development coincide with yours?

On the other hand, one good outcome of looking at all the job postings in development for which you do not qualify now is that you will get some idea of how big the field is and how many different kinds of professionals are needed.

There may come a time when listings like these help you, but many professionals will tell you that networking is a better way to find jobs. Networking simply means getting to know people, letting them get to know you, and trying to find what you are looking for through the people you know and the people they happen to know. For organizations looking for good employees, networks help find the best candidates. Job seekers use networks to learn who is hiring and what organizations might be looking for.

Networks definitely help open doors, but do not forget that you must still be a person of substance once the doors crack open. What kinds of people are successful in development? What process of formation and training do they undergo? Once again, we will rely on the experiences and wisdom of development professionals who know the field. If you aspire to become a successful development worker yourself, there is good advice here. One strong theme is that you should take stock of your gifts, study what you love, get involved as you are able, and take advantage of good opportunities that come your way. If you cultivate a set of useful capabilities and gain wisdom through your own experience, doors will open, probably through the networks you have entered. Before you know it, entry-level positions, and then others that fit you even better, may come your way. It can happen very quickly.

The chapter begins with two stories, one of a generalist and the other of a specialist, both of whom have become prominent development leaders. Their stories will lead into a discussion that interweaves two central themes, one being the virtues, knowledge, and skills that are especially helpful in development work, and the second being the difficult question of whether aspiring development workers should train to be generalists or specialists. The quick answer to this question is that you should be the person God intended you to be, because he can and does employ both generalists and specialists in his service. But stick around for the longer answer; it gets pretty interesting.

As you read about Dana and Michael, there might be a tendency to feel intimidated. Do not be. For one thing, Dana and Michael are obviously both gifted, but they began their journeys much like anyone else. They might well have been intimidated by their own stories had they been able to look ahead. Remember too that not all successful paths must be like theirs. Read these simply as stories of how God led two of his followers through a series of twists and turns to where they are now, and then let God lead you on your own path.

Meet Generalist Dana DeRuiter and Social Scientist Michael Woolcock

Dana DeRuiter liked to write, so she majored in English. It might come as a surprise, then, that ten short years later Dana found herself on a mountaintop in Hokkaido, Japan, advising top officials from the Bush administration on global health policy at the G8 meetings. How does one go from an English major in college to a senior policy position in global health in such a short time? Here is Dana's story.

It began on a semester program in Honduras.

> After that semester I found myself drawn to working on issues of poverty. I had been exposed to the complexities and wanted to learn and contribute more. Living in a developing country and grappling with all these issues in a hands-on way changes you. It certainly changed me.

Back at college for her senior year, Dana added a minor in international development to her English major and volunteered at CRWRC. Volunteer activities became an internship, which eventually turned into a full-time position. She worked for nearly five years at CRWRC, where her main job was writing field reports, funding proposals, and evaluation reports.

Aware of her writing abilities, CRWRC sent Dana to Bangladesh, Kenya, Haiti, and South Africa so that she could write about CRWRC's work. Those were great learning experiences. Dana's learning continued when CRWRC tapped her skills to assemble a manual of best practices.

After five years at CRWRC, graduate school seemed like a logical next step, and Dana began a master's program in public policy. Dana had avoided math and economics in college, a decision she came to regret in the face of her program's heavy emphasis on economics and quantitative research, but the intense academic workload and rigor was invaluable to honing her analytical skills.

During the summer between her first and second years of graduate school, Dana worked as an intern at the State Department in Washington, DC, which sparked a strong desire for future government service. She acted on this desire by competing to become a Presidential Management Fellow (PMF), a two-year federal program designed to attract graduate students into civil service. Dana was selected and went on to pursue her first government job as a PMF at the President's Emergency Plan for AIDS Relief (PEPFAR).

On staff at the State Department, and assigned to the PEPFAR program, Dana became a core team leader with responsibilities for Ethiopia and Uganda. Travel to Africa was common. After just three years with PEPFAR, she served on a detail assignment with the National Security Council as the director for global health. During this eighteen-month assignment, half under President Bush and half under President Obama, Dana strategized about global health policy with some of the US government's top leaders. It was during this time that she traveled to Japan for the G8 meetings. In 2009, Dana became a senior policy advisor for global health at USAID. As a policy advisor, Dana acts as a link between technical experts and the higher levels of policy formation in the executive branch of the government.

Dana describes herself as a generalist, which she sees as an asset. "What I have is a set of tools that allows me to think critically and analyze problems in many different arenas—tools such as knowing how to frame tough questions, exploring a wide range of policy options, communicating among a variety of stakeholders, and helping to bring the right people together to formulate policy."

Dana is not oblivious to the criticisms of foreign aid, but she often finds that these criticisms gloss over the complexities inherent to the field. She thinks the US government has an important role to play, and sees her own role as providing decision makers with the best information and processing tools for making good policy. She feels incredibly blessed to have this opportunity. "I definitely see this as a calling. Some people are called to live and work overseas. As for me, my calling is to be here in Washington."

Michael Woolcock is a senior social scientist with the Development Research Group at the World Bank as well as a director of the World Bank's "Justice for the Poor" initiative.[2] A significant part of his job is to research, write about, and consult on policy issues with governments around the world and with multilateral institutions like the World Bank.

Researching such vital global issues and becoming a recognized development authority on social capital and justice systems was hardly on Michael's mind in 1989 when he first felt the call to global service. As a young man, Michael hoped for a career in sports, but economic realities pushed him instead to become a high school English teacher. By age twenty-five he had taken a position at a small Australian vocational college where he taught about social impact assessment as it related to tourism in developing countries. It was his first significant encounter with the developing world, though he had still never been out of Australia. As he taught the course, Michael became concerned about the types of social interaction that tourism fostered between wealthy Australians and developing-country nationals.

With these thoughts going through his mind, he attended, as he had done for ten years, his "Monday night group," a gathering of Christian young people who met once a week for Bible study, book discussion, and fellowship. The group was highly influential in Michael's spiritual, intellectual, and general-character formation. That night a leader of the group argued that hunger and poverty in Ethiopia represented a major challenge to Christians the world over. Would the global Christian community take up the challenge? Michael pictured people around the world suffering so needlessly and dying so young. It was an epiphany for him, because he knew right then what he must do with his life and where he would put his energies.

Michael is the sort of person who, when he makes a decision, dedicates himself to it wholeheartedly. He knew he needed to start with learning, so he searched for a top-quality program and ended up in the United States. Over the next seven years, Michael studied for a PhD in sociology and took enough economics courses to be, as he puts it, "minimally trained and functional" in the academic discipline that was then dominating development thought and practice. He also spent time in India and Bangladesh, where he studied the interactions between social and economic aspects of microenterprise programs. It was this research and writing that brought him increasing recognition as one of the world's foremost authorities on the role and importance of social relationships, or what has come to be called "social capital."

Coincidentally, as he was finishing his degree, some leaders in the World Bank were at the same time beginning to recognize the tight relationship between the social side of life and economic development. They put out word that they were hiring researchers to explore these issues. One of Woolcock's colleagues alerted him to this position, and in 1998 Michael began working for the World Bank.

Since then Michael has continued his research, written many books and papers, and taught development at Harvard University in the United States and at the University of Cambridge and the University of Manchester in the United Kingdom. He has been at the forefront of important research and policy initiatives and is now a director of the $15 million "Justice for the Poor" program, where his focus is on improving systems of justice and governance.

Throughout Michael's vocational journey, his faith has played a prominent role. He did not know where development education would lead him, so he concentrated on simply being faithful. He realizes that his specific path, with all its unforeseen twists and turns, can't be held up as a step-by-step model for others, but he can commend his general posture of faithfully taking one step at a time. As he says, "one of the principles of our Monday night group was that what you do now is preparing you for what God has next in mind for you."

The Essential Triad: Virtues, Knowledge, and Skills

If we analyze these stories with an eye to discovering what allowed Dana and Michael to move so quickly through a succession of positions and to then become, at relatively young ages, highly respected development leaders, we will notice an interplay among three central aspects of life that make people effective: virtues, knowledge, and skills (or, to abbreviate, VKS). Dana and Michael were both motivated by their faith, which led them to care for people in need and gave them a desire to serve. Both put in time doing serious studying and learning. And both are highly competent in practicing their trades. Think of these attributes as three wheels on a tricycle (see fig. 5.1; you might note that I gravitate toward metaphors with wheels in them). When you ride, your virtues will power and direct your knowledge and skills. The trike will ride faster and more smoothly (i.e., it will achieve more) the sturdier and rounder the three wheels are. If any of the three wheels is deficient or missing, you will not get very far.

The virtue wheel is at the lead, following the biblical idea that virtues such as love and compassion come first. The apostle Paul puts it in this order in his letter to the Philippians: he prays that their love may lead to knowledge, their knowledge to action, and their actions to the fruit of righteousness (Phil. 1:9–10). It all starts with love, a love that leads to learning and action, which must be supported by knowledge and skill. All three wheels work together. For example, if you love someone and want to do something that will contribute to that person's well-being, then you must learn or come to know what will best help. If you come to know that the people you love need clean water, then it will be good to learn about water, how it contributes to health, how to obtain clean water, and the like. Once you have an understanding of the sources of clean water, it becomes important to learn how to work with people in a development context and how to dig wells, set up functioning water

Figure 5.1. Basic qualifications for development workers

Virtues/Character
- compassion
- identity
- purpose
- flexibility
- humility
- love of "the other"
- prayer
- perseverance

Knowledge
- culture
- language
- history
- development theory
- specialty field

Skills
- people skills
- professionalism
- technical experience
- networking
- communication
- listening

management systems, and develop water usage laws. Knowledge is thus put into practice through the development of skills.

Sometimes we emphasize knowledge and skills but forget love. When this is the case, Paul tells us in 1 Corinthians 13, we are like clanging cymbals and do not actually achieve anything good. If love is missing, we may even use our knowledge and skills in self-serving ways that actually harm others. All three wheels are necessary, and they must work together. If love combines with knowledge and skill, then the community may well be blessed with clean water and transformed lives, which Paul thinks of as "the fruit of righteousness."

What kinds of people, with what mixes of VKS, are best suited to development work, especially aspects of the work that put them in contact with people in developing countries? Allow me to tell you a negative story. Once, in Costa Rica, we invited a young missionary couple on a Sunday afternoon outing. As the day went along we naturally talked about our lives and the work we were doing in this foreign land. When it was the young man's turn to speak, he went through a rather long list of difficulties. He was having a terrible time with the language, did not like the food, found Costa Ricans rather unlikable, could not handle the government bureaucracies, and was seriously homesick. I appreciated his honesty, and there are probably days when any good missionary feels like this, but he seemed genuinely confused and distraught by it all. Someone finally asked him why he was in Costa Rica if it was so difficult for him. His answer? "Because God is calling me to be here." We did not know each other well enough for me to think that I might counsel him at that point, but had the opportunity arisen, I probably would have affirmed him in his sense of a general call to serve God and his people around the world but questioned him about his specific call to Costa Rica. I would probably have encouraged him to find a mission closer to his home in North America where there are also many opportunities to serve. I would have been thinking about his own well-being but also the well-being of the Costa Ricans he intended to serve.

When I asked development professionals what personal qualities are important for development work, the picture that emerged was much more positive. Among others, a virtue highlighted by development professionals is love and appreciation for the people, languages, and foreign cultures, including the food. A spirit of adventure and a willingness to live in distant lands help a lot too.

Based on what these development professionals said, a composite picture of the ideal development worker comes into view. Imagine you are reading a job posting for such an ideal person, which might read something like this (notice the overlap with what developing country nationals said in chap. 4):

The successful applicant must have the following qualifications:

Virtues

> *Love*—love for people from all cultures and all backgrounds, manifested by a deep respect for everyone and a desire to get to know them and be among them.
>
> *Humility*—the awareness that other people, even the very poor, are knowledgeable, skilled, and have much to offer and teach; being able to laugh at yourself; discerning God's plan instead of imposing your own.
>
> *Confidence*—willingness to contribute analysis and ideas while allowing others to critique you and even reject you if they so choose.
>
> *Patience*—resisting the temptation to analyze problems superficially and to expect results too quickly, and a willingness to move ahead in the people's time and in the Lord's time.
>
> *Persistence*—an abiding will never to accept the unacceptable and to continue striving for life-giving transformation, even in the face of adversity, minimal progress, or apparent failure.
>
> *Curiosity*—a love of lifelong learning about the people you work with, God and his world, yourself, best practices, new ideas . . . basically everything.
>
> *Professionalism*—seriousness about accepting only your best effort, recognizing that intense study and hard work must accompany the longings of the heart.

Willingness to grow—a capacity for self-reflection, personal growth, and character formation.

Areas of Knowledge

Self—including faith, strengths and weaknesses, purpose and motivation, and an awareness and appreciation of your own history and cultural identity.

God—a strong spiritual center, with a pronounced willingness to grow in understanding God's plan for you, his people the world over, and his world in general.

People you serve—their history, institutions, culture, language, ways of thought, belief systems, and unique, identity-defining stories.

Development theory—an awareness of the history of development and competing development theories and perspectives, the relationship between what happens in the community (micro) and global systems (macro), and the dynamics of constructive cross-cultural interaction.

Skills

People—an ability to relate, work, communicate, and cooperate with others across cultural, linguistic, and socioeconomic barriers.

Listening and observing—the ability to affirm others when they are speaking, to draw others out, to ask good questions, and to grow in your understanding of people, cultures, and organizations very different from the ones you are accustomed to.

Communication—especially writing and speaking at professional levels (in meetings, letters, proposals, etc.), but also in ways that allow you to take difficult concepts and speak about them in simple ways.

Self-assessment—the ability to capitalize on one's strengths and to find ways to either strengthen or overcome personal weaknesses.

Critical thinking and problem solving—the ability to see connections between goals and strategies, to discover causal links, and to see the pros and cons of different solutions; the ability to learn from mistakes and make improvements.

Some unique combination of knowledge and skill (more on this below).

No doubt this is a daunting list. First, no one person can possibly embody all these qualifications perfectly. Development workers are not superhuman, which is why Dana Bates, whose story is told in the next section, suggests that a key virtue in addition to the ones listed is the ability to forgive others as well as to ask for (and accept) forgiveness for yourself. Where love and humility are present, they will cover a multitude of sins, and forgiveness will come.

Second, the three components of the VKS trinity are deeply interconnected and very hard to sharply delineate. For example, one might know how to speak a language, but the ability to learn languages is a skill, and the love of language learning is a virtue closely linked with loving others. If you really love a people, then it follows that you will want to know them, which means that speaking their language is essential. Another example is the virtue of patience, which becomes part of knowledge if we understand that transformation may be a slow process. We can also train ourselves to be patient, such that it becomes something of a skill.

There is much about these job qualifications that is straightforward and self-explanatory, and maybe I do not need to say much more about it. But I would like to let you in on some especially delightful and instructive words from the development professionals I interviewed. Note the experience and wisdom embedded in these comments.

On the centrality of love

> Love is the most important virtue to bring to development work. We must love the people, the country, and the work we are called to do. Acts of love are what people remember long after we are gone. Love is the message of the gospel; we love people because God loved them first.
>
> —Dr. Milton B. Amayun, MD, MPH, family health team leader, USAID Benin

On balancing confidence and humility

> We have to be confident that we have something to share. At the same time it requires an incredible amount of humility. You are going into somebody else's culture and space with relatively little knowledge. That requires a certain amount of swagger and a large dose of humility.
>
> —Matt Van Geest, a community development worker with long experience in Haiti

On taking the time to learn

> I remember reading about Paulo Freire and how he was very slow to judge. He moved into a community and then spent at least three months listening and

observing. He hung out, observed people, and talked with them casually for a long time before making any suggestions about what the community might want to think about or how they might want to organize. Our tendency as North Americans is to move in and pass judgment on the first day. It is both a skill and a virtue to spend time in the observation phase, and even then you only start to scratch the surface. I have been in Nicaragua for twenty years, and there are still things I don't understand.

—Dr. Belinda Forbes, a missionary dentist working in Nicaragua (see her story later in this chapter)

On languages and relationships

Languages are really helpful, because language is the door to a relationship. If you have to communicate through an interpreter, then you are on one side of the door and the other person is on the other side of the door. It is like you are passing things to each other, but you are not in the same room.

—Duncan Boughton, agricultural economist at Michigan State University

On compassion

In development work we must continually ask what touches our hearts. I was in Cambodia when the earthquake hit Haiti. I saw it on the news, but it didn't impact me much. I finally sat down that Sunday and said, 'God, what's going on? Two hundred thousand people have been wiped out, and I'm approaching this from an organizational perspective, not from my heart.' I had to get this straightened out, which thankfully I did. A wise pastor told me that if you don't have the passion to deal with what is happening at the community level, then it's time to quit. If you think in terms of organization—putting numbers in the right boxes but not letting the pain touch your heart—then it's time to bag it."

—Andrew Ryskamp, United States director of CRWRC

On passion and preparation

The most important question I ask in an interview to a young person is how their undergraduate experience changed their outlook on life. I want to know how they grew from that experience and what the key influences in their personal growth were. We want people who can describe well a sense of passion and calling for the poor in bringing about change. I get more excited about a young professional who walks in the door and is well balanced, solidly rooted, and moldable than I do about somebody who comes in with all kinds of specialized training.

—Dirk Booy, partnership leader for global field
operations for World Vision International

On lifelong learning

In the last semester of my senior year of university, a guy left his last undergraduate exam screaming, "Yahoo . . . I'm done." But I thought, "that's sad, because it is just beginning. Sure, they have given us a fancy sheet of paper, and we have learned some things, but the real learning is just beginning. . . . We must always be learning."

—Roland Vanderburg, program director for CAUSE Canada

The discussion in this section has thus far intentionally avoided the last item on the list of job qualifications, the one about the unique combination of knowledge and skill. All the qualities up to that point are those that anyone working in development should strive to embody. It is wonderful to be a good, centered, generally capable person, but is that enough? This question leads us to the generalist/specialist dilemma, on which we need to spend some additional time.

Generalist or Specialist: More Real People and Some Words of Advice

When students enter college, one of the questions on many of their minds is, what will I be trained for when I graduate? The anxiety surrounding this question may be aggravated by that oh-so-common sequence of questions that college students suffer through time and time again. The first question is, what is your major? That is an easy one, but then comes the dreaded follow-up, what are you going to do with that? Though the questions can induce anxiety, we should admit that they are fair, especially when college costs tens of thousands of dollars and several years of your life. But they are not the best questions either, because so much of what lies ahead is unknown, and most people are just beginning to get a handle on who they are, what their beliefs and commitments are, what they are good at, and what they like to do.

However the question about a major is answered as the college years unfold, that second question rises to the forefront when students start getting infected with "senioritis." They may have studied history, philosophy, international relations, cross-cultural studies, or even international development, but many college graduates still feel as if their knowledge and skills have not advanced to the point that they can be considered specialists, much less an expert in a given field.

They are not yet health professionals, economists, human rights lawyers, bankers, agriculturalists, or professionals of any kind possessing advanced knowledge and skills that they could use to help others. They are generalists, and they wonder if they are employable and whether they should acquire some set of technical knowledge and skill.

What college graduates do not yet realize is that they typically know more and are able to do more than they think, but their awareness of this grows gradually over time and through experience. We will study this further in the next two chapters when we look at the college years and beyond. For the moment, it may help to hear more from people in the field about what they do, what kind of training they have, and what advice they have for young people on these issues. What we find is a diverse mix, with some people being generalists all their lives, some training early on to be specialists and then using those skills for a long time, and some people moving back and forth. One person starts out a generalist and then becomes a specialist; another trains to be a specialist but later becomes a generalist.

If you look back at the development professionals introduced in previous chapters, you will find an array of specialists and generalists. Lawyers, business people, and social scientists are among the specialists. The generalists include those who have turned their skills toward managing organizations, forming policy, and advocacy. The fact that such admirable people can serve in so many roles signals that answering the generalist/specialist question is not straightforward.

I would like to introduce you now to four more development professionals, two specialists and two generalists. I have three purposes in mind. One is to help you see how different combinations of VKS play out professionally. A second is to impress upon you the variability of vocational paths real people have followed. And a third is to provide you with some role models who might inspire you individually. We will start with an agricultural specialist.

Beth Doerr works in Florida as the internship manager at Educational Concerns for Hunger Organization (ECHO), which trains young people interested in agricultural missions.[3] Beth grew up in Georgia and gained a lot of helpful experience on her family's hobby farm, including gardening and many practical skills in, as she says, "fixing things." Beth grew up thinking about mission service but knew she did not have the gifts to be a preacher. She thought about agriculture instead and found a college offering a BA in agriculture. Upon graduation, Beth interned at ECHO and gradually specialized in drip irrigation, fruit tree orchards, and vegetable gardening. She took consulting jobs and some longer-term positions that allowed her to work in the field and have an impact in developing countries around the world. Back at ECHO since 2004, she now shares her gifts with today's interns, many of who will get out in the field like she once did. Early in her career, Beth chose not to get an advanced degree, though studying for an MA is still a possibility. She noticed that specialists with advanced degrees tended to spend their time in offices, and she wanted to "get out there" and be close to the people.

Specialized knowledge and skill have been important to Beth, and she has used them well, but she stresses they are not everything, maybe not even the most important thing. As an ambassador of Christ, she came to realize that building relationships with people was vital, and also that the way she lived was every bit as important as her specialized knowledge and skill. She saw how important modeling Christian life practices is, because "people are watching our attitudes and actions, not just what we are accomplishing."

Next, consider Dana Bates, a generalist who turned a desire to be active outdoors into an adventure-education and experiential-learning program in Romania. Dana is the founder and executive director of New Horizons Foundation Romania,[4] an organization that provides experiential education for youth in ways that encourage them to become agents in the sustainable development of their own communities. New Horizons combines adventure education and youth service clubs in an effort to help Romania's youth become moral, conscientious citizens committed to the common good. New Horizons' programs are proving to be so successful and inspiring that they are becoming a model for other organizations in other countries.

As is so common, Dana's path to New Horizons could not have been envisioned looking forward, though it does make sense when looking back. In college, Dana sensed that he loved thinking, so he majored in philosophy, a decision he has never regretted. Surprisingly, Dana sees his degree as highly practical.

> To build and lead an organization like this, you need to think well, communicate well, and be able to persuade people about your vision. . . . You can learn to tie knots for the ropes course later, but as a philosophy major, I learned to separate essentials from nonessentials, to abstract, to build bridges across ideas that do not seem related but that really do have shared assumptions. Being able to think well and to write well have been invaluable to me in my work.

At graduation, Dana thought he might become a pastor like his father, but weakness in public speaking and a lack of enthusiasm for his courses forced him to reconsider. During seminary, Dana and his wife Brandi got involved with a summer adventure-education program, which took them on LaVida expedition programs in the Adirondacks. In the mid-1990s they visited Romania and couldn't help but notice the social, political, and moral breakdown in the aftermath of communism. Sensing a call to do something about it, they resolved to bring adventure education to Romania and to thus help the nation's youth develop into the moral and visionary leaders it so desperately needed. They signed up with Young Life, raised support, settled in a poor, coal-mining mountain valley, and set up Romania's first high ropes course on the mountain above their little town, Lupeni.

There was a lot of learning in those first years, especially about local corruption. They also learned that one-week adventure programs were great, but that the youth would soon fall back into their same old patterns. As a solution, they developed IMPACT clubs that meet every week to plan and undertake community service projects. There are now hundreds of them across Romania, and they continue to spread in Romania and beyond. Their aim is to become the "Scouts" of the developing world.

Many Romanians work with Dana in this program, and he exercises little oversight or involvement in day-to-day program operations. Dana's primary tasks are what he calls "vision casting"—that is, writing and articulating the vision and mission to donors, influencing major policy directions, developing partners, and motivating staff, none of which require "specialist" training.

While it is sometimes lonely for Dana and his family in Lupeni, Romania, he feels strongly that he is living out his calling.

> The two greatest commandments tell us that we worship God through caring for our neighbor, who is the highest expression of God as we may ever see it. Development is about loving our neighbor, and both experiential education and service learning are powerful ways of teaching people how to love. My calling is to make both a practical and a theoretical contribution to that.

Roland Vanderburg is another generalist, and he is currently the program director of the Canadian organization Christian Aid for Under-Assisted Societies Everywhere (CAUSE Canada). This Christian NGO works with communities far off the beaten path and believes "development relates to the unfolding of people's collective imagination in defining not only who they are, but where they want to go."[5] Roland began to learn about needy people and development at a young age, when his father and he used to visit a hospital for the severely disabled. A growing desire to care holistically for the marginalized and his involvement in several inspiring economic development courses launched

Roland's career in community development, with somewhat of a focus on microfinance and microenterprise. Early in his MA program in international development, Roland evoked a round of snickering laughter when he confessed his hope to "start a bank for poor entrepreneurs." Fellow students seemed to think it a silly idea to dream so big. But Roland followed through on his dream when he worked with Opportunity International in Nicaragua in the 1990s. Today, the microfinance organization he helped organize, ASODENIC, serves over thirty-five thousand people.[6]

His experiences in Nicaragua were only one part of Roland's vocational formation. He also had internships and working assignments throughout Central America. He led skill training, supported development services, directed programs, and taught about economic development. In his current role at CAUSE Canada, Roland directs programs for Central America and West Africa that focus on transforming lives through women's empowerment. Literacy training and business and microfinance development are key components of the programs. The most fulfilling part of Roland's work is seeing transformational life changes, what Roland calls "the unfolding of the imagination," in women who are initially beaten down, ashamed, and powerless. "They hardly speak, and they will not look you in the eye. And then, a couple years later, I visit the communities, and these same women look you in the eye and walk with dignity. They sing and dance and tell you what they accomplished and what they want to do in the future."

Finally, Belinda Forbes is a dentist who lives and works in Nicaragua as a commissioned missionary for the United Methodist Church. She works full time with Acción Médica Cristiana (AMC), a Nicaraguan NGO that focuses on community health and development, especially the needs of women, children, and adolescents in poor and isolated communities.[7] As a dentist, Belinda does direct dental work and, together with Nicaraguan dental colleagues, trains others in some basic dental skills, including pulling teeth, health education, and preventive care. She has developed additional skills in translation, facilitation, and intercultural communication, which allow her to assist short-term teams that come to Nicaragua from other countries, manage AMC's English promotional materials, and act as a liaison between AMC and its many partner organizations around the world.

Belinda first felt the call to mission service shortly after becoming a dentist. She knew some Spanish, was willing to serve, and had been using her dental skills in Boston's immigrant community when she started to think about service to the poor in a Spanish-speaking country. Belinda sought out a mentoring relationship with her pastor and his wife who both had been long-term missionaries. They encouraged her to take a short-term assignment in Nicaragua with a church partnership. She arrived in 1991 with a one-year commitment, but has been there ever since. Belinda has worked with several churches and local NGOs, but since 2000 she has worked exclusively with AMC. Her dental skills are put to good use in Nicaragua, where there is only one dentist for every twenty thousand people and even fewer in the remote regions where AMC works.

Clearly, Belinda is a specialist, but she also wears the generalist hat when helping to manage the collaborative relationships between AMC and its Northern partners. Like most people on the AMC team, Belinda fills in where she's needed and in ways that take good advantage of her dental skills, her administrative capabilities, and her ability to be a bridge across cultural divides. In all these tasks, Belinda views her role as that of an accompanist rather than a protagonist. Belinda learned early on that being a good partner is a bigger part of development work than just applying a particular skill. "If you want to be effective in the long run," she says, "you must be a good partner," which is why she thinks of herself and her sending church as being in a covenant relationship with the people of Nicaragua.

The stories in this section, together with those earlier in the chapter, show that there are many vocational paths. They may be clouded when looking ahead but make more sense when looking back. They show how six people, in light of the way God made them and the opportunities he gave them, made choices to study, learn, and gain experience, all of which helped them become effective development leaders. Some of them trained early on to become specialists, while others followed general programs of study and allowed their special talents to rise to the top through experience. Unfortunately, there is no clear answer as to whether any one aspiring development worker should acquire a specialized area of knowledge and skill, though Michael Woolcock offers some helpful advice:

> God has gifted people in different ways, and they should follow their passions, strengthen their abilities, and contribute in areas they are really good at. Some people are brilliant in a narrow domain, like overcoming obscure diseases; others have the ability to see the big picture and connect different fields of expertise. The best advice is for you to follow your passions and skills, taking stock of what God has blessed you with.

As each of us follows such a path, we grow in our understanding of ourselves, our gifts, and our sense of calling. As we come to better understand both ourselves and the larger world, and as we apply virtues, knowledge, and skills to real life problems, we also grow in wisdom. This ability to discern what is going on and to respond appropriately helps us find our own unique talents as well as become effective development workers in whatever field we are in.

Growing in Stature and Wisdom

There is a time for everything, and a season for every activity under the heavens.

Ecclesiastes 3:1

As with any profession, working in development requires a particular set of VKS, but there is no magic formula for success. It is not like a recipe—add three parts humility, a cup of confidence, and a pinch of microenterprise knowledge, let it steep for a year, and—voilà!—out comes a transformed community. Knowledge and skills are important, but they have to be used in love and with wisdom. Knowing how and when to put certain skills to use, what mix to use, and when to exercise such contrasting virtues as patience and courage are abilities that turn development work into an art. Such wisdom is a gift that comes to us in different ways. Some people seem to be born with wisdom. Wisdom can also be taught—for example, in training exercises or through the analysis of case studies. But the main source of growth in wisdom is experience, first by working under the tutelage of wise mentors, and then by establishing the ongoing habit of intentional reflection and analysis of one's experience. This is why so many job postings in development require experience: because there is simply no way to exercise the requisite wisdom without going through real life situations, making decisions, seeing how they come out, reflecting on them, and learning from them. Like snowflakes, no particular situation is ever repeated exactly, and what works once might not work the next time, even though circumstances seem similar. Still, experience provides some artful leads toward knowing what works and what does not, what inspires and what deflates, what brings reconciliation and what causes division.

To complicate matters further, what works for one person in one situation might not work for another person in that same situation. Everyone is unique and needs to figure out how to work with his or her own talents and capabilities. In the world of teaching, for example, I have learned from some excellent lecturers. When I tried to imitate them, however, in spite of major effort on my part, I could not lecture as well as they did. Gradually, and over time, I have come to believe that I am more effective in an open discussion format. In reaching this conclusion I was helped by my own assessments of what went on in class, by student evaluations, and by the constructive comments of some master teachers who sat in on my classes.

One time in Nicaragua, I arranged for an agricultural specialist to provide a week of training to a group of farmers who had each received ten acres of land in a government land-reform program. As new and proud landowners, the farmers wanted to learn how to transition from slash-and-burn farming, a practice that required them to move every few years, to a productive, sustainable style of farming that protected their land for the future. The trainer's name was Mauricio, and the farmers thought he was coming to teach them textbook answers to farming. Mauricio did give them some ideas, but along with the first lessons came the assignment to doubt everything he said, to experiment, to build up their own wisdom, and to always ask if there was a better way. "If what I suggest does not work," he told them, "then you need to try something else. This land, the rainfall, the ecology, the seeds you use might all be slightly different and work in different ways, so you need to try different things, evaluate what happens, and be wise." I hope they got the message that day—I sure did. I have never forgotten this little piece of wisdom.

To give you an idea of some of the issues, dilemmas, and tensions you may face as a development worker, and to show how important wisdom is to working your way through them, I offer a sampling of situations, or dilemmas, that arise frequently in development work, though always in slightly different guises and circumstances. I think you will see how difficult some choices are and why wisdom is so important. As you read through these four situations, think about the VKS that are called for. Put yourself in the shoes of the people who must make the choices. What would you do?

A Time to Give and a Time to Receive

Nathaniel Veltman is a couple years into a community development position in Ethiopia with the Presbyterian Church. Soon after his arrival he was wrestling with the problem of when he should be the giver and when the receiver. A strong temptation for a young development worker is to take on too aggressively the role of the giver. If we overplay this role, however, we risk stripping other people of their dignity when they want to give something to us. As Nathaniel says:

> Empathy and compassion are important, but I can easily go astray if I come to believe that I am always in a position to provide. It is true that I am here to give, but I am also in a position to receive something from a partner church. Having the ability to discern when it is time for me to give and when to receive is something I must learn.

A few years ago I watched a community development training video in which a group of foreign, white missionary/development workers made a visit to a rural community in Bangladesh. They had never been there before. As the group gathered, the local people sat in a circle on the ground while community leaders set up kitchen chairs for the foreign visitors. They would be the only ones sitting on the chairs should they choose to receive this offer. What should they do? Accept the chairs and receive this gift, which might very well be given to honor them? Or turn them down so they can sit at the same level and thus attempt to empower local people by breaking down a hierarchical and paternalistic mindset? Of course by insisting on sitting on the ground, they might also publicly embarrass the leaders who brought them the chairs, and they would send the message that the visitors were in charge of the meeting. In the video the visitors turned down the offer and sat on the ground, which was portrayed as the right choice, but to this day I am not sure they made the right decision. Would you have accepted or turned down the offer? How would you come to know what the best choice is?

A Time to Stay and a Time to Go

I argued in chapter 3 against the notion that development workers are always "working themselves out of a job," but sometimes they are. Working in the Kibera slums of Nairobi as a Maryknoll missioner was emotionally and spiritually draining for human rights lawyer Christine Bodewes. She discovered that the evil forces in Kibera were so deeply entrenched that they would be incredibly hard to dislodge. Still, she worked hard even though many of her efforts seemed to fail. One day, thugs vandalized her office and destroyed years of legal work. It was the guidance and support she received from her spiritual director that helped her both keep the faith during these difficult days and start over.

Maryknoll has a guiding principle that missioners should go where they are not wanted but needed and should stay until they are wanted but not needed. The day when it seemed she was no longer needed came for Christine eight years after starting to work in Nairobi's slums. A fine Kenyan lawyer had left her own private practice and was now prepared to lead the human rights office that Christine helped establish. A short time later, the opportunity arose to do graduate study on the role of the Catholic parish in promoting human rights and the rule of law. Christine's spiritual director, a veteran Maryknoller, told her it was time to leave, both for her own health and well-being and for the good of the community. And so she left. Should she have stayed and continued her human rights work in a place where the road would still be long and hard? Or was it right to take up the new task of reflecting on her experiences, studying the role of the church in human rights, and sharing in an academic context what she had learned?

Sometimes it seems right to stay for a much longer time. Kurt and JoAnn Ver Beek started working in Honduras in the 1980s, came back to the United States so that Kurt could study for a PhD in development, and then moved back to Honduras in 1995 to teach a semester program on development studies to college students from North America. Kurt and JoAnn wonder sometimes if they should leave and work elsewhere, but in addition to the semester program, they have been influential citizens in a poor barrio where they live. Over the last ten years, they have helped establish a Honduran justice-advocacy NGO called the Association for a More Just Society and are now playing a facilitating role in Transformemos Honduras (Let's Transform Honduras), a national movement of Christian churches against corruption.[8] Kurt says, "many development workers come and go, but they never learn to speak the language well and they never really understand. Because I have been here twenty years, I have understood more of the Honduran history and mindset and have been able to build relationships that have made our work more effective. I love being here this long. I keep learning more and feel sometimes that I am just now starting to understand Honduran people and their politics."

Many development organizations move their foreign staff to new countries every three to five years. They do not want the people to get too embedded in the local culture. How would we know what the right length of time is for a foreigner to stay in one place?

A Time to Listen and a Time to Speak

Among the earliest lessons we learn in development is how important it is to listen, to encourage local ownership, to avoid taking over, and to resist imposing. Listening skills are thus among the essentials for effective work. But does there ever come a time to speak or make suggestions?

Mike Soderling, medical missionary in Guatemala, tells the following tale:

> A big problem in missions is that when foreign missionaries sit in a meeting with a group of local pastors, the ideas of the foreigners often dominate the discussion. I ran into this problem once when we wanted to help war widows. They had no place to live, so we thought it would be a good idea to build houses for them. The pastors agreed. We built the houses, but the pastors never identified the widows who would live in them. Finally, the pastors had to tell us that they would not look for recipients for these homes, because the women would not want to live in them. The pastors knew this all along, but did not want to tell us and be disrespectful. That experience taught us a lot about being better listeners and being more patient.

Here is another story told by Matt Van Geest, a community development worker with many years of experience in Haiti:

> Corruption is a big problem in Haiti, and there are times when you have to call people out for doing things that are really wrong, especially when local people are unable, perhaps for cultural reasons, to say anything. I was in a meeting once with forty farmers. It was obvious that one guy was engaging in corrupt activities, but nobody was willing to say anything because they go to church together or work next to each other in the fields. In this situation, when no one else could speak about it, I felt it was my place to call him out, uncomfortable as it was. Why could I do that? Because I had lived in the community for three years already and had built relationships and understanding. I respected the people I was working with, and I felt they had come to respect me, which is what allowed me to play this role. To be able to call people out for corruption in a constructive way is something that an outsider can sometimes do better than an insider. One has to be very careful about playing this role, but it is one that can be helpful.

There are times to be silent and listen, and times to speak up. Did you notice how both Mike and Matt reflect on their experiences and learn from them. Notice too how Matt, though he decided to speak out on this occasion, also cautions against getting too comfortable with this practice.

A Time to Fund and a Time to Refrain from Funding

In development, money, like uranium, can be a power-packed resource or it can explode and usher in disaster. The challenge of managing money is not new, neither in life nor in international development. The Bible, for example, is full of hopes for prosperity but also replete with warnings about how destructive money can be. In development work, money can help build schools and provide education, but it also fosters dependency and corruption. No issue in development work is as contentious or delicate, and because of its potentially destructive power, wisdom is absolutely vital.

For development workers new to the field, there is often an overwhelming temptation to rush in with financial resources. This temptation is strong because they are so obviously needed, but it may also be because rookies, not yet fully confident in what their other contributions might be, may rely too heavily on their connections to money, which is sure to please the people they work with. Unfortunately, funding can also be like crack cocaine, making you feel good for a little while but then destroying you from the inside over the long term.

Andrew Ryskamp, director of CRWRC in the United States, is well aware of the dual nature of money. He has learned that communities and nations must start working productively and wisely with their own assets, which is why he is a big fan of asset-based community development (ABCD).

> Doing good work in development is a tricky process because we come in with resources. To promote sustainability, CRWRC partners with likeminded organizations in developing countries. Understandably, our partners are always on the lookout for resources to keep their organizations going. How do we support these structures without funding them? If we provide all the funding from the outside, where is the sustainability? That's the dilemma, because you think development can go more quickly if you put some resources in. In some ways that is exactly right, but then the sustainability piece comes into play. The desire for resources among our partners complements the fact that people in North America have resources and want to give them, so there is pressure on that end too. Our policy is not to provide a lot of funding, and I judge that part of success is when our partners accept that CRWRC may not give them much money but [still] value our relationship because of the time we spend with them and the work we do together.

Donors in North America want their money to go directly to people in need. Some of CRWRC's partners pressure CRWRC to give them more financial help. It would be easy to give in to these pressures, but Andrew has worked in development for forty years now, and he knows that sustainability would then be hard to achieve—penny wise and pound foolish. Is he making the right choice to be cautious with funding?

Concluding Comments

The most successful development workers have love in their hearts for people in need, are able and willing to gain the virtues, knowledge, and skills necessary to really help, and have the humility and discernment to grow in wisdom in the midst of difficult and uncomfortable circumstances. There is room for generalists and specialists of all types, but everyone needs to love, to know themselves and the mission, to strengthen their VKS, and to grow in wisdom. It is now time to consider how you can become this sort of person.

Further Reflection and Action Steps

1. Check out www.devex.com and www.reliefweb.int. Find a position that appeals to you and identify the VKS you would need to develop in order to qualify for it.

2. Identify a development issue or problem you are familiar with and discuss with others what virtues, areas of expertise or knowledge, and skills might be most needed to work in the context of this issue.

3. Review the job qualifications listed earlier in this chapter. Compare them to the qualities that nationals look for in a North American as these were presented in chapter 4. Are there any surprises?

4. Matthew 25 contains the parable of a master giving "talents" to his servants and charging them with being good stewards. What special talents or resources have you been blessed with due to circumstances of birth and upbringing, and how might these prepare you for international development work?

5. Show the list of job qualifications to some people who know you. Let them rank you on all VKS categories. Do you agree with their assessment? What are your strengths and what are some areas you could work on over the next few years? Identify one in each category, set some goals, and make a plan.

6. This chapter introduces you to six development workers. Discuss which of these resonates most with your own life and dreams for the future?

7. From the section on wisdom, pick one of the situations and determine what kinds of VKS are needed to make the best choice. List the likely consequences (pro and con) of your decision.

Finding Your Way

The College Years

I am the vine; you are the branches. If you remain in me and I in you, you will bear much fruit; apart from me you can do nothing.

John 15:5

Get your feet wet, and then get them a little wetter, and then decide when you are going to dive in.

Kurt Ver Beek, professor, development worker,
twenty-year resident of Honduras

I need to surround myself with mentors who I can trust and who are a few steps ahead of me.

Faith Wise, global mission director
for Providence Church in Westchester, PA

Learning, Growing, Becoming, and Serving: Powerfully Positioning Your Pieces

As a college professor for almost thirty years, I am continually amazed by the power of the formative processes that shape us during the college years. Sure, everyone is different, but what I see over and over again is young people entering their first year of college as teenagers who are joyfully energetic and enthusiastic, but also rough-edged, uncertain, insecure, and, dare I say it, somewhat immature. Four short years later, they graduate as adults. They carry themselves with confidence, relate to me and other older folks in a more horizontal way, increasingly channel their energy constructively, own their faith commitments, and have a growing understanding of who they are and want to be. The process of building their identities and their life missions is still ongoing, but the foundations are laid and the shape of the structure is definitely coming into view.

I hope this chapter helps some of those college-aged young people begin to work out their calling to global service, particularly in the broad arena of development work. Though everyone is called to transformative service in some corner of God's world, not everyone is called to work directly in international development. Moreover, those who are called may be called to do this work at different stages of their lives. For those who at a young age are ready to get their feet wet and to explore where they might fit in the world of international development, how can they prepare while in college? What should they study? What else should they do?

When I began doing the research for this book, I assumed that the development professionals I interviewed would share a trove of valuable advice about the college years, and they did. I asked what experiences from their college years were especially helpful to them, as well as what advice they would give to college students today. But then I made the mistake of thinking I could get some additional information by asking them to talk about what they would do differently if they could go back and start college again. For about the first fifteen interviews, I kept getting the same answer, which was that they would not trade away anything they had done, no matter what they had majored in or what other activities they had been involved with. In other words, there were few regrets. The only regrets I learned about were criticisms of themselves—for example, wishing that they had been more focused or more involved. At some point I revised the question and started getting more informative responses; instead of asking what they would do differently, I asked what they wished they would have done in addition to what they actually did.

Before rushing ahead and sharing what they said, I would like to make three brief points about the significance of their not wanting to exchange any of what they had done for something else. First, everything they studied and did turned out to be helpful. Whether they studied international development, political science, biology, urban ministry, sociology, or something else, they were happy with what they had studied because they learned a lot that they still value today. Second, all of these different college experiences turned out to provide that foundation of general virtues, knowledge, and skills (VKS) that they continue to value. No matter what they had studied, they talked about how they learned to think critically, read carefully, write and speak coherently, work with others constructively, do research efficiently, and reflect thoughtfully on their own faith and place in the world. World Vision International's global partnership director, Dirk Booy, says that college is a time to "prepare professionally, experientially, and spiritually"; it seems there are many particular paths to such preparation. Third, a consequence of the other two, one should not worry too much about making exactly the right choices with regard to which courses to take, what to major/minor in, or what activities to engage in. It is much more important to embrace your choices with diligence and joy and to learn what there is to learn, rather than fretting about getting exactly the right combination of courses and experiences for that much-talked-about résumé. This is one situation where it is wise not to let the best be the enemy of the good. Take good courses, do good things, and trust that God will use you. Julie Peterson, vice president at American World Services, describes how this works:

> In God's kingdom it is like we are standing on a train platform waiting to go out into the world. But which train should I get on? There are ten thousand trains passing by, but which one is for me? I used to think God had a special train marked "Julie." How egotistical! I finally heard God telling me: "Here are all these trains going places, so get on one. You are not getting your own train." Instead, God was telling me to join some work that was already being done in the world. This realization really freed me from my anxiety about getting on the right train, because I was not going to get on the wrong train ever. Get on with it. Study something good, join an organization that engages and energizes you and that is addressing something broken in the world.[1]

I used to imagine myself becoming a good chess player, and to that end I did some reading about how to play better. My imagined chess proficiency is still only a dream, but I learned something that I often refer to when discussing programs and career paths with college students. One book said that beginning chess players often think the grand masters have plans in their heads early in the game about how they are going to attack the other king and win the game. Not true at all, said this book, which talked about the opening, the midgame, and the end game and how to play wisely at each stage. As I learned more about these three stages, I came to see that the opening is like the college years, when personal choices start to define one's life mission. The most important goal of the opening in a chess match is to get your pieces into good places on the board. You want each piece to cover many squares. For example, it is not a good idea to stick your knight over on the side of the board; it covers only four spaces, whereas in the middle of the board it covers eight. If the pieces are well positioned in the opening of the game, then they are poised to take advantage of opportunities as they arise during the midgame. The masters do not know exactly where those opportunities will turn up, but their pieces are ready when they do.

This chapter will help you think about getting your pieces in powerful positions so that your hopes of serving and making a difference are not just dreams of what might be, but real transformational events. There are three main parts. The first is a brief overview of what the "pieces" are and how you can shape, strengthen, and position them. The second is a direct look at college programs, focusing especially on what to study, and the third covers all those extracurricular activities you can participate in during the college years.

Virtues, Knowledge, and Skills Redux: Preparing for Global Service

Metaphors help our understanding, but they always break down, because nothing is exactly like anything else. Thus, the chess game comparison breaks down. Chess pieces are what they are. You cannot change them and make any one of them bigger, smarter, or more powerful than it is. Pawns never go backward; bishops cannot go straight across the board. In real life, however, not only do we position our pieces, but we also shape and strengthen them. Maybe you are not a good writer now, but you can become one. Maybe you cannot speak Spanish now, but you can learn. Maybe your intercultural experience is limited, but you can get more. Unlike lifeless chess pieces, you can both increase your virtues, knowledge, and skills in quantity and improve them in quality.

How does such shaping and strengthening actually take place? The first step is to take stock of the raw material you have to work with, which in this case is the genetic material God gave you and the life situation where he placed you. You have no control over that. He gave you a unique genetic makeup, knowing you when you were yet in the womb, making you a male or a female, giving you some inherent characteristics from your mother, some from your father, and others that are entirely your own, such as athleticism (or not), musicality (or not), natural social skills (or not), and so on. And then there is your context. Some are born to single mothers, some to working families or business leaders, some rich, some poor, some light- and some dark-skinned, some in small towns, some to parents living overseas. Though we are all unique, we get so used to living with ourselves that we come to think of our own inherent abilities and our contexts as ordinary, nothing special. We focus more on what we cannot do and what we do not have. Whatever your contextual circumstances—language abilities in Swahili, for example, or a big church family that might support you on your first overseas learning trips—they shape you in unique ways and open the door to particular opportunities.

While in college, work at understanding your own uniqueness. Take the famous Myers-Briggs test. Listen carefully for how your teachers, pastors, and friends affirm you. Be honest with yourself about what you love to do, what you are good at, and what may be some weaknesses. Try things out. Engage in an intentional process of identifying your capabilities and start thinking about how you can use them to take advantage of opportunities to learn, grow, and serve.

A second major source of VKS is education and training, one major source of which is your college experience. Education and training come from many other sources as well, including the guidance of parents, coaches, mentors, pastors, and peer groups, as well as what you learn from books, magazines, video games, the internet, television, popular media, and advertising. As you can perceive, some educational experiences are constructive and edifying, while others steer you in less helpful directions. But good educational resources can instruct us on virtues (e.g., a group counseling session that reveals how other people respond to your words and actions), on knowledge (e.g., a video about Papua New Guinea), and on skills (e.g., a how-to manual on participatory methods that your community development class studies).

The third major source of VKS is experience. You can read about the Masai of East Africa, and you should, but that will never replace being there and living among them for a time. You can take classes on participatory methods, but you will never master them until you practice them for a number of years. You can do Bible studies on love, but you will never "get it" until you are in real relationships.

There is a fourth resource that intersects with the other three, and that is your own will. You can sit in a language class, but you must choose to engage. You choose whether to read a book or to play a video game in your free time, whether to apply to this or that college, and whether or not to sign up for the off-campus program in Uganda. Once in Uganda, you choose whether to eat the local food or to demand hamburgers, fries, and pizza. When encountering someone who is poor, you choose whether to love or to turn away.

These four elements—raw material, education and training, experience, and will—interact in mutually reinforcing ways to build and shape a certain pattern of VKS that you embody within your person and that builds, grows, changes, and evolves throughout your life. It is different when you are twenty than when you are thirty. It is forming and reforming all the time through a combination of who you are, the choices you make, how you are educated, and the experiences you have.

Working in development requires certain types of VKS, some of which come naturally, but all of which require a long period of education, training, and experience. Just as it is essential for medical doctors to go through four years of medical training and then three years of residency before being certified, development workers also need to go through a long training period. How important this is was brought home to me by Susan Van Lopik, a long-term career development worker. Susan used to lament that young people would go overseas, do six years in the field, and then return home. She noted that "development is so much about relationships, yet after six years of trust building and learning how to work together across cultures, just when people are starting to get effective, that's when they burn out and return to North America." Six years is not a magic number, but Susan's comment reminds us that development work messes with people's lives, which calls for serious training if we really love and want to serve. How many years would you want your physician to be in training before you allowed her to operate on you? How many years should someone be in training before she imagines herself wise enough to work on transforming people's lives, cultures, and ways of life in an African community?

What to Study: So Many Good Options

Among the most basic educational choices students must make is what to study. If you are wondering whether you have a specific call to work in international development, I would like to steer you toward taking three types of college courses. First are courses that help you get to know and understand people around the world. Second are courses on the history and theory of development work. And third are major and minor programs that prepare you in specialized fields of study.

And Who Is My Neighbor?

As in the story of the good Samaritan (Luke 10:25–37), development work is about helping people in need. This particular story highlights a disaster victim whose immediate needs are pretty obvious. The Samaritan addresses three basic ones: bandages, travel to a safe place, and money for convalescent care. Jesus concludes the story by commending the Samaritan for having mercy on his "neighbor" and then telling us, "Go and do likewise."

Our job is to apply the lessons of this story to how we live in our world today. If we hope to do as the Samaritan did and have mercy on our neighbors, then we must get to know them, develop relationships with them, learn about their lives, and discover with them the causes of their sufferings. If you really want to know your neighbor, you must learn about and appreciate their histories, religions, cultures, geographies, governance patterns, economies, and ethnicities. Just as an orthopedic surgeon should not repair a knee without having sufficient understanding of the circulatory, nervous, respiratory, digestive, and other biological systems, so too the development worker should gain familiarity with the historical and holistic environments in which children are embedded before taking on the task of improving child nutrition.

There are three primary curricular strategies for growing in this broad type of understanding. The number one strategy by far is to *study abroad* in developing countries. The opportunities for getting close to people—for eating, communicating, worshiping, and living with them, thereby getting to know them—are unsurpassed by any other learning strategy. Virtually all colleges and universities these days offer multiple opportunities for semester- or year-long study in developing countries. When asked what advice development professionals would give young people, an oft-repeated suggestion was, "tell them to get as much overseas experience as possible, to go on as many study abroad programs as they can."

Semester programs influence participants in three powerful ways. First, minds are expanded as students come into contact with an entirely new reality. They start to understand the similarities of all people across cultures as well as the significant differences. Hayden Hill, who participated in two programs, one with the Roma community in Romania and another in Uganda, says, "exposure to the poor and oppressed led me to build relationships with real people and helped me understand what life was like." Naturally, students learn much about "the other" on these programs, but they also come to see themselves through the eyes of others. As a result, their understandings of their own cultures, governments, and histories change. Second, students are placed in cross-cultural relational contexts, like living with host families, such that their abilities to interact across cultures and languages are enhanced. Third, students often talk about how their own lives are changed—in particular, their sense of what their life mission is and what they feel called to. Some encounter their first sense of calling to global service, others have their calling affirmed through their experiences, and some discover they are not cut out for international work. Brit Steiner, now in the Office of Civilian Response at USAID, went on a semester program to Cairo, Egypt, in her sophomore year and had this to say about it (similar comments could be heard from many others):

> I volunteered to work at Mother Teresa's Sisters of Charity orphanage in Cairo, where I helped take care of abandoned children and elderly folks once a week.

In Cairo I was amazed by how many people there were, how much noise there was, and how busy everything was. It was a bit overwhelming, but over the four months I got used to it and even came to enjoy it. What I saw and experienced there totally changed my life. I would not be doing international development work if I did not have that experience.

Nathaniel Veltman, a community development worker in Ethiopia, did a semester program in Ghana and then a semester-long internship with an NGO in Malawi. Nathaniel remembers both experiences for how helpful they were in "building relationships with the people. In Ghana I went to the market for breakfast, bought food from the vendors, and talked with them. I talked a lot with my host family too, as I did in Malawi. All those experiences helped me more fully understand my call to work overseas and how important it is to build relationships with the people."

Strategy number two for getting to know people is to *take courses that teach about the peoples and regions of the world.* These come in many packages, and the best guide to which one is best for you is your own heart and interests. Many colleges feature area studies programs (for example, Latin American studies) that combine history courses with area-focused courses from other disciplines, including geography, economics, and religion. Anthropology courses are another good option for learning how to understand people from all different walks of life in their own cultural contexts. Such courses are often offered on campus but can also be part of study abroad programs. Exactly how many such courses you should take is impossible to say with precision, but it would look odd if in a job or internship interview you professed a lifelong interest in Latin America but had spent little time in the region and had no relevant coursework.

Strategy number three is to learn how to converse with your global neighbors in their own *languages.* On-campus classes are an obvious option, as are study abroad programs where language learning is emphasized. Another option is to spend a summer or longer in one of the many immersion programs offered in countries the world over.

Kris Ozar is program quality manager for Catholic Relief Services in Ghana. Like many students, Kris thought other college courses would be more important than language courses. After he graduated, Kris landed a position in Kenya with Maryknoll missions, working mostly with microfinance programs. Before starting, however, Maryknoll sent him for six months of intensive language training in Kiswahili, which allowed him to communicate well with the members of the microfinance groups. Four years later Kris studied for an MA in sustainable development management at the School of International Training in

Vermont. He hoped to return to Africa one day, but many of the placements in Africa require fluency in French. Kris was fortunate to find a position in English-speaking Ghana, but he wishes he would have learned French when he had the chance. As he reflects on his college years, Kris says that "every off-campus program helped me realize I wanted to contribute to the positive development of human beings, but I managed to avoid learning language in college. Looking back it was a major oversight. I sincerely regret not taking advantage of the opportunity to learn French when I was younger. As I look ahead in my career, not being proficient in French is a major deficit in my toolbox, something that will become more and more difficult to remedy as the years go on."

Vernon Jantzi, with the Center for Justice and Peacebuilding at Eastern Mennonite University, also highlights the importance of learning other languages. He suggests that students "learn as many languages as possible. Language exposes you to different cultures and creates cultural sensitivity. If you can get so far in a language that you are able to read literature and other forms of artistic expression, then you can get tuned in to how people express their deepest commitments and desires. Even if you go to Africa, where English is often an official language, learning the local languages is important if you are serious about developing constructive working relationships."

There is no easy answer to the question of which languages you should learn and how you should learn them. If Latin America is your focus region, either Spanish or Portuguese makes sense. For sub-Saharan Africa, French or Portuguese might rise to the top of the priority list, though learning a major African language, such as Kiswahili, would also be an excellent choice. Happily, the benefits from learning one foreign language spill over into others, because language experts say that learning one language makes learning additional languages easier. Studying language at school is an excellent way to get started, but to achieve fluency and internalize the language, do your best to spend time in an immersion environment—in an off-campus semester, for example. Once there, if you avoid the temptation to hang out with people who speak your native language, the gains you make will be impressive and you will build some real cross-cultural relationships in the process.

Understanding Development

In the college classroom, one surefire way to induce drowsiness is to tell students it is time to talk about theory. For some reason the word weighs heavy on the eyelids. It seems there is a tremendous drive among us to be practical, to get to the action, and to do something instead of "wasting our time" talking about it, which is what discussing theories seems to imply.

Despite our preference for action, however, we must humbly confess that practice without theory is destined for trouble, and the world of development has known a great deal of such trouble. Among the most tragic stories of development work gone awry is the one told by Peter Uvin in his study on the Rwandan genocide of 1994, *Aiding Violence: The Development Enterprise in Rwanda*.[2] Uvin argues persuasively that most development workers in Rwanda focused on their own narrow areas of interest and failed to understand the racial and ethnic dynamics that were marching toward genocide. In a word, their theories were wrong, and so their practices did not address what needed to be addressed. As Uvin tells it, not only did development organizations in Rwanda ignore the forces building toward genocide, but they actually contributed to those forces.

This is a worst-case scenario, but failure to pay careful attention to development history and evolving development theory leads to serious consequences. First, the same mistakes are repeated over and over. Second, and maybe worse, people in the aid enterprise, from rich donors in the North to community people in the South, are conditioned to expect development to be badly done. As an example, one of the frustrations development professionals often encounter is that communities become conditioned to expecting NGOs to just give them things. Third, failure to attend adequately to theory leads people to head in entirely wrong directions at community, national, and international levels. For example, it is easy to see that international trade is a major factor in economic well-being, but which way does it play? Does it make poverty worse, or does it help the poor escape their poverty? To answer this question requires, in part, a careful study of economic theory, but as most of us discover, understanding these theories and their implications for policy is hard. Some advocacy organizations, anxious to make pronouncements about trade policy, are too willing to skip the hard work of studying theory and jump instead to policy formation that might ultimately be quite misguided.

As a reminder of how important development theory is, including the world and life views our theories are based on, take a look again at chapters 1, 2, and 3. We might summarize those chapters with two simple words: theories matter.

So where and how do we learn our theory? This is one of the strong suits of college. It is a wonderful place to read, discuss, and think things through. If you imagine a future for yourself in international development, this is the time to take advantage of this intellectually rich environment to study and wrestle with ideas. What courses might you take for this? Some schools now have specific courses in international development, which are an excellent place to start. Other obvious possibilities include courses in intercultural communications or missions that are oriented toward holistic development. Many other excellent theory courses can be found in the social sciences: anthropology, economics, geography, political science, and sociology. Pick the courses that wrestle with explaining how the world works, and especially how the developing countries and marginalized people worldwide fit into that world. Religion, history, and philosophy courses often wrestle with how to explain or interpret the human condition. Take some of these courses, choosing the ones that have an international orientation, are theoretically rich, and challenge you to think hard.

The first three chapters of this book point out that theories matter for what we actually do in development work. They also make the point that theories are tightly intertwined with faith and worldview. Some students attend Christian colleges where the conversation about the significance of faith is ever present, from chapel services to classes to dorm life. For students attending secular colleges and universities, where faith is not addressed as explicitly, you should take the same theoretical courses in development, economics, philosophy, and so on; but beyond that, be sure to find a community of Christian scholars with whom to reflect on these theories. Either in a group like this or on your own, read some works by Christian scholars.

Picking a Major: No Regrets—Study What Fits You Best

Not one of the over fifty development professionals I interviewed would change their major in college if they had a chance to do it over. Any regrets they expressed related to what they might have done in addition to what they actually did, such as learn a language. This finding may be surprising considering the wide variety of programs that people majored in. Majors ranged over some twenty fields, including agriculture, art, biology, business, history, intercultural studies, philosophy, and sociology. It is also striking that many of these professionals are now in positions quite unrelated to their majors. In some cases there is an obvious connection, as with Greg Matney, who studied business and now works in promoting business development; but often there is no obvious connection at all, as with Dana DeRuiter, who majored in English and is now a senior advisor in global health at USAID.

Does this mean that what you study is irrelevant? No, what you study is hugely important, but it is not determinative. Let me try to explain. First, much of what we learn in college and carry with us into the future has to do with general qualities that make us good and competent people. Throughout four or five years of learning and growing, college students make great strides in learning to learn, thinking critically and analytically, discussing, writing, speaking, working in teams, solving problems, researching, planning, budgeting time, meeting deadlines, and even coping with stress. Every well-managed college program helps you grow in these general skills that professionals often identify as the qualities most important in their own work. Wherever you pick them up, these skills are highly transferable, allowing people to move into new areas of work as situations change and opportunities arise. The more you shape and strengthen such qualities, the more your "pieces" are positioned powerfully. Carl Stauffer, now a professor of peacebuilding at Eastern Mennonite University, affirms this when he says that "the people who thrive on the field are not those with a particular line of study (e.g., sociology or even development). Some of best people come out of the arts or English literature; they can think laterally and bring in lots of information that is outside of social disciplines."

Why then is it also hugely important what particular field you study? For two reasons: If you study something you are really interested in and find fascinating, your own investment in it is all the greater. You learn more because you care more. The second reason is that particular courses of study do indeed prepare you for specific types of positions; they help you gain VKS relevant to specialized fields. To get into peacebuilding, majors related to understanding human behavior would be helpful. Majoring in geography, geology, or environmental science might help you contribute to the protection and provision of clean water.

It is impossible to be comprehensive here, because there are so many ways to prepare and so many ways to be involved. Check out the sidebar for an illustrative list of majors and some (only some!) of the work areas and career options closely related to these majors. If, for example, you love to learn about accounting, business, or economics, you may be preparing for a career in microenterprise systems or NGO management.

The list in the sidebar is only illustrative. Psychology majors might be especially well prepared to address the trauma by conducting recovery therapy for trafficking victims or child soldiers. And English majors often possess well-honed writing skills, which is notable since four professionals in the survey landed their first positions after college because of their ability to write.

Charlotte Keniston double majored in art and intercultural studies. After a stint with the Peace Corps in Guatemala, Charlotte is pursuing a master's degree in documentary film and photography. Charlotte says, "I want to continue working in development, but using creative tools. Documentary media has huge potential as a tool for social change and also as a way to let the poor document their own experiences and stories."

Many more stories could be told about how majors that do not seem directly related to international development actually turn out to be highly useful. The

International Development Studies Career Connections Related to Different Academic Fields

Major Program of Undergraduate Study	Career Focus
Accounting, business, economics	Microfinance/microenterprise
	General business promotion
	Market development
	NGO management
	Government policy
Geography, environmental studies	Natural resource management
	Cartography and map analysis
	Forestry and reforestation
	Urban and regional planning
	Water and sanitation hydrology
Political science	Public policy and/or administration
	International law and human rights
	Conflict transformation and peacebuilding
	Promotion of civil society
Biology, nursing	Public health management
	Lab research on tropical diseases
	HIV/AIDS specialist
	Nutrition/health education
Anthropology, sociology, social work	Community development
	Gender issues/women's empowerment
	Humanitarian relief
	Capacity building in NGOs
	Refugee support and resettlement
	Conflict transformation and peacebuilding
	Social policy

bottom line is that if you are interested in getting into international development, virtually any major can be a good choice. This relates back to several development principles from chapter 3. Development is deep, wide, holistic, inclusive, and transformative. If development is about every part of life, then it should be no surprise that all college majors apply.

So which one should you choose? Do not force it, and do not fret about it, because the answer is fairly simple. Pick the major/minor combination that best fits who you are, what you are especially good at, and what types of knowledge and skills you enjoy learning and using. There are many books on vocation and careers that go into helpful detail about assessing your gifts and discovering your calling,[3] but I honestly think we should all be wary of making too much of this choice. If most people turn out to be happy with what they studied in college, and if what they studied in college varies so widely, then perhaps the college experience as a whole is more important than the particular major one chooses.

Whatever you choose for a major, I have two follow-up pieces of advice: First, invest in it wholeheartedly, which is what God expects us to do with our talents and the opportunities he has given to us. Second, trust that God will take you to a good place with what you learn. One of the common themes among all the professionals I interviewed is how God is there with them every step of the way. Christine Bodewes captures both of these ideas when she says, "follow what you are good at and what you love, and God will provide the path. We do not have to create the paths. . . . God does that part. All we have to do is say yes to God's call. Be the best lawyer, teacher, or architect you can be, and get the best professional training available to you. When you have skills, expertise, and language, you are in a position to go almost anywhere in the world and make a contribution."

Packaging and Timing

Study abroad, regional courses, international development theory, and fully investing in at least one major: is it possible to pack all this in during a four-year college program? The answer is yes and no, and the key to understanding this is that college was never meant to be the final chapter in anyone's education. Yes, you can get much of this during college, but you can never get as much as you really need. There is always more to do and more to learn. Remember that one of the best pieces of wisdom on making choices is not to allow the best to become the enemy of the good. There is no perfect package and no perfect timing; focus on doing something worthwhile rather than stressing about whether it is the best. Four years of college go by very quickly, and you cannot do it all. If you prioritize majors and minors during college and do not manage to learn a language, you can volunteer in a developing country after college and learn a language then. If you feel a strong need for study abroad programs during college and are not able to get all the major/minor coursework you might like, there are many ways after graduation to keep on learning.

The Extracurricular Realm: All the Other Stuff You Can Do in College

The classes we take are a big part of our college experience, but no one should spend every waking hour studying; there are too many other good things to do. Some of these are strictly knowledge-oriented—for example, an evening lecture by a visiting speaker. Others are highly experiential and provide opportunities to serve, learn, and improve our skills.

Until 2011 Jason Fileta was national coordinator for the Micah Challenge. His job required leading, organizing, motivating, encouraging, and communicating. When Jason started college, he was not very good at any of these, and he was not much interested in them either. What changed Jason was his study abroad semester in Honduras, including the classes he took, but even more his interactions with new and different people. He says, "I started to listen to them and get to know them, and these people gradually became a very important community for me. You could say that I "reconverted" to Christianity, and along with this new community I started to ask God what he wanted me to do about all the injustice in the world."

Returning from the Honduras semester, Jason felt a new energy to get involved, so he joined the social justice coalition student group. His involvement led him to an awareness of some of his own gifts in leadership, organizing, and communication, and it put him in a community of caring that embraced people both close to home and around the world. His spiritual life took a turn for the better too. He learned how to pray and to rely increasingly on God. "We would talk about things, pray about them, and think through what we could do about them."

As Jason's story reminds us, a huge part of any student's training, preparation, and formation happens outside of the classroom. When you engage and get involved, you also gain insights into your own specific calling. Some of your experiences will go well and others not so well. You will discover whether you really do have a passion for working directly with the poor, and whether your own inherent capabilities are more oriented to personal interaction or administration. As Julie Peterson reminds us in her story about the trains at the beginning of this chapter, it matters less which particular ways you get involved and much more that you do something worthwhile with the time and talents God has given you and the opportunities he puts in your path.

What kinds of experiences and activities should you seek out? I have gleaned the following suggestions from the collective wisdom of the development professionals I interviewed for this book.

Volunteer in the Community

Rest assured that there are needs in the community where your college is located. Wherever there is a community of people, there are needs. What are they, and how could you help address them? Most likely there are children who need tutoring, minimum-wage workers who need help filling out tax forms, rivers that need to be monitored or cleaned up, homeless people who need a friend, poor people who need help developing job skills, refugees who need help learning English or looking for work, hungry people who need help getting access to food, and young people embraced by gangs who need alternative friends and activities.

There are several benefits to be gained from local volunteering that also apply to working overseas. Among the most basic is that you learn how to serve, and in the process of serving you also learn. You learn who people are, how they got where they are, what their fears and hopes are, and what obstacles face them as they try to improve their lives. As Hayden Hill points out, if you get to know people at this level, and if you listen to their stories, you learn how to build relationships with people in need even as you also improve your understanding of how important relationships are to development work. As you learn such things, you also gain a better appreciation for how to serve in ways that really help. Service and learning go together so tightly that we now call it "service-learning." Many colleges are getting on board with official service-learning programs that help you find productive ways to volunteer. Take advantage of them.

How important is it for you to get involved in these ways? Mary Ann Weber, who until recently was the human resources coordinator for MCC in Goshen, Indiana, answers this questions poignantly with some leading questions of her own.

> Get involved in your own community right now. You do not have to wait. You do not have to go international. Even in Goshen there are places to serve, like a soup kitchen and health clinic. Why would you go international if you are not helping where you are? If you are not involved in trying to make a change or trying to relate to people in need right now, what makes you think you could be effective in a place where you do not even know the language or the culture? You need to start now, volunteering and working in your own backyard.

Join Student Organizations

Student organizations of all types provide basic training in leadership, followership, communication, and organizing, all of which are good in a general sort of way. Some of these organizations focus on development-related issues like sex trafficking or HIV/AIDS. Others form relationships with development organizations, such as the International Justice Mission or World Vision, whose Acting on AIDS program was started by students at Seattle Pacific University.[4] Getting involved in such an organization puts you in a position to learn but also to have an impact now. At Calvin College, students with business and global affairs interests organized a chapter of Global Business Brigades, an organization that sends a group of about fifteen students to Panama twice a year to share business knowledge with some of Panama's indigenous peoples who are trying to get business activities started.[5]

If you volunteer in the community or join some student organizations, you will have a good start on the following recommendations.

Build your networks

One question I asked the development professionals was how they came to the positions they occupy today. The overwhelming conclusion is that networks are the magic formula. In more than 90 percent of the cases, people found their way to internships, then to careers, and then to transitions in those careers through networks. When workers took new positions, they were often already known to their new employers. It is of course common to use networks to find such opportunities, but networks are also helpful for fundraising, providing emotional support, and connecting people who have needs with others who can meet those needs.

In 2011, recent graduate Derek Hoogland was in a two-year internship with Partners Worldwide in Liberia. He was amazed at how powerful networks were once he arrived in Liberia and started interacting with development workers: "Just getting out here is all I needed to do to learn about positions—posted on an expat Listserv here or spread by word of mouth."

Among numerous networking stories I heard, Ryan Musser's stands out. It might be that Ryan is a born networker, and perhaps that is just part of his God-given personality, but there are lessons to be learned from his experiences.

It probably started for Ryan in middle school, when he embarked on what would become a series of church-based mission trips. To make these trips possible, he built up a support network through his church, school, and general community to finance the trips and serve as a general source of encouragement to him. During his college years, Ryan did a summer internship with World Relief in Baltimore, worked as an election monitor for two weeks in Sierra Leone, did another summer internship with the Enough Project in Washington, DC, and then did a study-abroad semester in Uganda and Rwanda with Food for the Hungry, who shortly thereafter invited him to do another internship in Thailand, this one for a full year. Upon his return to the United States, he continued working for them in their response to the Haiti earthquake. Ryan was then offered a paid internship with the International Foundation for Electoral Systems (IFES) in Washington, DC. With the exception of his first internship, all the other activities came through networks he had cultivated over the years.

So far Ryan's story might be interesting, but not exceptional. It is when you probe just a bit deeper that you see the real power of networks. None of Ryan's internships offered substantial compensation, so how did he manage to do them all? For one thing, when appropriate, he continued to use the support network from his hometown. He also started developing and taking advantage of other networks. For his internship in Baltimore with World Relief, he had a friend who lived there, so he asked about housing in Baltimore. Before long, he found himself a guest at his friend's house for the whole summer. He had to pay for the metro but otherwise had no living expenses. The following summer, interning with the Enough Project in very expensive Washington, DC, Ryan says,

> I went on my college's alumni network and sent emails to all the people in the DC area. I told them I was a student at their college and doing an unpaid internship. I told them I needed a place to stay and asked if they would house me or if they knew someone who would. I got several offers. The offer I ended up taking was with a family I did not directly contact. Someone I had contacted passed my name on to someone else, who passed it on again, and that is how I found a place to stay. The man of the house worked at the State Department on security issues in Africa and he knew the director/founder of the Enough Project. That is how they knew it would be a good fit. All they asked for was fifty dollars per month to pay for utilities. They fed me for free. In addition, one of the other people I had contacted happened to receive free metro passes that he never used, so he gave them to me. I did not spend one dollar on transportation all summer.

Ryan has been blessed thus far with an incredible array of experiences, with multiple organizations, both overseas and in the United States. He teaches us about the importance of getting to know people, being willing to ask for help, and finding creative ways through one's networks to make it all possible.

Here is another story on the power of networking. After returning from a semester in the Middle East, Brit Steiner did an off-campus semester in Washington, DC, where she landed an internship at USAID. Making the most of this great opportunity, Brit took the initiative to ask over a dozen of her colleagues to sit down with her and talk. As Brit remembers,

> I did not have any trouble getting people to meet with me over coffee because all the people I wanted to meet with had at some point been in my position. I wanted to know why they were here (USAID) and how they got here, but I would also get to know them on a personal level by asking them about their weekend and their families. I would let them get to know me on a personal level too. That kind of vulnerability is somewhat rare in the working environment, but most

people found it refreshing. I didn't only want to know how people got into the kinds of jobs I thought I wanted but also what kinds of people they were and what kinds of lives they led. Choosing the right career is a very personal journey.

For Brit, this sort of relationship building was not just a strategy to get a job. Still, after she graduated, she had to wait only a few months before USAID called and offered her a position as management and program analyst in the Office of Civilian Response.

BE INVOLVED IN YOUR CHURCH—NURTURE YOUR FAITH

We have already seen how being involved in a church community can provide a support base for internships and overseas experiences that require fundraising. Being part of a community that is willing to send you "out" with its blessing and support can be deeply motivating, comforting, and empowering, but it is also a relationship that keeps us accountable to others and, ultimately, to God. It is for all of these reasons that David Bronkema, now director of development programs at Eastern University, encourages college students to be intentional about joining a church community. Find a community that enfolds you, challenges you, nurtures you, engages you in ministry, and holds you accountable for who you are and what you do. That type of relationship will stand you in good stead when you are out in the field, distant from a supportive community, facing difficult circumstances, and trying to stay true to your calling.

For most of the people I interviewed, it is their faith, their sense of identity and purpose, and their relationship with God that keep them going when they encounter the terrible pain of seeing young women trafficked, children orphaned by AIDS, bodies missing limbs due to war, or women on street corners selling candies as a way of getting enough food for their children. For Duncan Boughton, who spends much of his time studying and trying to improve agricultural markets in Africa, this is so important that he puts it above everything else.

> The most important thing is to focus on growing in your knowledge of God, because you do not want to make a split between your faith and career. God will take care of your career, but you need to take care of your relationship with God. Maybe that is an oversimplification, but you must not neglect your relationship with God. Development is messy and confusing and we really need the Lord to guide us into the good works he has prepared for us to do. That is exciting. My goodness, I mean that is amazing! He invites us to participate with him in finding useful things to do, trying to make a contribution, and not despairing when things are hard. Truth be told, they are always hard. We must come to trust God with the outcome, and growing in a relationship with God is key.

Cut the branches off the vine and the branches wither. Being part of a community of faith helps you grow in the understanding of your faith and your calling, gives you opportunities to pray, worship, and serve, and may well provide you with a community of support in the future. Your church involvement may also make a great contribution to the formation of your own worldview. All good reasons to become part of a church community now.

ATTEND PRESENTATIONS, LECTURES, AND EVENTS, BOTH ON AND OFF CAMPUS

College and university campuses bubble over with opportunities that you must balance with your studies. National and international speakers come through, professors give presentations on their latest research, organizations invite you to join them in advocacy for this or that cause, and conferences on global development issues take place regionally and nationally. Many of these events make special efforts to get students to join in. True, you cannot do everything, nor should you try to. Everyone needs to find appropriate balance, but it is worth asking how much slack or wasted time you have programmed into your schedule. When Hannah Marsh looks back on her college days after just a few years in various postings at USAID, she wishes she had been more active:

> I look back at my college experience and wish I had taken advantage of more of the opportunities provided. My school had tons of really valuable extracurricular events and activities. Now I see clearly the value in connecting with individuals actively working in the field. Some of the speakers who came to colleges like mine are now my colleagues. I wish I had valued those opportunities more and participated in them when I had the chance. They are definitely excellent preparation for the future.

To all this we could add the advice to work harder at getting to know your professors outside of class. Like Brit Steiner did with her colleagues at USAID, meet with your professors and get to know them better. Get another student or two to join you. Ask about their families, their weekends, how they got to be where they are today, and what struggles they have had to face. Tell them who you are, what your dreams are, and what your own struggles are. The benefits abound. Among them are that your professor might know you well enough to recommend you for a special activity, as happened with Ryan Musser when his professor recommended him to be an elections observer in Sierra Leone. Another is that you might get more invested in your classes. As Hannah Marsh explains: "I wish I had talked more with my professors, sat closer to the front of class, and asked more questions. The few times I did that, I also did exponentially better in those classes."

Find a Mentor or Mentors

Everyone needs mentors—wise counselors who have traveled similar paths before, picked up some experiential wisdom, and are now willing to listen to us, guide us on our way, and serve as role models. Joshua had Moses. Mary had Elizabeth. Timothy had Paul. In other familiar arenas Luke had Obi-Wan and Yoda, and Frodo had Gandalf. For people planning to go into foreign cultures and hoping to have an impact on foreign ways of life, mentors are especially crucial, and your college years are a good time to find one. Mentors can help you know what to expect, save you from unnecessary errors and wrong turns, give guidance on how to resolve dilemmas, share in your joys and sorrows, and nurture your spirit.

Notice the value some of today's development professionals place on their mentoring relationships:

> My advice is to gain a lot of mentors—professors, older students you can learn things from, people in business. Build those relationships. I still have contact with two professors on a quarterly basis. For everything I do, I cherish input from others and consult many people before making decisions.
>
> Greg Matney, regional facilitator for Partners
> Worldwide, Hyderabad, India

> As a college student, I was concerned about hunger and poverty and volunteered in food kitchens and building houses. I also had this great mentor who was good at cutting you off at the knees, though in a loving way. She made me realize that helping like this was good, but that we also needed to address the upstream issues. That is when I was introduced to advocacy as a Christian alternative to direct service.
>
> Sarah Rohrer, field organizer with Bread for the World

> What skill set are you developing that will help you address the passions on your heart and the needs of the world? How do you put those three together? My strategy was to identify the smartest person I could and find a way to work with them.
>
> Julie Peterson, vice president at American World Services

Consulting with lots of knowledgeable people, allowing yourself to see new possibilities, being open to change, and walking alongside someone you respect—this is all the stuff of mentorship.

When Dr. Belinda Forbes first thought about applying her dental skills in the developing world, she sought out experienced and respected missionaries to guide her. This experience proved to be extremely helpful, which is why she now advises young people to

> find a mentor, someone with mission experience, who can ground you and point you in the right direction. It took me almost three years to find my way into missions. During those years, I spent time nurturing the call, acting on the call, finding opportunities, and discerning where I should go. I made visits, wrote letters, and made phone calls. Having a mentor in such a time is particularly helpful. Find someone who has been in missions or someone who is actively involved in cross-cultural work.

Now comes the big question of how you actually find such a wise mentor. Some colleges have mentorship programs. Sign up. Some college programs in development or missions offer to help you find a development or mission professional as a mentor. If so, sign up. If these options do not exist, then find a mentor, or several, on your own. Maybe there is someone who has been working in the field for many years and is now living in your community. Use your professors and other networks (e.g., your church) to find the sort of person you would like to spend some time with. Call that person and indicate who you are and what you would like, suggesting a casual relationship in which you might meet for coffee once a month or so. You are right to think that the people you might have in mind are busy, but they are also good people who almost certainly care about the formation of the next generation. My strong hunch is that they will make time for you. Go ahead, make the call.

Intern with a Variety of Organizations

As we review ideas of what to do in college, you will notice multiple virtuous circles as one activity might relate to and reinforce others. You might find a mentor in your church community who tells you about a volunteer opportunity, and your mentor and the people you meet volunteering might become members of your network. Internships are another element in the circle.

Local internships can be done during the semester, and both local and international internships can be done in the summer. Local internships put you in situations where you might interact directly with people in need, and they also help you gain a better understanding of how organizations function in the civil society sector and how they are managed. If you get an internship in a government or private sector organization, you learn something important about that kind of organization and the people who work there. In any internship, you learn a lot about yourself, what you are good at, what motivates you, what you like doing, and what you need to improve.

Dana DeRuiter, Brit Steiner, and Hannah Marsh all work at USAID. They came from different colleges and majored in different fields. But all three had internships either in USAID itself or in the State Department, and all three credit those internships with paving the way to their current positions.

Tim Bollinger did a semester-long internship with CRWRC in Zambia in his senior year and after graduation took a full-year internship in Mozambique, again with CRWRC. His experiences were incredibly enriching and eventually led to his current position with a Mozambican health-oriented NGO. One thing he learned is that in the early years it helps to play the field, work with different organizations, and experience and learn from a diversity of sources. Like Ryan Musser, who had interned with four different organizations by his first year after college, Tim encourages people to check out different organizations and opportunities during the college years, a period in your life when you still have the freedom to try things out at a relatively low cost.

Closing Thoughts

College is a time for testing—not just taking tests in classes but testing yourself to see what you are good at, what you like, and what kind of a person you are. It is a time to test your faith, abilities, commitment, and willpower. As Paul tells the Thessalonians: "Test everything. Hold on to the good" (1 Thess. 5:21). In those four, short college years, you have incredible opportunities to develop your virtues, knowledge, and skills, and to discover and shape your own mind and heart. To return to the chess analogy, college is a time to build, shape, and strengthen your "pieces" and to get them in good places. All too soon, the college years are over, you graduate, and it is time to move on.

What comes next? A job? More schooling? Internships? The Peace Corps? Chapter 7 gives some clues as to what to expect during what chess players might call the midgame. A lot can happen in the midgame, as the stories in chapter 7 from recent graduates attest.

Further Reflection and Action Steps

1. Take an inventory of the capabilities that are part of your "raw material." Start with the ones that relate closely to the job qualifications listed in chapter 5. Which are inherent in your internal makeup, and which are contextual?

2. Once, during an event led by an experienced missionary, we were asked to imagine we had died and could compose our own epitaph. We each wrote down the epitaph we hoped would grace our gravestones. We then read our creations, all of which spoke of exemplary lives of service and love. The lesson came when we were told that if these are the epitaphs we envision, that is how we must start living today!

   Let's do this exercise for college. Outline the recommendation letter that you would like your professors to write to a potential employer on your behalf when you graduate. What virtues, knowledge, and skills do you want them to highlight? Draw up a tentative plan for what you will do and how you will live until graduation so that a professor might actually write such a letter.

3. Review Dana DeRuiter's story in chapter 5. Dana majored in English. Discuss how this major helped her get to where she is today. What are the special VKS that your current major is helping you cultivate?

4. Make a list of the courses you've taken that meet each important area of study for someone preparing for development work: (1) getting to know your neighbors, (2) theory courses related to development, and (3) a relevant major concentration. Do you have a good balance? If you currently feel unbalanced, do you have plans to restore the balance either in college or in graduate education?

5. What extracurricular activities are you currently involved with? In what ways are these shaping you? What capabilities are you becoming aware of and what capabilities are you nurturing? How many of these activities are oriented toward serving others? In what ways?

7

The Early Years after College

Getting from Here to There

If you sense a calling to international development, don't give up. Never give up. Do a lot of reading. Network like crazy. Talk to everyone you can imagine [that] might have something to say about these things. Pursue your calling and work to define it. Pray, seek God's will, and then move in that direction. God will open and close doors in a way that's very extraordinary.

Roland Vanderburg, program director for CAUSE Canada

Development is a challenging field and hard to break into when you have only a BA and little experience. But I have high hopes for those who have a passion for development work, and my advice to them is to keep at it, keep at it, keep at it.

Jacqueline Klamer, writer/project coordinator
for Partners Worldwide

Sow your seed in the morning,
and at evening let your hands not be idle,
for you do not know which will succeed,
whether this or that,
or whether both will do equally well.

Ecclesiastes 11:6

For about four years your path is clear. Go to school fall and spring, get a summer job, worry a bit about the student loans that are adding up, wonder about whether you are studying the right things, and head back to school the next fall. There is comfort in such a known and familiar path, but then comes graduation, and the path grows foggy. You think there is a way ahead, partly because you know there are thirty-year-old professionals in your field who were liberal arts majors like you, but you cannot see clearly and you wonder how to get from here to there. What should your next step be? The loans are coming due, parents looking over your shoulder make you uncomfortable, you are in a relationship that might lead to marriage (or maybe not), and the confidence you had built up by your senior year takes a hit.

To get started on a career in international development, there are lots of options right after college, most of which revolve around gaining experience and further education. There are many ways to get experience and many graduate programs from which to choose. Which ones, and in which order, are right for you? This chapter presents six ways to get experience, three international and three domestic, and then shows how these may interweave with choices about graduate school, a fourth domestic option. Along the way, I offer some advice on two daunting issues that many aspiring development workers encounter: fundraising and student loans.

So what do you do? Your first thought might be to find a paid, entry-level position in a development-related field, preferably overseas, but you run into what might be called the "experience pickle." When you look for a position, all the paid ones seem to require two or more years of experience. Hence the pickle, as 2002 graduate Luke Hamstra laments: "How do you get two years of experience if nobody hires you unless you already have two years of experience?"

Your thoughts turn toward other potential options. Maybe the Peace Corps (for Americans) or an internship through CIDA (for Canadians) would be good options. How about an internship with an NGO? You would probably have to raise your own financial support, but then what happens with the loans? The fact that you have not yet developed a specialty comes to mind, and you start wondering about grad school. Is now the time for that, or should you get some experience first? But this avenue leads you back to the experience pickle. Another option is to find a volunteer placement through your own personal networks, or perhaps through one of your denomination's mission agencies. An AmeriCorps placement might be good, though it would not be overseas. Another possibility for the truly adventurous is signing up for an immersion language program in a developing country. Once there, you learn the language, get culturally acclimated, and perhaps enter a local network that links you to a longer-term development position. Teaching English in Asia for a couple years is yet another option. Or maybe you should just take a "regular job" for a while.

Fortunately, all of the above options can be good ones, and this chapter tells stories of recent graduates who have taken steps along a variety of these paths. But there is no hiding the fact that a fair amount of anxiety can follow you through these steps. That is why Roland Vanderburg and Jacqueline Klamer both feel a need to tell you to keep at it, not to give up.

One piece of good news is that your first assignment might bring a good deal of happiness and satisfaction to counterbalance the anxiety. The last few years, I have received the results of an alumni evaluation of our college programs. As director of Calvin College's International Development Studies (IDS) program, I naturally checked the results for IDS majors, which were compared in the data with all other majors. On average, IDS graduates in their first five years after college reported making less money than other Calvin graduates but also enjoyed much higher levels of happiness and job satisfaction. Some anxiety mixed with good job satisfaction, while being involved in rewarding service—a pretty good overall mix.

As I will try to show, finding a way to get international experience is not that hard—if you are really committed to it. Once you manage that, as Professor David Bronkema at Eastern University puts it, "all sorts of opportunities open up." What you need to be prepared for is a few years of low income, perhaps even subsistence level. There are plenty of opportunities with organizations that pay minimally and/or expect you to raise your own funds. Read through the following options and consider which one fits you best.

Three Ways to Solve the Experience Pickle: International Opportunities

Option 1: The Peace Corps (for Americans) or a CIDA Internship (for Canadians)

These are among the first options most students consider. Both are government-funded programs with the express purpose of finding means to get young people in the field in ways that contribute to development, train them for future careers, and promote intercultural communication and good will among nations. Both programs pay all program-related costs and provide a small but adequate living allowance. One major difference is that the Peace Corps places its volunteers directly in communities in developing countries, whereas CIDA works directly with Canadian NGOs that take the volunteers and integrate them into their work overseas. Another difference is that Peace Corps placements are twenty-seven months while the typical CIDA placement is only six months.

For example, Charlotte Keniston and Luke Hamstra were both placed by the Peace Corps in different Guatemalan communities and assigned to work with municipal governments. Charlotte worked on women's rights and Luke worked on urban development, especially housing, water, and sanitation. Alisa Buma and Jillian Baker, both Canadians, found internships through CIDA. Alisa was placed in Kenya with Samaritan's Purse, and Jillian was placed in Honduras with CRWRC. Placements with both programs can differ greatly, some being in urban settings in Eastern Europe, others in isolated rural communities of Africa. Most people who join the Peace Corps will tell you something like the following: Peace Corps does a great job placing you in a community but then pretty much leaves you alone to figure out how you can best contribute. Volunteers typically partner with a local NGO, government office, school, or community group. One person from the partner group is assigned as the volunteer's counterpart to help the volunteer adjust, live, and work effectively. In practice, the quality and effectiveness of these placements and relationships vary greatly. Volunteers often find it helpful to seek out other relationships and other specific projects to get involved with in order to make the most out of their time and experience. Some of the best overall experiences come to volunteers who seek out relationships and opportunities other than those to which they have been assigned. For volunteers with an independent spirit and low need for structure, the Peace Corps is an excellent option, not only because they are put into a culturally rich environment in which they can learn a language, be among the people, and get two years of valuable experience, but also because they are given much latitude in using their time and experiences. If you are the sort of person who needs structure and specific, assigned tasks, the Peace Corps is probably not your best choice. As volunteer Luke Hamstra describes the experience, "after a few months of training, you are all on your own. Peace Corps lets you do what you will with it. If you want to work hard every day, you can. If not, nobody is there to hold your hand. You make of it what you want."

Luke also has some advice for Christians wondering what the faith implications of going with the Peace Corps are: "Christians should know that the Peace Corps is not necessarily un-Christian or anti-Christian. If you are a Christian and feel like emphasizing that in your work, nobody is going to know or pay attention. As a Christian, you should not feel like you must be in a Christian NGO."

When Luke went to Guatemala he was placed in the municipality of a small town. He arrived with high hopes, which suffered a major blow the first day when his coworker indicated to him that their primary job for that day, and days to follow, was to put their feet up on the desk, pull their cowboy hats down over their eyes, and rest until the work day ended. Luke was distressed about the prospects of making a positive contribution in such a setting, but the prospects changed a short time later when the whole corrupt mayoral administration was swept out due to political changes in the nation as a whole. The new mayor and his administration really did want to work to improve the community, and they were happy Luke was there to help.

Although he was no IT expert, Luke was nevertheless gifted with a computer, so he helped to create an interactive computer program that showed where all the houses in his town were, how many people lived in them, which had water and sewer lines, which were up to reasonable standards, and how the roads were laid out and which were paved. The program was then used to apply for national and international funding to improve these aspects of the town's infrastructure and housing. Quite an accomplishment and quite a contribution!

Luke's time in the Peace Corps opened up many additional possibilities. He received numerous development-oriented job offers, which he has thus far turned down, and he received a major scholarship for a master's program in international political economy and development at Fordham University. After completing his master's degree Luke focused on building and supporting a promising new community development NGO in Kenya called Omwabini (Rescue Steps). Luke had begun to work with Omwabini when he was in college and commmitted several additional years to its development at the conclusion of his Peace Corps service in Guatemala. Luke's postcollege story is less than ten years old, but it already has many chapters, with the Peace Corps experience comprising an important early one.

Beyond the experience of living and working in a developing country, the Peace Corps also offers other excellent benefits, such as deferment of student loans, a transition stipend of around $7,500 provided at the end of the term, access to scholarships for graduate programs, and a certain status that seems to pave the way to government jobs. Hannah Marsh has not done a careful study, but she says it seems like a majority of her coworkers at USAID have Peace Corps experience in their background.

On the other hand, there are three significant disadvantages of working with the Peace Corps, one of which is its lack of structure. The second is that the process of interviewing, vetting, and placement can take more than a year. The third is the lack of mentors. When you are out in the field for the first time, there is a strong need for wise mentorship. You might get lucky and find one in your official placement, but you may very well need to find one on your own, perhaps by connecting with a respected Christian NGO worker nearby. Sometimes, too, the volunteers themselves organize to form a helpful mutual support group.

A relatively new option with the Peace Corps is to integrate a volunteer experience with master's degree study in a development-related field. Over eighty United States universities participate in this program.[1]

Option 2: Overseas Internships with NGOs

Another excellent option for gaining experience right after college is to intern with an NGO. There are plenty of Christian and secular organizations that offer such internships, some international and some local. You will not have a problem finding such an opportunity, though finding the right one may require some careful research. Based on her experiences in Mozambique, Rebecca Vander Meulen has seen that

> almost every community or small town here has some sort of association responding to issues of HIV, poverty, or the environment. If you can pay your own way, there are plenty of these organizations that would be willing to host you. You will learn more about community development, make friends, and maybe find your way into a longer-term position, as happened with me.

I am sure you noticed the kicker in this statement, which is that in many cases you must be able to "pay your own way," about which we will say more shortly, particularly regarding fundraising. For the moment, let me say that raising your own funds is not as impossible or as scary as it might first sound.

What I most want to communicate is that if you really want that international experience, you can get it. Once you have a few years of experience, as David Bronkema suggests and as the stories of many young development workers attest, career opportunities start to open up. Here are two stories of college graduates who found placements with international NGOs.

Tim Bollinger graduated with a BA in international development and immediately began a yearlong internship with CRWRC in Mozambique. Tim had already spent a year in Brazil after high school on a Rotary International exchange, a college semester in Ghana, and then another college semester interning with a local NGO in Zambia. Gifted in language learning, Tim's year in Brazil helped him gain fluency in Portuguese, which is also Mozambique's official language. CRWRC got to know Tim during his internship in Zambia, so they offered him the yearlong placement in Mozambique, a position supported partly by a government grant and partly by Tim's own fundraising. As that year came to an end, there was discussion of a longer-term position, but Tim had come to desire more independence than the formal procedures of

Fundraising Works

Most of us resist raising our own support. We are not very good at asking for money, and we have the idea that our employer should pay us. To counter these thoughts, I want to say loudly and clearly that there is nothing wrong with raising your own support. If you think about it, anyone being paid by a mission organization in the voluntary sector is receiving funds that have been raised. Many long-time missionaries have raised their own support their entire lives. You should not fear raising your own support for an important, kingdom-building opportunity. If you are committed, can explain well what you are doing, and are carrying out a compelling mission, you will almost certainly find supporters who would like to encourage you, pray for you, and provide financial support.

Like many graduates, Nathan Dowling was "absolutely afraid to fundraise," so he applied to Food for the Hungry (FH) hoping for a salaried position. FH offered Nathan a position, but it was a "mission" position that required raising $20,000 in less than two months. That seemed impossible, but he decided to give it a try. He spoke to his parents' church and then his grandfather's church and was amazed at how much support he got. In one month he had raised over $11,000, enough to get started.

Stories like Nathan's abound. Here is one more: Emily Romero did a yearlong internship in Honduras and then studied for an MA in cross-cultural studies. Having married a Honduran teacher, Emily and her husband, David, returned to Honduras to start a new school for children in a marginalized barrio. The school opened with ninety students. Student fees cover some of the expenses, but Emily and David must also raise funds. They started with their personal contacts and the churches they have relationships with, and things are going well. Emily firmly believes that "if God calls us to this work, then he is also going to give us a way to do it. If you share who you are and what you are doing, people will see that passion and want to join you in ministry."

See chapter 9 for some tips on fundraising.

North American–based NGOs allowed, so he opted to go a different direction. As so often happens, during the internship in Mozambique Tim met people, and they led him to take steps that are still unfolding.

First, he met an enterprising woman from Peru who shared his vision to develop a new model for community-based tourism that allows visitors to learn about local culture in respectful ways rather than in the exploitative, transactional patterns of cultural tourism that are so typical. That led him to spend four months (expenses paid but no salary) exploring this possibility in Peru. The idea and the possibilities are still on the front burner as they wait to see if some grants are approved. Second, he met a committed British physician whose successful community health organization was having trouble with its own sustainability. She needed someone to help her and her coworkers imagine and create a different organizational structure. Having gained familiarity with the project, the people, and the situation, and believing that success was possible, Tim took a short-term expenses-paid assignment, turning down a fellowship opportunity with Kiva, the highly popular internet lending site for microenterprises around the world. In Mozambique he consults with the local organization and works with them to forge a plan to keep the organization viable. One possibility for Tim's future is a position within the new structure of the organization. This would be a position that pays a local salary, which for Tim would be more than enough. Tim's financial needs for all these activities have been low and have been mostly covered. He enjoys living and working with local people and feels little need for a North American type of salary.

Jillian Baker, a Canadian, graduated with an English major, an international development minor, and a desire to get out in the world and serve. Unsure of how to get her first placement, she returned home to study French, which she knew was an important international language. As she studied French, she also continued to search for a good internship. Her search led her to Idealist.org, where many service opportunities are listed, both paid and volunteer. Jillian found a "green revolution" type of organization in Mexico that was looking for a good writer. Jillian did not speak Spanish, but they were interested in her English writing skills. It happened that the person interviewing her knew French and was intrigued that Jillian was working on her own to build up her French skills. As Jillian discovered, the science courses that she had originally taken in college were of help, too, because some of the writing required a reasonable familiarity with natural science.

That is how Jillian joined up with the International Maize and Wheat Improvement Center, or Centro Internacional de Mejoramiento de Maiz y Trigo (CIMMYT), for a one-year internship.[2] Because CIMMYT was well funded with UN and foundation grants, Jillian was paid about $1,000 per month in addition to receiving a car and housing. This is not the sort of internship most people can expect, but it was the product of much searching and intentionality on Jillian's part. She had grown up in a Christian community and had expected to work for Christian organizations, but was delighted to find caring, thoughtful, and motivated people in the secular world too. This in itself made the experience a growing one.

Returning to Canada, Jillian searched for and found a ten-month CIDA internship with a Christian organization in Honduras. Afterward, with a few years of experience under her belt, she decided it was time for more schooling and obtained a master's degree in communications and development from a British university. When she graduated with her MA, Jillian had reason to hope for a longer-term position, and that's what happened when she was offered a position with World Vision Uganda to work in the general area of capacity building.

How about Those Student Loans?

An unfortunate wake-up call for many graduates is the letter from your banker informing you that it is payback time. A $20,000 to $30,000 debt is quite normal for graduates from private colleges. Fortunately, there are excellent options that allow you to manage your payments while you get that all-important international development experience.

If you go overseas with either the Peace Corps or CIDA, federally supported loans will likely be deferred, and interest will likely not accrue either. When you return from Peace Corps service of twenty-seven months, your transition allowance can be used for loan repayments.

If you work with an NGO, there are four good options. (1) A few NGOs actually pay you enough to make monthly loan payments. (2) Some NGOs (the Mennonite Central Committee's SALT program is one) provide loan repayment assistance during your time of service. (3) Other NGOs, such as International Justice Mission and Partners Worldwide, have significant fundraising expectations but also provide stipends, part of which can be used for loan repayment. It helps that living costs in many developing countries are low.

You may wonder whether money you raise should be used to pay off loans. I would say—yes! Here is why: First, most employees in charitable organizations are paid with donated money. Naturally, those employees decide how to use their income in all the normal ways that people steward the incomes God provides to them. If some is used to pay off expenses from earlier years, such as student loans, there is simply less to spend on other things. This is the way everyone lives. Second, when supporters contribute money to you and your mission, they know you have financial needs. Donors understand that you need an appropriate stipend—some for rent, some for food, and some to pay off whatever financial obligations you might have.

(4) The fourth option is the Public Service Loan Forgiveness Program, which is for US citizens and residents who (a) graduate with a significant amount of federal loans (most commonly Stafford loans) and (b) work in a relatively low-paying public service job with a US-based NGO (the legal term is a 501(c)(3) organization). If this fits, you may very well be eligible to take advantage of the College Cost Reduction and Access Act of 2007. If you qualify for this program, your payment is calculated as a percentage of your income. If you make these reduced payments for ten years, whatever principal remains is forgiven. For example, if you spend five years doing low-paid internships for NGOs, your payments may be much lower during those years than they would be under the normal repayment plan. If your income rises in your sixth year, your payments are recalculated. This program may allow you to take low-paying internships with NGOs in your early years after graduation. Check it out at www.finaid.org/loans/publicservice.phtml or at the government site, http://studentaid.ed.gov/PORTALSWebApp/students/english/PSF.jsp.

Before you reach the conclusion that international service is out of the question because of a heavy student debt burden, be sure to consider these options.

Tim and Jillian both found yearlong internships that propelled them on their way. Though both of these were at least partially paid, most such internships are unpaid and require volunteers either to raise funds or to provide them from their own personal resources. CRWRC, Hope International, International Justice Mission, Partners Worldwide, Samaritan's Purse, World Relief, and many other Christian and secular organizations make such overseas internships available. One popular program for recent graduates is the Serving and Learning Together program (SALT) of the Mennonite Central Committee. SALT places interns with local partner organizations and in local homes. Costs are low, and in 2011 the fundraising requirements were below $5,000 for the year. Most organizations have higher fundraising expectations, but most also provide fundraising guidance. More detailed information about programs and fundraising, including some tips on how to go about it, is included in chapter 9.

Option 3: Teach English Overseas

A number of graduates I know have spent a year or two teaching English overseas. You thus provide an important service and make enough money to live on while gaining international experience. China is one common destination, though opportunities abound in many other developing nations as well. You might also consider teaching English in a wealthier country such as Korea, Japan, or an oil-rich nation in the Middle East. Salaries and benefits can be quite high, and costs relatively low, so you can get a year of international cross-cultural experience while earning enough to make some significant payments on your loans.

Carly Miller graduated with a psychology major, an international development minor, and about $30,000 in student loan debt. Here is how Carly, who is currently teaching English in Korea, sees it:

> I figured that teaching in Korea for a year or two would be a good way to chip away at my debt! But it also seemed like a fun way to do that. I don't know if teaching is really my future calling, but my love of traveling and desire to experience life in another part of the world made this job really appealing to me. [It] felt a little bit like I wasn't really pursuing my passions by coming here, because I'm much more interested in the developing world, but I felt like I needed to deal with my loans so that I wouldn't be carrying around this debt with me for forever.
>
> I got connected with a recruiting agency that set me up with a *hogwan*, an afterschool tutoring [program]. My hogwan offered me about $1,560 a month. They also cover my rent, found my apartment, and provided me with a cell phone. My living expenses are so low here that I can put over half of my income toward loans and savings. I feel really blessed with my situation! At first I had

doubts about whether this experience would line up with my passions, but now that I am here, I am blessed to discover that the experience itself is rich and practical. Learning about Korean culture—their way of life, the food, and the language—has been so rewarding. I'm confident that I'll carry this experience with me always, and I'm sure it will be really helpful for any experiences abroad I might have in the future.

Carly suggests Dave's ESL Café as an excellent place to learn about these opportunities.[3]

In a few pages I will tell you about Alisa Buma, who also spent one year teaching English in Korea and managed to pay down $12,000 of her debt that same year. The whole experience for Alisa was excellent, but she stresses the importance of signing on with a reputable organization. It is worth noting, for example, that Dave's ESL Café is a for-profit site that does not research or stand behind the organizations offering jobs. Be sure to do due diligence regarding the integrity of any organization you are considering. Alisa's strategy was to take a course in teaching English as a second language (TESL), after which her program guaranteed placement with a reputable school or program.

Domestic Experience Is Good Too: Four Excellent Options Closer to Home

The next four options are all domestic and might be just what you need right now. For example, maybe you have a strong sense of global calling but prefer to live and work in North America. That is fine, because like the beehive in chapter 4, the bees that go out into the world depend on many support bees back in the hive. Others would genuinely like to work abroad one day, but maybe a personal situation requires them to stay in their home country for the time being. It is also possible that a great domestic opportunity comes your way when the international opportunities you pursued are not coming through.

Even if the domestic organization is not globally focused, such service can still provide excellent training and experience for international positions later on. You might gain knowledge and skill in an area such as conflict resolution, organizational management, job creation and microenterprise, community organization, or advocacy. You might become familiar with poverty-stricken urban environments, which wrestle with similar issues, whether in Cleveland or Rio de Janeiro. Or you might work with immigrant or refugee communities, learning about their lives here and in their home countries, about the dynamics that drove them to migrate, and about their country in general. You might even improve in a foreign language. All of these things are good.

Option 4: AmeriCorps or Domestic NGO

AmeriCorps is a US government program that facilitates placement of some seventy thousand volunteers every year with a national or local organization. Volunteers work in any of a number of areas, including education, youth formation, public health, income generation, refugee assistance, disaster relief, and community development. Public service organizations apply to AmeriCorps to fund their volunteers, but they recruit them directly, though approved positions are also listed on the AmeriCorps site.[4] With an AmeriCorps placement you have a position with a clear job description that is supervised by someone within the organization, which is quite different from the Peace Corps. As in the Peace Corps, volunteers are paid a living stipend, are eligible for loan deferral or forgiveness according to the Public Service Loan Forgiveness Program (see the sidebar above, "How about Those Student Loans?") and receive an end-of-service stipend. Most terms of service are nine to twelve months and can often be renewed.

Alicia Clifton began learning about international development during a semester program in the Middle East, after which she returned to college wanting to study more about development.[5] When she graduated with an intercultural studies major, Alicia wanted to take the next step, which she thought would be either an international experience or graduate school. Her inquiries led her to discover another version of the experience pickle. Alicia found that "it was difficult to get experience if you did not have a graduate degree, but it was difficult to be accepted to graduate school without any experience."

Resisting the temptation to give up, Alicia took an AmeriCorps Vista position in Buffalo, NY, with Jericho Road Ministries, a faith-based organization that works with refugees and low-income families. As an AmeriCorps volunteer, Alicia experienced organizational operations on many levels, including programmatic work for pregnant refugee women, volunteer coordination, research, church relations, organizational development, and grant writing. After two years, Alicia was hired as the full-time director of health and family services and program support. During three years at Jericho, Alicia learned about nonprofit management and some of the complexities of human development in general. She also identified and improved her own skills and passions, which include human interaction and participatory development processes. The experience was both motivating and formative, and it also contributed to her acceptance to the master's program in development practice at Emory University in Atlanta.

To work with a domestic NGO, it is not necessary to go through AmeriCorps. You can find a local organization, review its openings, and apply directly.

Finding the Right NGO

National and international NGOs come in many shapes and sizes, with different missions and different perspectives. To take some obvious examples, some are Christian and some not. Some work with youth and some with the elderly. Some take government funds and some are financed by a dedicated membership. While you might be trying to encourage NGOs to take you on in some way, remember too that you must "interview" them and be sure you would really like to work there. Listed below are some questions to ask. Answers to some can be found on the organization's website. You will have to ask others in face-to-face conversations. Probably no organization will line up perfectly with your own views and sense of mission, but try to find one you would be proud to work for, and avoid the ones you find problematic.

What is the organization's mission?

What is its perspective on development?

What types of development strategies are employed?

What is the organizational structure?

How do they honor human relationships?

Who is on staff in field offices?

How do they operate cross-culturally?

What is the source of the organization's finances, and how is the organization's money spent?

How will your existing virtues, knowledge, and skills contribute to the organization's work?

Every community has civic organizations that work with the homeless, youth who are at risk, students who need tutoring, single parents, returning citizens (i.e., released prisoners), immigrants, refugees, and the jobless. If you choose to stay close to home for a while, inquire about positions with such organizations. You will gain virtues, knowledge, and skills that serve you well in the future, should you make a transition to the international arena. You will learn about how NGOs function and how they are, and ought to be, managed. You might also gain expertise in a specific area that prepares you well for international work later on.

Option 5: Entry-Level Position (or Internship) in the National Offices of an International Organization

You might recall that Dana DeRuiter worked for five years at CRWRC, first as a volunteer and then as a full-time paid employee, before she did her master's degree and took a position with PEPFAR. Finding a domestic position with an internationally focused organization involves you directly in international development, even though you are not overseas yourself. It may also open up opportunities for working overseas later on. On the other hand, if you are like

Dana and find that you are better suited to live in North America, then this is an excellent way to begin a career that does not require living in a distant land. Here are the stories of two college graduates who took on such domestic positions, one with a Christian NGO and the other with USAID.

Mark Kaech got interested in international affairs when he traveled to Egypt right before starting college. This new interest led Mark to major in intercultural studies, which then led him into the ideas and practices of development. In his senior year he landed a summer internship in Bangladesh with Food for the Hungry (FH), and he began to think further about a career in development. Like so many others, Mark graduated with a lot of student debt and felt uncomfortable raising funds for an overseas position that would have to be used to pay back his loans. Fortunately, his internship had helped him develop a relationship with FH, and when FH offered him the position of recruiter for FH's various student programs, he quickly accepted. Three years later, these student programs fell victim to the economic recession, but Mark transitioned within FH to several other marketing-related positions in the Phoenix office. Mark soon became FH's media specialist, because of his gifts in telling people about FH's work in a number of formats (e.g., spoken word, written word, visual, web design).

Mark's work at FH has helped him improve his skills in communication, strategic direction, and general nonprofit management, which he could certainly continue to use in the home office; but he also has a longing to serve in a developing country. After working five years in FH's central offices, Mark's wife Mary was offered a four-year position with FH's team in Cambodia. It is not clear yet whether Mark will work with FH while in Cambodia. Either way, he sees it as "a breath of fresh air" and the beginning of a new chapter. As they transitioned to Cambodia, Mark was looking for organizations in Cambodia that he might be able to serve. Mary's responsibilities revolve around photojournalism and marketing, fields in which Mark is also capable and interested. For Mark, his work in the main offices of FH was a great start, and he is now looking forward to a lengthy international placement. At this point only God knows what service opportunities lie ahead in Cambodia and how the next chapter in Mark's story will read.

You may be wondering how to search for such a position. The networks you have built up may be one fruitful resource, but you can also check out job postings directly. A good place to search is the member lists of NGO associations. Many Christian organizations in North America are members of Accord (formerly the Association of Evangelical Relief and Development Organizations). Christian development organizations oriented to health issues can be found at Christian Connections in International Health (CCIH).

Other Christian and many secular development organizations are members of InterAction. Tens of thousands of organizations with some connection to international development are listed in the web-based *Directory of Development Organizations*, which can be searched by country.[6]

Entry-level positions can be found in government too, as happened with Hannah Marsh, currently a liaison specialist at USAID, though she cautions that getting a position at USAID right out of college is rare. Hannah studied international relations and Latin American studies at a large, private university, graduating with the hope of working in international development. Hannah believes it was God who laid on her heart the desire to serve globally, so she had faith that God would help her find a way to be involved. For Hannah it was network connections that led a USAID division head to hear about her and offer her a position. One can trace out these connections, Hannah says, but "there is no other way to look at it than to credit it to the hand of God."

Hannah's first position at USAID was entry level and administrative instead of the program- or policy-oriented position she had studied for, but she worked faithfully and has been promoted several times. Over the last five years she has worked in the Center for Faith-Based and Community Initiatives and in programs related to Latin America and the Caribbean, partner outreach, and volunteers. One of the major steps for Hannah was becoming a "direct hire," a long-term position, leaving behind the short-term contracts she was on for her first couple of years.

Though she found her position through network channels, Hannah points out that most people working with USAID come in through two programs, the Development Leadership Initiative (DLI) and the Presidential Management Fellows (PMF) program. The DLI is the means by which college graduates can enter into the Foreign Service and be placed with USAID. The PMF program is primarily for people with graduate degrees, but it is one you should know about. It was through the PMF program that Dana DeRuiter started out with PEPFAR.[7]

Hannah is not at all sure where the future will lead, but right now she feels called to be at USAID. She has thought a lot about her vocational path and offers the following sage advice:

> Where I am now may not be the summation of my life's vocational purpose, but I believe that every season of one's life and every position one holds is a piece of the larger calling God has for us. Where you are now may not be your sweet spot, but it is where you are now, so do not waste it. Maybe you will make photocopies for a while, but even here there is something you will learn, whether it is meeting someone or learning humility. I do not believe I have reached that

sweet spot yet, but I do believe that the lessons I have learned in all the positions I have held have fed into who I am today and what God is calling me to be and to do in the future.

Hannah has very much enjoyed her time at USAID, which is why she has been searching for a master's program that allows her to continue her studies while also keeping her position at USAID.

Option 6: Graduate School

Not everyone has plans to go to graduate school, and it is certainly not a requirement, yet it is a very common step for international development workers to take during the first ten years after they graduate. There are two main—and interlaced—reasons for getting a graduate degree. One is that there is so much more to learn, and once people are out in the field, they soon realize they really do need to know more about, well, almost everything—but maybe one thing in particular stands out, such as how to manage an organization, create income-generating jobs, resolve conflicts and find ways to work together peacefully and productively, plan flourishing city neighborhoods, reforest barren lands, and on and on. The second very practical reason is that graduate degrees are increasingly expected. As reviewed in chapter 4, there are many ways for foreigners to serve, but a common one is to contribute expertise and skills gained through a combination of experience and graduate education.

Those considering this path rightly wonder when to study and whether to get experience first and then the degree or vice versa. Other important considerations include where to study, what to study, and how to pay.

Let's take a look at each of these.

WHEN?

If everything else were equal and no other constraints intervened, then the near unanimous advice is to get a few years of experience first, and in the process discover where your personal passions and capabilities meet the needs of the world. Then make the choice about which graduate school to attend and what to specialize in. Because graduate schools know that experience enriches further education so abundantly, they often make it a main criterion for acceptance. A few years of relevant experience followed by a graduate program was a path taken by many of the development workers you are meeting in these pages.

Of course nothing really is equal, so there may be some excellent reasons for going to graduate school sooner rather than later. Maybe you are in a romantic relationship at a crucial stage. Will it flower or wither? Leaving the country for a couple years might not be the wisest choice right now. Maybe you have unhealthy parents who need you nearby for the next few years. For Nathaniel Veltman, it was the need to get used to a cochlear implant that would help him cope with hearing loss. In order to more fully adjust to the new implant and provide an opportunity to receive a second one, he postponed going overseas. Instead, Nathaniel took a master's in international development, with a focus on Africa. It worked out well for him because at the conclusion of his program he received a job offer in community development with the Presbyterian Church (USA) in Ethiopia.

When college graduate Bernard (Ben) Haven looked for entry-level positions, he discovered that many of the attractive jobs required both a graduate degree and experience. He was doubtful he could get the type of experience he needed, and he wondered instead whether an academic career might be his true calling. After all, he had assisted a professor doing research in college, liked it a lot, and thought research and teaching might be a good career path. Were he to follow this path, a doctoral degree would be essential.

Whether becoming a practitioner or an academic, Ben knew a master's degree was necessary, which led him to study for a master's in development studies. Like Nathaniel, Ben had also spent two of his college semesters in Africa, but even with a freshly minted master's degree no job fell into Ben's lap. So he taught English in China for four months and then, back home again, found work in the quality control department of a local factory. He kept looking for an opening into international development. His strategy was to take a general civil service position with the Canadian government. Now on the inside of government networks, Ben watched for openings at CIDA, the Canadian International Development Agency. Less than a year later, he found one, applied, and was hired, with responsibilities for Canada's HIV/AIDS programs in West Africa. After two years, and wanting to serve internationally, Ben volunteered for a position in Afghanistan as a "stabilization planner," in which he works with civil and military wings of the Afghan government to build a more representative and stable government in Kandahar. It was a combination of experience, graduate school, and strategy that got Ben to where he is today.

Where and What?

There are so many schools and so many possible specializations to choose from that I make no attempt to offer anything other than general advice. Many universities have multiple programs spread across multiple departments. Among all the development professionals I interviewed for this book, no two attended the same school. What I would like to offer is some questions to ask and a bit of guidance as to what kind of answers you might find helpful.

Are you ready for graduate school? Being ready means (1) that life experience has led you to have some questions about development that you need to have answered but that you are clearly not equipped to answer on your own; and (2) that you are motivated to study seriously and to spend the time necessary to learn well.

Will the program help answer your questions? Your questions may be big (e.g., which overall development theory best addresses poverty?) or detailed (e.g., what are the best low-cost and accessible diets for poor households?). Ask whether the courses offered address your questions and to what extent. Check to see how many of the required courses address questions that are not at the forefront of your mind.

What is the school's perspective? It is a mistake to talk about grad schools as if they are "good" or "not so good." Unfortunately, that is often the approach we take. Before asking whether a school is good, it is worth asking whether the school is modernizationist, Marxist, postdevelopment, capabilities approach, or something else. Many schools have a clearly defined orientation, and you should find out what it is. Some schools are eclectic, with scholars from a variety of perspectives. Be sure the school's perspective is one in which you really want to immerse yourself.

Should you attend a Christian graduate program? Working in human development implies deep commitments to life's basic questions. Christian development workers need to be able to think through their goals and their actions, no matter their development specialty, in the context of their Christian understanding of these basic questions. That said, Christians can learn a lot from people and programs that do not share the same foundations. I have noticed that Christians who have studied in only secular schools and worked in secular organizations often have difficulty articulating a clearly Christian vision of what they are about. I have also noticed that Christians who work and study only in Christian institutions and interact only with Christians have a tendency to insularity and small-mindedness.[8]

I have also noticed that development workers who went to secular colleges and then to a Christian graduate program felt greatly enriched by their graduate experience. The reverse also seems true, with the conclusion being that intentional interaction with lots of ideas and practices is good for everyone. Hence, my guarded advice is that if you have spent your whole life in patterns of secular thought and practice, consider a Christian graduate program. On the other hand, if you have gone to a Christian college that steeped you in a Christian perspective, and if all your experience thus far is with Christian organizations and communities, consider a secular program.

Does the program have a regional focus? Remember that programs often specialize in regions. If you anticipate working in Central or South Asia, find a program that specializes in this region and that has professors with ample experience and connections there.

Who are the students? Among the richest and longest-lasting impacts from graduate school are the learning you engage in with fellow students and the relationships you develop with them. Find out what the culture of student interaction and joint learning is like. Will students come from many countries, ethnicities, and religions? If so, conversations are likely to be lively, challenging, and formative.

What are the professors like? One of my favorite search strategies is to find out who the professors are in a given program and then use Google Scholar or another relevant database to find out what these professors write. If you are attracted to what they write about, you will likely appreciate learning from them. Another good strategy is to find out where some of your favorite development writers teach and check out the rest of the program and the other professors who are there. When you talk with current students, ask if the professors are good teachers who are accessible and enjoy engaging with students.

Master's or doctorate? Typically, master's degrees are more practical and assume students will become practitioners. Doctoral degrees, on the other hand, are more oriented to those who plan to do research and teach. The following is not a perfect division, but it generally holds true: if you want to work in development, think about a master's degree; if you want to explore, investigate, learn more about what works, and perhaps even teach, then a doctoral degree makes more sense.

What do program graduates do? Ask the professors and program representatives about the job prospects for their graduates. Be specific. Ask what happened with last year's crop of graduates. Find out where they have gone and ask yourself if those are the sorts of things you envision for yourself in the near future. And be sure to get beyond official responses by asking the students themselves. Graduate programs tend to be small enough for students to know what happens to their graduating colleagues. Moreover, they will generally be willing to tell you the unglossed truth.

How Will You Pay for It?

One of the things that surprised me when I started thinking about applying to graduate school is that many programs offer tuition waivers and living stipends. These might be straight scholarships or linked with research or teaching duties. In many cases you are actually paid for going to school. Programs are funded for different reasons and in different ways, but one common reason is that donors and foundations realize that the world needs educated and knowledgeable people in particular areas. They respond to this need by funding scholarships in programs that might be the same ones you are interested in. The donors want to encourage you to study, learn, and, eventually, contribute to the well-being of others in the world.

A second major source of funding is the government and various foundations, which make grants to universities so they can conduct direct research on questions of interest. There may be a grant, for example, to study food distribution channels in developing countries. The grant is given to a professor or group of professors at a particular university, who then distribute that money to graduate students who help them do the research expected in the grant.

Another source of government funding in the United States is the Foreign Language and Area Studies (FLAS) Fellowships program. FLAS works through many major graduate programs to provide significant financial support for language learning and area studies in the global South.[9]

Not all programs can offer this type of funding, but many do, so be sure to learn what kind of financial assistance you might receive before assuming that grad school is financially impossible for you right now.

Remember too that many student loans can be deferred if you are back in school full time.

Option 7: Just Work

The final option revolves around working in a "regular" job. This option may seem at first like a rather defeatist, fallback alternative, but just working has some distinct advantages. An easy and obvious example is someone who works in a domestic business for several years and then uses knowledge and skills gained there in microenterprise, leadership development, team building, or general business development. Greg Matney and Julie Peterson, introduced in chapter 4, both used their business training in North America when they got more involved in promoting business in a development context. A similar example comes from the popular new book by Jacqueline Novogratz, *The Blue Sweater*. Jacqueline tells how right after college she worked for high-profile Wall Street banking firms and then built on that experience when she entered development work. Eventually, her work experience contributed to the creation of the Acumen Fund, a program that invests in and generally supports promising socially oriented enterprises around the world.[10]

It is not hard to imagine other applications. Working in a school setting might do a lot to help one learn about teaching or educational administration. If you work in the medical field, you learn about health, disease, family medicine, patient care, and health-care systems. A job in local or national government might generate a lot of experiential insight into good governance. While there are differences in the way things are done here and in developing countries, there is enough commonality in our shared human experience that what you learn in one setting may also be of value in others.

I must add a cautionary note. All such experience can be of great value in development contexts, but there lurks a serious danger, which is that we start to think that the way we do it here is the "right" way, and we get the idea that development work is about teaching others around the world how to imitate our own society's practices. Such approaches to development are the source of many a development disaster throughout the world and throughout history. We have to be able to find a wise balance between appreciating the knowledge and skills that we learn in our own societies and accepting that others may go about things in different ways that are also good. Finding such a balance and respectfully working together allow us to share ideas and practices, learn from each other, and together decide what strategies to try in a particular context.

Because it is such a strong human tendency to see one's own ways of life as being superior to others, it might be wise for us all to err on the side of the advice shared by a Sierra Leonean who spoke to a class that Roland Vanderburg was leading. He told them that "when you go overseas, please, the first thing you must do is reach in and remove your Canadian brain and set it aside and listen and learn again, as if from zero." The statement is strong, but it is a powerful image that may remind us to balance what we know from our own society with what we learn in a new one.

There are other benefits to be gained from working that can also be helpful in the long run. Consider the example of Sarah Rohrer, a field organizer for Bread for the World (BFW), a Christian advocacy organization that tries to influence US policy in ways that are beneficial to the poor. Sarah grew up caring about and volunteering in behalf of the poor, the hungry, and the homeless. She graduated with a degree in religion and sociology and hoped to find work that allowed her to respond to poverty. Nevertheless, "real world reality" set in quickly for Sarah. Even though her heart told her to work on these social issues, the passage of time with no job led her to feel that she needed to accept any paying job she could find. Thus it was that she began a series of minimum-wage and low-paying jobs, including selling medical uniforms and loading trucks.

There came a moment Sarah well remembers when she "felt [she] was being wasted," but then she started realizing how valuable these experiences were. She was actually living among the poor and interacting with the people who themselves slipped in and out of poverty. She came experientially to know what life felt like in this predicament, especially how low-wage workers were treated by their workplaces, governments, and society in general. Working several years in these types of jobs helped Sarah become a much better advocate for the people who struggle daily with life issues associated with poverty.

Sarah has thus come to believe that "even a job that is not vocationally focused can be a central part of one's formation." Still, there came a day when Sarah decided on graduate school in a seminary program that helped her study advocacy and faith-based direct service. In seminary Sarah reconnected with Bread for the World, an organization she had first been involved with in college. She resonated with the organization's mission and kept informed on their activities. When she finished seminary, Sarah worked for a while in a drop-in center for the homeless before applying for a position at BFW. Sarah then became a field organizer for BFW, a position that allowed her to organize people in Christian churches to advocate for programs that help poor, hungry, and homeless people the world over.

Option 8: A Combination of Options 1–7

This is probably an obvious alternative, but it is worth making explicit. Some of the stories above focus on one option, but many times the first few years after college comprise a series of several options. There is no set of user instructions that tells you precisely where particular activities will take you and what order they should take, and there is no predetermined timeline for how long you must engage in temporary, low-paid, or self-funded assignments before you can expect a "real" job to come along.

Alisa Buma's story illustrates how important it is to take opportunities as they arise, to be persistent, and to get a variety of experiences. Alisa's first seven years after graduation are hard to keep track of, but they eventually led to a contract position with Samaritan's Purse, working in some of Africa's intense conflict zones. Alisa is enthusiastic because this is what she has prepared for, where she feels called, and the kind of situation where she wants to make a contribution.

Here is how Alisa's adventures unfolded. Right after college she applied for and received a CIDA (she's Canadian) internship through Samaritan's Purse in Kenya. It lasted only six months, and when she returned to her home in Canada, she realized she still had neither the experience nor the education to get a long-term job. There was also the matter of $40,000 worth of loans, which had been deferred during her Kenya internship but were now coming due. She took a TESL course and headed off to Korea, where she had a great intercultural experience, engaged in lots of regional travel, and managed to pay down $12,000 on her loans. Returning home after one year in Korea, she studied for a master's degree in conflict resolution. With even more international experience and now a master's degree, she could still only find an internship position that paid a living stipend. Alisa thus began a year-and-a-half assignment in northern Liberia for Right to Play, a Canadian-based NGO focused on using sports and games in the development of youth.

As her position in Liberia was coming to an end, Alisa searched for positions at ReliefWeb[11] and learned about a small French NGO working with displaced women and youth in Khartoum, Sudan. The organization is called Enfants du Monde—Droits de l'Homme (EMDH).[12] Alisa applied and then accepted a position with them that paid living expenses and offered a reasonable stipend besides. When she arrived in Khartoum, Alisa discovered that EMDH was in crisis. For the next seven months she found herself stepping into leadership roles that caused a good deal of stress but that also greatly added to her learning. While in Sudan, Alisa happened to meet up again with Samaritan's Purse staff, and the organization eventually offered her the two-year assignment in Sudan.

Over the last seven years, Alisa completed a CIDA internship, taught English in Korea, worked with three NGOs in three different African countries, studied for a master's degree, and worked odd jobs at home in between all these other activities. Alisa's story is instructive in many ways but perhaps mostly in demonstrating the importance of not giving up, of pursuing a variety of opportunities, and of dealing constructively with life realities such as a heavy loan burden. Alisa notes that her experiential learning through all these activities was broad and profound, and it is learning that she carries with her in her new position.

Alisa's varied experiences with NGOs lead her to the following practical suggestions:

> There is a vast spectrum in the quality of programming and ethical motivation among the hundreds of NGOs you might consider working with. There are differences in size, national origin, operational methods, and donor influence, all of which impact effectiveness. There is no sure way to know what an NGO is like before signing a contract, and you may find [that] the in-country leadership

plays a huge role in defining organizational culture, regardless of what they might say at the organization's main international offices. Know too that working in conflict zones can be extremely stressful, and different organizations help their staff cope with such stress in different ways. Sometimes, whether an organization is Christian or secular makes a big difference. The bottom line is that you should be sure to learn as much as you can about the organization before signing on. Talk with or email people who have worked there before, or even people from other NGOs who have worked with the NGO in question.

Still, though field work can be unpredictable, and sometimes you feel like you take two steps backward for every step forward, it is also true that some of the expected, and even the unexpected, impacts can be extremely rewarding, motivating, and life changing. Positively impacting people's lives—empowering individuals to make a difference—can have a remarkable ripple effect in families and communities. It truly is a vocation and not just a career!

On the Way

During the first few years after college, the "real world" hits graduates full in the face. For one thing, you realize the world is not just waiting for you to finish school so it can put you to work. You may have a profound sense of calling, but you must also pay the bills. Finding ways to honor your calling while paying the bills requires the perseverance that Roland, Jacqueline, and the author of Ecclesiastes remind us about in the opening quotes to this chapter. "Keep at it" and "don't give up," they entreat us. The stories on these pages and in earlier chapters testify to the reality that those who choose to keep at it find a place.

Reality strikes in other ways too. Development workers in the field for the first time quickly realize how hard development work is and how flexible, patient, and persistent they must be. After a year or two of development work, it is common for people to descend into the "sophomore slump." The excitement and the hopefulness of the first year wear off and the realization dawns that it will be a long and sometimes painful slog.

You may also have to wrestle with your youth. Paul tells Timothy, "Don't let anyone look down on you because you are young" (1 Tim. 4:12a). Paul's advice is good for young development workers too, but self-confidence must be blended with humility and a learning spirit. In developing countries it is often extremely unusual for a young person to hold a position of authority. Yet sometimes your wealth, education, and Northern origins may lead you to have such authority. This can be a delicate situation. Add to this mix that young people often have a need to prove themselves, and the results can be explosive. To help you through these situations, Paul's follow-up words to

Timothy offer wise advice: "set an example . . . in speech, in conduct, in love, in faith and in purity" (1 Tim. 4:12b).

Do you remember Julie Peterson's story from chapter 6 about all of God's trains? During your first few years, you will likely get the chance to try out several of them. As you engage in volunteering, internships, graduate education, and short-term assignments, you get chances to put things to the test, to evaluate your own abilities for living in cross-cultural environments, to struggle with the distance from friends and family back home, and to discover where your capabilities respond to real needs. These can be hard years, but they are also good. As Hannah Marsh says, embrace them and do not just look to the future. Serve in the moment even as you prepare to serve in the future. As Paul tells the Thessalonians, these are years to "test everything. Hold on to the good" (1 Thess. 5:21). There will be low points. But there will also be mountaintop experiences in which you see the power of God at work in the lives of others: well-nourished children studying in school, healthy people free of disease, formerly illiterate women who now read and carry themselves with dignity, peace where conflict once reigned, workers who now provide for their families. You will witness glimpses of transformation. Know that you serve a good God whose plans for you and the people you work with are bigger and ultimately more secure than you could ever fathom.

Further Reflection and Action Steps

1. If you were going to look for an internship with an NGO, how would you go about it? One place to start is by reviewing the websites of consortia and of organizations themselves to learn about the internships they might offer. Using the resource pages from chapter 9 and the websites listed there, find at least one internship that might be a real possibility for you.

2. Assuming you need to raise financial support for a yearlong internship with an NGO, develop a plan that briefly addresses the following:

   • how you will describe your internship to potential supporters,
   • the means by which you will communicate your message, and
   • the people or institutions you plan to contact.

3. Compare what for you would be the most likely international option with the most likely domestic option. Make a list of the pros and cons of each.

4. Of all the stories of real people in this chapter, explain which one you most resonate with or find most attractive and which one you find the most troublesome.

5. Do an analysis of your personal situation, including your capabilities, relationships, loans, general obligations, and preferences, with an eye to discovering which of the seven options might be best for you in the next two or three years.

Into the Future

Continue to work out your salvation with fear and trembling, for it is God who works in you to will and to act in order to fulfill his good purpose.

Philippians 2:12–13

It's not about you.

Rick Warren,
Purpose Driven Life

This book began with a young person responding to Christ's call to be his ambassador to a suffering world. Chapters that followed offered guidance about training for a career as a development worker. Now, at the close, I would like to point out that once the training period transitions into a career, development workers continue to face pressing issues throughout their lives.

During the period of intense training, which I am loosely thinking of as your college years plus the next five years, you are mostly in learning mode. You will definitely make important contributions, but the scale tilts toward learning. As you gain experience, the learning continues, but your contributions also increase as you put that learning into practice. Over time, contributions become more significant and gradually overtake learning, though the learning continues for as long as you live, whether through ongoing experience or periods of study. See figure 8.1 for a visual representation of this relationship.

I want to emphasize this point, because you will face difficult decisions throughout your vocational life, especially if you are privileged to work, live, and travel with frequency in developing countries. In your early years, when there is so much to learn, it is normal and respectful to follow the lead of more

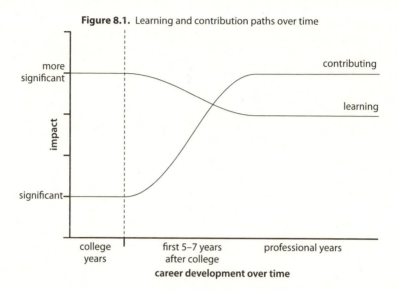

Figure 8.1. Learning and contribution paths over time

experienced colleagues, even if at times you might question their judgment
and the choices they make. Before you know it, however, you move into one of
those positions and become a part of a new generation of mentors and leaders.
In the early years, you learn the profession from others, but as you progress
through your professional life, you increasingly shape the way development
work is done and the way development workers live.

In this closing chapter I would like to briefly identify two major issues you
may very well wrestle with your entire professional life. I dare not give you
pat answers to them, and there is no *Development Work for Dummies* guide
that will provide them either. In fact, you can expect a good amount of fear
and trembling as you work through them. They are issues we need to resolve
in faithfulness, in community, and in praxis. The issues are (1) redeeming the
real-world development establishment and (2) keeping body, soul, family, and
community together.

The Development Establishment

Development workers tend to have high ideals, as well as high hopes for helping to improve the lives of people who are suffering. They look forward to
working with like-minded people from all cultures and making a discernible
impact. Thankfully, effective work is indeed being done across the world. Get
connected with the people who are doing this work, learn from them, and, if
opportunities arise, join them.

It is also true that you are likely to witness early on the harsh reality that the real world of development assistance demonstrates a lot of brokenness. For example, standard development theory teaches that development is supposed to be bottom-up and participatory, but you quickly realize that much of the development establishment seems powered by a top-down bloc of donors and money. You may see a project fail and hope that the next one will be better designed and managed, but the next thing you know the same program design is being implemented again, with virtually no changes.

If you are overseas, you will encounter the expatriate community in the capital city of a developing country, sometimes even the leaders of Christian organizations, and realize that many of them do not seem motivated by the same values you hold. They run down the local culture in condescending ways that strike you as disrespectful, and they live their lives largely distant from the people they are there to serve. You may also discover that many of the staff in the local NGOs you partner with care more about their wages than the mission. You wonder if you are really helping if you care more about the mission than they do. Sooner or later, probably sooner, you run into locals who seem to think that you owe them money and who are willing to take it from you and the organization you work for when you are not looking. In the midst of all these realities, it is easy to become jaded and cynical.

A former student of mine, Sarah Baker, who gained experience in several organizations after graduation, ran into some of these challenges. In an email exchange, she proposed a solution to this dilemma that seems just about right. She said that we must surely get over our youthful idealism but must be careful not to replace it with pessimistic cynicism. Instead, we need to find a balance of what she called "hopeful realism." A hopeful realist seeks out development workers, organizations, and programs that are effective in their work, of which there are many, but that may not catch our attention and press coverage the way failures and brokenness do. Seek them out. Surround yourselves with people who really care and who are striving every day to be more effective. A hopeful realist acknowledges mistakes and brokenness but also takes on the redemptive process through continuous evaluation, learning, and innovation.

Keeping Body, Soul, Family, and Community Together

Most of this book focuses on the work to be done and the type of people who actually do this work well. But how about the well-being of the workers themselves? Challenges faced by development workers include the familiar ones of burnout, workaholism, office politics, and any number of others, but development work in foreign lands presents unique challenges in addition to these, such as the trauma associated with witnessing suffering up close and personal, or the loneliness from feeling isolated in a foreign culture. As we face these unique challenges, Bryant Myers argues that, in addition to helping others thrive, development workers must also attend to their own care. One suggestion Myers makes is that development workers get away now and then, to allow for both physical and psychological rest. He says that "people who work on the front lines need time on the side lines."[1] One common and helpful practice is for groups of missionaries/development workers to gather periodically in retreats to fellowship, share stories, have some fun, and pray and worship together.

Here are just a few of the challenges you can expect to face, many of which arise around relationships and family. Young development workers who go into the field single must inevitably address how to resolve their need for personal intimacy. Some young singles encounter loneliness in the field. They are far away not only from family and old friends but also from other young singles. Sometimes young development workers find a sense of community where they are placed, but other times the socioeconomic, cultural, and educational divisions between them and young singles in the local culture are too difficult to span. I will risk saying that this issue can be more difficult for young women than men, mostly because the behavioral standards many cultures expect women to live up to are higher than those for the men.

Some development workers make the deliberate choice to remain single and organize their lives around that choice. Others enter cross-cultural dating relationships. If and when that happens, they discover that courting expectations are very different than in North America. Foreign development workers must know that they are being watched and that their integrity and ministry is on the line as locals evaluate their behavior patterns. Such relationships often do lead to marriage, as indeed they did for me. I met my wife in the home I was assigned to live in during my year in Guatemala. We married a year after I returned to the United States and have now been married for over thirty years. We can both attest to the joys and the special challenges of such a relationship. How this all works and what it means for you personally, for your broader family, and for the work itself are worthy topics for reflection, discussion, and prayer. Such issues are generally highly contextualized for the cultures, work, and individuals in question. For all such choices, mentors and supportive communities play vital roles.

For young couples, a big issue is the joint acceptance of a specific calling. If your work involves traveling or living overseas in difficult situations, taking spouses along implicates them too. What you both do and how you support each other are questions to consider early, often, and with the help of a supportive community. Sooner or later children may come along. How will they be raised? Will they go to English-speaking schools? As they approach middle school, will you send them to boarding schools in other countries or look for schools that integrate your children with the local community, language, and culture? It is not necessary to have all such questions answered before you enter the field, but you should know they are out there waiting. In anticipation of the days when such decisions must be made, watch what your colleagues do and talk with them about their choices.

Where will you live, and where will you find a nurturing faith community? Both of these choices are weighty in terms of living out your ideals with integrity, working effectively in your calling, and ultimately keeping body, soul, family, and community together. You might faithfully choose to live in a walled community and attend church with other North Americans. For the young idealist, this may sound like selling out, but there are sound reasons that push foreign workers in these directions. One deeply committed North American development worker with long experience explained to me that he and his wife chose to live in a gated community for the simple reason that his work required frequent travel. That meant that his wife would be home alone. They were well aware of the security issues associated with living in a poorer neighborhood, where she would feel quite exposed and vulnerable, especially when he was away from home. If they were required to live in such a neighborhood, he said he would have to leave the field, because he simply could not ask his wife to subject herself to that level of fear and danger. In addition, they made the decision to educate their children in English-speaking private schools, thinking it best to allow their children to experience some of both cultures and to be prepared for college in North America when the day arrived.

On the other hand, you may together make the decision to live in a modest home right in the middle of a poor urban community and join a local church fellowship there. That is what Kurt and JoAnn Ver Beek did in Honduras, where for the last nine years they have lived in Nueva Suyapa, a poor hillside barrio built on a covered-over municipal dump. Here is how Kurt describes their choice:

> As we thought about our witness and work in Honduras, we saw it as our duty to live with the poor. We had two young children, but decided to give incarnational living a try. The very first night someone kicked in the door of our neighbor's home. It took them about ten minutes, and the entire time our house was shaking. We did not sleep that entire night and very little the next couple [of] days. A week later somebody got shot about a block from our house. I went to buy

sugar and there he was, bleeding all over. This was shocking. Both these things happened in our first week. Yet in the nine years since then, nobody has gotten shot or tried to break into our home, and we have come to love where we live. We like our neighbors and the neighborhood. We are close to our local church, and I think we feel safer now than when we were in a nicer home.

Choices about personal lifestyle intersect with another touchy issue—namely, your financial package. You may receive a salary that is low by North American standards but that will put you on easy street in a developing country. You and the people you work with will inevitably compare your income with theirs and wonder how that affects the work you are doing together. The salary and benefits package you receive will be a major point of practical tension.

These personal-life issues intersect with your immersion in a sometimes alarming reality, one in which precious children suffer horrible abuse and people die of hunger or preventable diseases right in front of you. In the midst of this, you may be saddened or angered by what appears to be the callous disregard with which much of the world reacts to such suffering. When you face such trauma yourself, you must of course address the needs in front of you, but you must also tend to your own needs for healing. At a recent vocational retreat for international development students, Elizabeth Schepel, who has worked with suffering children and other victims of abuse, offered the following helpful advice: "Self-care does not mean that we avoid suffering. It means we must acknowledge that we are impacted by what we see and experience. To stay healthy and to be able to work long term, we must actively care for ourselves and recognize the signs that we need to take a break and process what we're going through."

As I hope is evident, development work is not only about the work that we do but also about our Christian witness in every area of our lives. You will do much better at keeping body, soul, family, and community together if you find a supportive faith community in which you can reflect, share, pray, fellowship, and worship together.

In Closing: Development Work Is Hard, but It's Good

In a classic passage from *The Lion, the Witch and the Wardrobe* by C. S. Lewis, Lucy learns that Aslan, the king of Narnia, is a lion. Aware that Aslan is "on the move," Lucy asks the beavers if Aslan is safe. Mrs. Beaver responds, "'Course he isn't safe. But he's good."[2] Development work can also be described this way. Maybe this is how kingdom work is in general—not safe, but good. Think of Paul on his missionary journeys. He had great successes, but it wasn't safe. He suffered beatings, floggings, shipwrecks, incarcerations, and, finally, execution.

Surprisingly, the Bible offers a fascinating and highly instructive story about development work: the story of Nehemiah. The work is hard and there are dangers all around, but God is with the work, and success is ultimately gained. Read the story and you will find out how Nehemiah, a "foreigner" in Persia, discovers that Jerusalem has fallen into ruins, resolves to do something about it, and eventually travels as a development worker to Jerusalem to help them restructure their society and rebuild the walls. The first thing Nehemiah does is weep. Right after that he prays. He confesses his own brokenness, reminds God of his love for and promises to his people, and then asks for God's help. This is a very good way to start.

As the story unfolds, Nehemiah prepares, plans, organizes, and then travels to Jerusalem. Once there he carefully surveys the situation, interacts with the people in participatory ways, facilitates their organization into building groups, and helps them resolve conflicts that arise in the process of the rebuilding. The Bible does not use this word, but Nehemiah's development work is what we would today call "holistic." The story addresses security, production and distribution, urban planning, spiritual life, land distribution, inequality, food, governance, and more.

The Jerusalem community struggling to rebuild their walls and their community faces enemies who would love to see the work undone. Some of the enemies are within the very same community Nehemiah is working with. Some people do not want to work. Others want the benefits of a new wall but are taking advantage of their own people for profit and even enslaving some of them. Nehemiah must work through such internal discord and unite the community in both its identity as God's people and its mission.

External enemies are never far away either. They mock the Israelites and threaten them with physical harm. They send messengers to the king with nefarious lies about the work being done and then plan a military attack. A savvy and wise leader, Nehemiah anticipates these attacks and helps the people prepare for and repel them. Eventually the walls are built, an event followed by rejoicing, celebration, and recommitment to follow God. It is a wonderful story.

In the first lines of the preface to this book, lawyer Christine Bodewes says that her work in the Nairobi slums was hard. She lived in difficult circumstances, faced threats to her work and to her person, had her office vandalized, and saw many of her coworkers arrested and jailed. And still she considers it to be the best job she ever had. She loved every minute of it. Somehow, that is what I think Paul and Nehemiah would say about their work too.

If you hear the call and respond to it by becoming a development worker, you will, like Nehemiah, need to weep, pray, plan, prepare, and even celebrate when things go well. And you will love it. True, there are powers and principalities out there that will threaten you on every side. The attacks will come. Prepare for them and be ready to face them, but rest assured that God is with you and that, as we are promised in Philippians 2:13, "it is God who works in you to will and to act in order to fulfill his good purpose." This is a wonderful blessing and promise and one you can depend on wherever your journey takes you.

Resources for the Road

This chapter provides you with some resources that can help you be more efficient in your searches and decision making. Here is what you will find in the chapter:

> Consortium websites that list development organizations and/or vocational opportunities
>
> Websites for Christian NGOs that offer internships and fellowships
>
> Websites for selected secular organizations that offer internships and other experiential possibilities
>
> Tips for fundraising
>
> A listing of members in the Council of Christian Colleges and Universities (CCCU) that offer undergraduate programs in fields closely related to international development
>
> A listing of CCCU schools with graduate programs in fields closely related to international development

These are offered as starting points for your search. The resources listed here are not intended to be exhaustive.

Consortium Websites

Some of the following sites provide job postings and/or internship and volunteer possibilities for a wide variety of organizations. Other sites provide member lists of organizations that can be searched individually for jobs and internships. Quotations below are taken from the associated websites.

www.accordnetwork.org

Accord is the former Association of Evangelical Relief and Development Organizations.

www.ccih.org

Christian Connections for International Health promotes global health and wholeness from a Christian perspective.

www.idealist.org

"Idealist connects people, organizations, and resources to help build a world where all people can live free and dignified lives."

www.interaction.org

"InterAction is the largest alliance of United States–based international nongovernmental organizations (NGOs) focused on the world's poor and most vulnerable people."

www.reliefweb.int

"ReliefWeb serves the information needs of the humanitarian relief community."

www.devex.com

Devex is "the largest provider of . . . recruitment services to the development community."

www.internationalpeaceandconflict.org

Peace and Collaborative Development Network "is a free professional networking site to foster dialogue and sharing of resources in international development, conflict resolution, gender mainstreaming, human rights, social entrepreneurship and related fields."

www.devdir.org/index.html

The Directory of Development Organizations lists over sixty-five thousand NGOs in the global community.

Faith-Based Internship/Fellowship Opportunities

The Christian NGOs listed below have defined internships and/or fellowship programs for recent graduates.

www.bread.org

Bread for the World offers yearlong Washington, DC–based advocacy internships focused on poverty and hunger issues worldwide.

www.crwrc.org and http://crwrc.org/pages/servicelink_opp_intlind.cfm

Christian Reformed World Relief Committee (CRWRC) offers volunteer international internships.

www.echonet.org

Educational Concerns for Hunger Organization (ECHO) provides yearlong agricultural internships that prepare individuals for subsistence and urban farming in developing countries.

www.hopeinternational.org

Hope International provides domestic and international business internships in microenterprise development.

www.ijm.org

International Justice Mission offers field and domestic internships aiming to protect individuals from violent forms of oppression, with a specific concentration on human trafficking.

www.mcc.org and http://salt.mcc.org

The Mennonite Central Committee offers general volunteer opportunities and yearlong cross-cultural immersion experiences for Christian young adults.

www.partnersworldwide.org

Partners Worldwide offers yearlong field and local internship opportunities focused on alleviating poverty through business development and job-creation activities.

www.samaritanspurse.org

Samaritan's Purse provides five-month international internships oriented toward training successful relief workers.

www.tonyblairfaithfoundation.org

The Tony Blair Faith Foundation Fellows program increases global awareness on basic development issues through interfaith dialogue and mobilization planning and activities.

http://worldhungerrelief.org

World Hunger Relief offers sustainable-farming and holistic-development internships through their Texas farm, and extension internship opportunities in a developing country.

http://worldrelief.org

World Relief provides community-development internships.

Selected Non-Faith-Based Opportunities

This is a list of some selected non-faith-based programs and websites that provide internships or information about internships and related opportunities.

www.americorps.gov

AmeriCorps is a one-year US-government service program that places individuals in nonprofit or local government agencies focusing on poverty alleviation.

www.fsdinternational.org

Foundation for Sustainable Development (FSD) typically offers community-development internships of two months to a year in underserved communities around the world.

http://ghcorps.org

Global Health Corps (GHC) offers one-year domestic or international fellowship opportunities that partner a North American with a country national for the advancement of global health equity.

www.peacecorps.gov

Peace Corps is a two-and-a-half-year US-government volunteer program that places individuals in developing countries across the globe in promotion of world peace, friendship, cross-cultural understanding, and development.

www.peacecorps.gov/index.cfm?shell=learn.whyvol.eduben.mastersint

> Peace Corps Master's International is a collaborative program with over eighty US universities that combines Peace Corps service with study for a master's degree.

www.peacecorps.gov/index.cfm?shell=learn.whyvol.eduben.fellows

> Peace Corps Fellows USA is program for returned Peace Corps volunteers, found in over forty universities, which allows the integration of community service with a master's degree program. Participants receive financial aid for their graduate studies in return for community service.

www.worldteach.org

> WorldTeach offers year-round eleven-month volunteer teaching opportunities in developing countries.

www.eslcafe.com

> Dave's ESL Café is a list of English-teaching programs (though it does not investigate the programs or guarantee their character).

Below are two additional non-faith-based programs and websites geared especially toward Canadians.

www.cuso-vso.org

> CUSO-VSO is a Canadian NGO that links volunteers to one- or two-year opportunities in developing countries around the world. United States citizens may also apply.

www.acdi-cida.gc.ca/internships

> International Youth Internship Program (IYIP) offers one- to three-year internship opportunities for Canadian citizens with the Canadian International Development Agency (CIDA). Interns collaborate with CIDA partner organizations in supporting local development priorities in developing countries around the world.

Tips for Fundraising

If you are new to the development field and searching for opportunities to gain experience, you may have to raise your own funds. Some organizations expect you to raise a specific amount in order to participate in the internship/

fellowship opportunity. Listed below are some tips, advice, guidelines, and activities commonly used to raise funds and spiritual support.[1]

Whom to Ask

Friends and family. The people who know you best are most likely to support you financially. Be inclusive and do not assume that a particular person will not give. Even if they cannot give at the time, if they care about you, they may want to know what you are doing and could support you in other ways.

Churches. Your church is a great community to tell about the work you will be doing and to recruit both financial and spiritual supporters from. Make sure to share with all the churches you may have a connection with or that may have a connection with the organization or work you will be doing. Ask family members in other churches if you can share your ministry plans with their churches.

Local businesses. Many small businesses set aside money each year to give to particular causes, organizations, or individuals in need. Check with the businesses you visit often to see if such programs exist. This may be a great way for the organization to give back and for you to share your message and raise some funds. Even if a business cannot support you directly, the owners may be willing to cooperate in sponsoring a fundraising event.

College or university. Some colleges and universities have scholarships or alumni funds to support individuals in public service activities.

Philanthropic organizations and corporations. Many large organizations and corporations have established grants that support individuals in volunteer and global service. Search for these opportunities. Also, some chain restaurants offer event opportunities that allow you to receive a designated percentage of total sales of the day.

How to Ask

Support letters. Letters are a great place to start and reach a large number of people in various locations and they are the most common means of raising funds. Be mindful, however, that letters are easy to set aside and forget about. It is a good idea to follow up letters with a timely phone call. The more personal the letter, the more people are likely to support your work. Keep letters brief and easy to read.

Phone calls. The phone is a more personal way of getting in touch with potential donors. They allow you direct contact with an individual and leave room for further discussions and questions about your work and support needs.

One-on-one conversations. Taking directly to another person is the most personal way you can share your passions for global service and explain your fundraising needs. When you are face-to-face, the people you talk with can experience firsthand your enthusiasm and interest.

Public speaking. Share your message with large groups of people (e.g., at a community event or in church).

Events. Fundraising events help you get in touch with potential donors, educate others on your work, and join in community. If you are especially gifted in music, dance, storytelling, or the visual arts, or if you have friends who could help you with this, consider organizing a festive and entertaining benefit event that encourages attendees to join in supporting you in the work ahead.

Technology. The internet and social-networking websites allow you to connect with a lot of people in a short time. Although this is probably one of the least personal methods of raising funds, social-networking strategies could help grow your donor base.

Things to Remember

Thank-yous. Whether someone supports you financially or in some other way, make sure to thank them. This is polite, keeps you connected with your supporters, and may lead to ongoing support in the future.

Don't be discouraged. Not everyone can or will give financially. Continue to be inclusive and allow even those who are unable to give monetarily an opportunity to learn about your work and support you in different ways.

Stay in touch. Through blog entries, emails, and letters, share your experience with the people who helped make it possible. When you return, you can have people over for dinner and share your pictures and stories, or maybe bring back a small token of appreciation. By sharing your experience, you continuing to educate people on the issues you care about and increase the likelihood that they will also care and join you in service.

Enthusiasm. If you take the time to raise funds for a particular type of work, you probably believe in the cause. Share your enthusiasm with others. Allow people to see why you are passionate about a particular issue or organization.

Prayer Support

One of the most important ways your community can support your endeavors is through prayer. Listed below are some helpful ideas for building prayer support.

Prayer groups. Start a prayer group that meets to pray about global issues and for global servants worldwide, including you. Keep in touch with the group and let them know your prayer requests throughout your term of service.

Prayer cards. Create a personal prayer card. You may want to include a picture, a Bible verse, and some prayer requests. Distribute these to donors, family members, and friends.

Topical prayer requests. Create a list of different prayer requests that you would like people to focus on while you are away. Give each interested individual a different request to focus on.

Christian Colleges and Universities with Development-Related Undergraduate Programs

The following is a list of selected members from the Council of Christian Colleges and Universities (CCCU) website. These schools have programs that may be of interest to young adults wanting to be involved in global service. Of course, this is not an exhaustive list, and there are additional Christian undergraduate institutions you should explore, such as many of the Roman Catholic colleges and universities. Programs offered by the following institutions include international development, intercultural communication, global missions, nonprofit management, and global economics. For additional CCCU member schools, visit www.cccu.org.

Abilene Christian University (Texas)

Anderson University (Indiana)

Asbury University (Kentucky)

Azusa Pacific University (California)

Baylor University (Texas)

Belhaven University (Mississippi)

Bethel College (Indiana)

Bethel University (Minnesota)

Biola University (California)

Bluffton University (Ohio)

California Baptist University (California)

Calvin College (Michigan)

Campbellsville University (Kentucky)

Colorado Christian University (Colorado)

Corban University (Oregon)

Cornerstone University (Michigan)

Covenant College (Georgia)

Eastern Mennonite University (Vermont)

Eastern Nazarene College (Massachusetts)

Eastern University (Pennsylvania)

Evangel University (Missouri)

Fresno Pacific University (California)

George Fox University (Oregon)

Gordon College (Massachusetts)

Goshen College (Indiana)

Greenville College (Illinois)

Hope International University (California)

Houghton College (New York)

Indiana Wesleyan University (Indiana)

John Brown University (Arkansas)

Kentucky Christian University (Kentucky)

Lee University (Tennessee)

Malone University (Ohio)

The Master's College (California)

MidAmerica Nazarene University (Kansas)

Milligan College (Tennessee)

Moody Bible Institute (Illinois)

Mount Vernon Nazarene University (Ohio)

North Greenville University (South Carolina)

North Park University (Illinois)

Northwest Nazarene University (Idaho)

Northwest University (Washington)

Northwestern College (Minnesota)

Nyack College (New York)

Olivet Nazarene University (Illinois)

Oral Roberts University (Oklahoma)

Seattle Pacific University (Washinton)

Shorter University (Georgia)

Simpson University (Florida)

Southwest Baptist University (Missouri)

Spring Arbor University (Michigan)

Taylor University (Indiana)

Toccoa Falls College (Georgia)

Trinity International University (Illinois)

Trinity Western University (British Columbia)

Union University (Tennessee)

Vanguard University (California)

Wheaton College (Illinois)

Whitworth University (Washington)

Graduate Programs in Christian Institutions of Higher Education

The following Christian universities offer concentration options, certificate programs, and master's degrees in areas relevant to international development.

Anderson University (Indiana) — intercultural service

Azusa Pacific University (California) — global leadership; teaching English to speakers of other languages (TESL); transformational urban leadership

Baylor University (Texas) — international economics; international journalism; international relations

Biola University (California) — anthropology; applied linguistics; intercultural studies; missions; TESL

Campbellsville University (Kentucky) — TESL

Cornerstone University (Michigan) — TESL

Eastern Mennonite University (Virginia) — conflict transformation; development and peacebuilding; nonprofit leadership; organizational leadership and peacebuilding; restorative justice and peacebuilding; social entrepreneurship; strategic peacebuilding; trauma healing and peacebuilding

Eastern University (Pennsylvania) — economic development; international development; nonprofit management; organizational leadership

Fuller Theological Seminary (California) — global leadership; global Christian worship; intercultural studies

Goshen College (Indiana) — environmental education

Hope International University (California) — global business management; international development; nonprofit management

Moody Bible Institute (Illinois) — intercultural studies

Northwest Nazarene University (Idaho) — missional leadership

Oral Roberts University (Oklahoma) — nonprofit management

Trinity International University (Illinois) — cultural engagement; social entrepreneurship

Trinity Western University (British Columbia) — cross-cultural ministries; international business administration; leadership; linguistics; TESL

Union University (Tennessee) — intercultural studies

Wheaton College (Illinois) — intercultural studies; TESL

Whitworth University (Washington) — international management

Notes

Preface: Servants at Work in International Development

1. I personally interviewed forty-four development professionals. Emily Daher, my student assistant in the summer of 2010, interviewed thirteen. Most interviews were oral. Five were by written correspondence. Small modifications for grammar and clarity have been made to these transcripts.

Introduction: God, You, and the World Out There

1. Timothy C. Morgan, "Purpose Driven in Rwanda: Rick Warren's Sweeping Plan to Defeat Poverty," *Christianity Today* 49, no. 10 (Oct. 2005): 32–36. The PEACE acronym stands for the proposed method of achieving the plan: Promote reconciliation, Equip servant leaders, Assist the poor, Care for the sick, Educate the next generation. To learn more about the PEACE Plan, see www.thepeaceplan.com.

2. My friend John Suk tells me this is the real job title we should all have. It covers who our boss is, where he sends us, and what our mission is.

3. An address by Monsignor Ivan Illich to the Conference on InterAmerican Student Projects (CIASP) in Cuernavaca, Mexico, on April 20, 1968. Available at www.swaraj.org/illich_hell .htm. There are many books on the market with a similar message, including the 2009 book by African economist Dambisa Moyo, *Dead Aid: Why Aid Is Not Working and How There Is a Better Way for Africa* (New York: Farrar, Straus and Giroux, 2009).

4. As told in Luke 10, a similar moment leads to the big question, "And who is my neighbor?" which leads into the story of the good Samaritan. An excellent study of who our neighbor is in the modern, globalizing world, and how we should live together as neighbors, is found in Douglas A. Hicks and Mark Valeri, eds., *Global Neighbors: Christian Faith and Moral Obligation in Today's Economy* (Grand Rapids: Eerdmans, 2008).

5. Pope Benedict XVI, *Caritas in Veritate (Charity in Truth)*, 1.

6. N. T. Wright, *Surprised by Hope: Rethinking Heaven, the Resurrection, and the Mission of the Church* (New York: HarperOne, 2008), 184.

7. I have heard Haugen say this in several public presentations. It is a powerful line. The concept is developed in more detail in Gary A. Haugen, *Good News about Injustice: A Witness of Courage in a Hurting World* (Downers Grove, IL: InterVarsity, 1999), 92–105.

8. Roland Hoksbergen, "North American Christians in the Third World: How Best Can They Serve?" *Bulletin of the Association of Christian Economists*, Spring 1987.

9. People who rush in really can do a lot of damage, which may be why many books and articles sport phrases like "beyond good intentions" in the title. Two books in this genre, both by Christians, are Mary B. Anderson, *Do No Harm: How Aid Can Support Peace—Or War* (Boulder, CO: Lynne Rienner, 1999), and Steve Corbett and Brian Fikkert, *When Helping Hurts: Alleviating Poverty Without Hurting the Poor . . . and Ourselves* (Chicago: Moody, 2009). One story of such harm is that of evangelist Bruce Wilkinson's experiences in Africa. Read about it in Michael M. Phillips, "Unanswered Prayers: In Swaziland, U.S. Preacher Sees His Dream Vanish; Mr. Wilkinson Hits Wall Trying To Push 'Orphan Village'; Rodeo Stars, Safari Guides; Feeling Snubbed by the King," *Wall Street Journal*, December 19, 2005.

10. In the last few years, economists like William Easterly and Jeffrey Sachs have engaged in some pretty vigorous arguments about foreign aid: whether it works, how it should be given, etc. It is worth noting that both are united in their view that the main goal of development is basically for people to have more stuff. They are of course right that many people in the world actually do need more stuff, but not just any stuff, and maybe not everyone. It is interesting that for Easterly and Sachs, economic growth is really the overarching objective of development, for everyone, all the time. See Jeffrey Sachs, *The End of Poverty: Economic Possibilities for Our Time* (New York: Penguin, 2005), and William Easterly, *The White Man's Burden: Why the West's Efforts to Aid the Rest Have Done So Much Ill and So Little Good* (New York: Penguin, 2006).

Chapter 1: What to Do and Why

1. For a thoughtful study of the first three perspectives, plus a chapter on feminist perspectives, see Richard Peet and Elaine Hartwick, *Theories of Development: Contentions, Arguments, Alternatives* (New York: Guilford, 2009).

2. See Jeffrey D. Sachs, *The End of Poverty: Economic Possibilities for Our Time* (New York: Penguin, 2005). The "ladder of development" is a concept used throughout the book.

3. Lawrence E. Harrison, *The Central Liberal Truth: How Politics Can Change a Culture and Save It from Itself* (New York: Oxford University Press, 2008). This is one of many of Harrison's books that first attempt to discover the values that lead to prosperity and democracy and then to identify strategies for transferring these values to cultures that need to adopt them.

4. W. W. Rostow, *The Stages of Economic Growth: A Non-Communist Manifesto* (Cambridge: Cambridge University Press, 1960). See esp. chap. 2.

5. Think, for example, of a modern-day textile plant in a developing country where workers may produce something worth $10. Ignoring other costs, the powerful business owner, aided and abetted by government leaders, may get away with paying a wage of only $1, while making a $9 profit for himself.

6. Among the more horrifying accounts of such colonial practices is the story of what is today the Democratic Republic of Congo. See Adam Hochschild, *King Leopold's Ghost: A Story of Greed, Terror, and Heroism in Colonial Africa* (Boston: Houghton Mifflin, 1998).

7. His most famous book, still widely read, is Paulo Freire, *Pedagogy of the Oppressed* (New York: Continuum, 1970).

8. Precise terms for rich countries and poor countries are elusive because the issues are about a lot more than a nation's GDP per capita. When the main debate was between liberal capitalism and Marxism, it made sense to think in terms of West (capitalist) and East (socialist/communist). When postdevelopment thinking criticized both East and West, it became more common to use the terms "North" for the relatively rich and "South" for what was variously called the "third world," "developing countries," or sometimes even the "two-thirds world" (to emphasize that most of the world's people lived there). In most of this book I use the terms "North" and "South."

9. Peet and Hartwick, *Theories of Development*, 228–29.

10. See David Korten, *The Great Turning: From Empire to Earth Community* (Bloomfield, CT: Kumarian, 2007). *Yes! Magazine* is a periodical and website inspired and supported by Korten that provides up-to-date analysis about the movement. See www.yesmagazine.org.

11. Such organizations hold a global meeting, called the World Social Forum, every year in Brazil. It was organized to provide an alternative to the World Economic Forum, which is held every year in Davos, Switzerland.

12. Amartya Sen, *Development as Freedom* (New York: Anchor Books, 2000).

13. This is a much-cited phrase from Sen's *Development as Freedom*, 285.

14. Many prominent Christian development organizations engage in microenterprise work. Opportunity International and Hope International focus on it almost exclusively. In the next two chapters we will see how Christian beliefs and values influence this strategy.

15. See, for example, "Science as a Vocation," in Max Weber, *Essays in Sociology*, trans. H. H. Gerth and C. Wright Mills (New York: Routledge, 1998), 129–58. One contemporary modernizationist very similar to Weber, Lawrence Harrison, is quite open about how important it is for developing societies to trade in their religious values for ones more in tune with reason, science, and technology. See Harrison, *The Central Liberal Truth*.

Chapter 2: For God So Loved the World

1. In Tim Stafford, "Imperfect Instrument," *Christianity Today*, February 24, 2005, www .christianitytoday.com/ct/2005/march/19.56.html.

2. Steve Garber, *The Fabric of Faithfulness: Weaving Together Belief and Behavior during the University Years* (Downers Grove, IL: InterVarsity, 1996), 42. The follow-up question is one I heard him put to students in a class we taught together.

3. Of course there are more traditions than just these four, including the Lutheran, Anglican, and Orthodox traditions. It is also true that there are different wings or subtraditions within each broad tradition. My intent here is not to be exhaustive but rather to highlight four prominent traditions in the mainstream of Christianity that have all been thinking through how to be involved in international development.

4. Pope Paul VI, *Populorum Progressio (On the Development of Peoples)*, 3.

5. Pope Paul VI, *Populorum Progressio*, 13.

6. Pope Paul VI, *Populorum Progressio*, 14.

7. Pope Paul VI, *Populorum Progressio*, 81.

8. Pope Benedict XVI, *Caritas in Veritate (Charity in Truth)*, 11.

9. Pope Benedict XVI, *Caritas in Veritate*, 15.

10. Edward P. DeBerri and James Hug, with Peter J. Henriot and Michael J. Schultheis, *Catholic Social Teaching: Our Best Kept Secret*, 4th ed. (Maryknoll, NY: Orbis, 2003), 30.

11. Church denominations in the Reformed (Calvinist) tradition have gone by many different names, sometimes with links to a particular national origin. "Presbyterian" was the name taken in Scotland, "Congregational" in England, and "Covenant" in Sweden. Of course there are many churches too with "Reformed" as part of their name. Churches in the Netherlands tended to take on the name "Reformed." Today, the World Communion of Reformed Churches membership list gives some idea of the names and locations of Reformed churches throughout the world. See http://wcrc.ch/node/164.

12. John Hesselink, *On Being Reformed: Distinctive Characteristics and Common Misunderstandings* (Ann Arbor, MI: Servant Books, 1983), 94. Italics in the original. Hesselink is quoting Emile Doumergue, noted biographer of John Calvin, as translated and quoted in M. Eugene Osterhaven, *The Spirit of the Reformed Tradition: The Reformed Church Must Always Be Reforming* (Grand Rapids: Eerdmans, 1971), 101.

13. When Calvinists address the passages that talk about the importance of belief (such as John 3:16), they note that such belief itself is a gift of God and not a matter of our own choosing. Belief itself is an act of God's grace (see, for example, Question and Answer #65 of the Heidelberg Catechism). Accepting God's sovereignty in this matter also ends the stress that surrounds many difficult questions, such as whether unborn babies, or people who have never heard the name of Jesus, are saved. The Calvinist has an easy answer for this: it is a matter for God, not us.

14. Quoted in James D. Bratt, ed., *Abraham Kuyper, A Centennial Reader* (Grand Rapids: Eerdmans, 1998), 488.

15. See Genesis 1:28 and Genesis 2:15.

16. Bryant L. Myers, *Walking with the Poor: Principles and Practices of Transformational Development* (New York: Orbis, 1999), 3. This term is also being increasingly accepted by other Christian traditions.

17. One of my own personal favorites on how we think and theorize is Nicholas Wolterstorff's small book *Reason within the Bounds of Religion* (Grand Rapids: Eerdmans, 1984).

18. Richard A. Yoder, Calvin W. Redekop, and Vernon E. Jantzi, *Development to a Different Drummer: Anabaptist/Mennonite Experiences and Perspectives* (Intercourse, PA: Good Books, 2004).

19. A good source for the general history reviewed in the next few paragraphs is Cornelius J. Dyck, *An Introduction to Mennonite History: A Popular History of the Anabaptists and the Mennonites* (Scottdale, PA: Herald, 1993).

20. Yoder, Redekop, and Jantzi, *Development to a Different Drummer*, 86.

21. Two respected sources for a brief history of evangelicalism are George M. Marsden, *Understanding Fundamentalism and Evangelicalism* (Grand Rapids: Eerdmans, 1991), and John Stott, *Decisive Issues Facing Christians Today* (Old Tappan, NJ: Fleming H. Revell, 1984), esp. chap. 1.

22. Two of many books that review these developments are Philip Jenkins, *The Next Christendom: The Coming of Global Christianity* (Oxford: Oxford University Press, 2007), and David Martin, *Tongues of Fire: The Explosion of Protestantism in Latin America* (Cambridge, MA: Wiley-Blackwell, 1993).

23. See www.lausanne.org for a wealth of information on the Lausanne Movement, including the Lausanne Covenant itself, plus many thoughtful papers that have continued to explore the mission of the church in today's world.

24. Richard Stearns, *The Hole in Our Gospel: The Answer That Changed My Life and Might Just Change the World* (Nashville: Nelson, 2009), 1–2. Other books by evangelical Christians that highlight the holistic nature of the gospel message include Gary Haugen, *Good News about Injustice: A Witness of Courage in a Hurting World* (Downers Grove, IL: InterVarsity, 1999), and Donald E. Miller and Tetsunao Yamamori, *Global Pentecostalism: The New Face of Christian Social Engagement* (Berkeley: University of California Press, 2007). An insightful article that explains how evangelism and mission fit together is David J. Bosch, "Evangelism: Theological Currents and Cross-currents Today," *International Bulletin of Missionary Research* 11, no. 3 (July 1987): 98–103.

Chapter 3: Common Ground

1. This is the figure cited by the Christian advocacy organization Bread for the World. See www.bread.org/hunger/global/.

2. Statistics are hard to come by, but this is a figure used by UNICEF. See www.unicef.org/protection/index_exploitation.html.

3. See the collection of *New York Times* stories on the Congo at http://topics.nytimes.com/top/news/international/countriesandterritories/congothedemocraticrepublicof/index.html.

4. Steve Corbett and Brian Fikkert explain this very well in *When Helping Hurts: Alleviating Poverty without Hurting the Poor . . . and Ourselves* (Chicago: Moody, 2009).

5. Douglas J. Schuurman, *Vocation: Discerning Our Callings in Life* (Grand Rapids: Eerdmans, 2004), 17.

6. Pope Benedict XVI, *Caritas in Veritate (Charity in Truth)*, 12.

7. See http://wordnetweb.princeton.edu/perl/webwn?s=holistic.

8. James F. Engel and William A. Dyrness, *Changing the Mind of Missions: Where Have We Gone Wrong?* (Downers Grove, IL: InterVarsity, 2000), 93.

9. Bryant L. Myers, *Walking with the Poor: Principles and Practices of Transformational Development* (Maryknoll, NY: Orbis, 1999), 88. Italics added.

10. Jeffrey Sachs, *The End of Poverty: Economic Possibilities for Our Time* (New York: Penguin, 2005), 75–78.

11. See their websites at www.transparency.org and www.amnesty.org.

12. Economist Richard Easterlin has studied the relationship of wealth to happiness for much of his life. See, for example, Richard Easterlin, "Explaining Happiness," *Proceedings of the National Academy of Sciences of the United States of America* 100, no. 19 (Sept. 16, 2003): 11176–83. Christian psychologist David Myers has also written much on this topic. See David G. Myers, *The Pursuit of Happiness: Who Is Happy—and Why* (New York: Morrow, 1992).

13. Terrence L. Jantzi and Vernon E. Jantzi, "Strengthening Civil Society for Rural Development," in *Local Ownership and Global Change: Will Civil Society Save the World?*, ed. Roland Hoksbergen and Lowell M. Ewert (Monrovia, CA: World Vision Publications, 2002), 303–28.

14. See David Livermore, *Serving with Eyes Wide Open: Doing Short-Term Missions with Cultural Intelligence* (Grand Rapids: Baker Books, 2006).

15. Michael Woolcock, "Getting the Social Relations Right: Towards an Integrated Theology and Theory of Development," in *Globalization and the Good*, ed. Peter Heslam (Grand Rapids: Eerdmans, 2004), 41–51.

16. C. S. Lewis was a master at creating memorable images. In his Narnia tale *The Last Battle*, the children go through the stable door and find themselves in heaven, which is the beginning of a brand new and wondrous journey ([1956; repr., New York: HarperCollins, 1984], 211).

17. This is one weakness of the Millennium Development Goals (MDGs), which intend to ensure that everyone enjoys the basic life conditions from which they can embark on their own process of development. Note that the first seven goals focus on particular ends rather than on process: http://mdgs.un.org/unsd/mdg/Host.aspx?Content=Indicators/OfficialList.htm.

18. Much has been written on both of these participatory strategies. I recommend the following two overviews to get a good idea of how they apply to international development: On ABCD, see Alison Mathie and Gord Cunningham, "Who Is Driving Development? Reflections on the Transformative Potential of Asset-Based Community Development" (Occasional Paper Series, No. 5, Coady International Institute, St. Francis Xavier University, P.O. Box 5000, Antigonish, NS, Canada B2G 2W5, www.coady.stfx.ca/resources/abcd/Who%20is%20Driving%20Development .pdf). On appreciative inquiry, see Graham Ashford and Saleela Patkar, *The Positive Path: Using Appreciative Inquiry in Rural Indian Communities*. International Institute of Sustainable Development and Myrada, 2001, 1–43. Accessed at http://myrada.org/myrada.

19. Unfortunately, another "normal" response is for people to retreat into their own views and ways of life. Instead of tolerating others, they just shout at them about how wrong they are. There is no attempt to listen or interact.

20. I am ignoring the reality that Christians themselves do not always agree with each other. Instead of highlighting such disagreements, I would rather focus our attention on the common ground that mainstream Christian traditions share and then contrast that with secular perspectives.

21. For a redemptive reading of the meaning and character of postmodernism, I suggest the Christian philosopher James K. A. Smith's *Who's Afraid of Postmodernism? Taking Derrida, Lyotard, and Foucault to Church* (Grand Rapids: Baker Academic, 2006).

22. Lesslie Newbigin, *The Gospel in a Pluralist Society* (Grand Rapids: Eerdmans, 1989), 10. This is a point that Newbigin explains and persuasively analyzes in a book that is becoming a classic.

23. Bradshaw's life is spread over several Christian traditions. For many years he worked with the evangelical organization World Vision. His written work is filled with references to Reformed writers and ideas, and he is now pastoring a Mennonite congregation in Kansas. He has written two insightful books about how Christian development workers can and should bring their faith into cultures very different from their own. See Bruce Bradshaw, *Bridging the*

Gap: Evangelism, Development and Shalom, Innovations in Missions Series (Monrovia, CA: MARC, 1993), and *Change Across Cultures: A Narrative Approach to Social Transformation* (Grand Rapids: Baker Academic, 2002).

24. Myers, *Walking with the Poor*, 111–12.

Chapter 4: How Many Niches Are There?

1. This diagram builds on the development wheel created by Bill Essig, who contributed the wheel idea to a project on the role of civil society that we worked on together in the late 1990s. See Melissa N. Rose and Lowell M. Ewert, eds., *Civil Society: A Foundation for Sustainable Economic Development* (Washington, DC: Mercy Corps International and the Council for Christian Colleges and Universities, 1998).

2. There are many ways of organizing microfinance/microenterprise work, some of which include the use of solidarity groups.

3. See www.micahchallenge.us. The Millennium Development Goals target measurable improvements in poverty rates, education, the life situations of women and girls, health (especially related to children, women, and HIV/AIDS), and environmental sustainability.

4. See www.partnersworldwide.org.

5. See www.ijm.org.

6. See www.awscorp.com/index.cfm?page=personnel for an introduction to Julie and the work she does at American World Service.

7. Accord's website is www.accordnetwork.org. In Canada there is a similar type of umbrella consortium called the Canadian Council of Christian Charities (CCCC), which includes both domestic and international organizations. See www.cccc.org.

8. See www.ccih.org.

9. See www.interaction.org.

10. Paul Collier, *The Bottom Billion: Why the Poorest Countries Are Failing and What Can Be Done About It* (Oxford: Oxford University Press, 2007).

11. The Mennonites are among the Christians who pay the most attention to relationships and kingdom community. It is one of the main themes in Richard A. Yoder, Calvin W. Redekop, and Vernon E. Jantzi, *Development to a Different Drummer: Anabaptist/Mennonite Experiences and Perspectives* (Intercourse, PA: Good Books, 2004).

12. I received comments from Martin Mutuku, Partners Worldwide partnership manager, Kenya; Davis Omanyo, CRWRC East Africa team leader; Chinyere Nwachukwu, CRWRC constituency bridger, Nigeria; Cherie M. Espino, CCT technical assistant to the president, Philippines; Pamela Mumbi, IJM country director, Zambia; Irene Murillo, CRWRC country director, Honduras; Kelia Garcia, AJS administration and projects coordinator, Honduras; and Augusto De la Torre, World Bank chief economist for Latin America and the Caribbean.

Chapter 5: Becoming an Effective Foreigner

1. Denis Goulet, *Development Ethics: A Guide to Theory and Practice* (New York: Apex, 1995), 193–94.

2. See www.worldbank.org/justiceforthepoor.

3. See www.echonet.org. ECHO runs a highly regarded internship program, and alumni are in high demand, though some suitors are mission organizations that require personal fundraising.

4. See www.new-horizons.ro.

5. See www.cause.ca.

6. See www.asodenic.org.ni. ASODENIC stands for the Nicaraguan Association for Economic Opportunity and Development.

7. See www.amc.org.ni.

8. See www.ajs-us.org and www.transformemoshonduras.com/EN/englishpage.php.

Chapter 6: Finding Your Way

1. Julie first heard the train story in a talk by Jim Skillen, retired president of the Center for Public Justice.

2. Peter Uvin, *Aiding Violence: The Development Enterprise in Rwanda* (West Hartford, CT: Kumarian Press, 1998).

3. One helpful general book on Christian vocational direction is Gordon T. Smith, *Courage and Calling: Embracing Your God-Given Potential* (Downers Grove, IL: InterVarsity, 1999).

4. To learn about IJM's Campus Chapter program, see www.ijm.org/ItMatters. For Acting on AIDS as part of World Vision's ACT:S program, see www.worldvisionacts.org.

5. For some information on the Calvin College club, see http://calvinbusinessbrigades .wordpress.com. For the general site on Global Business Brigades, see http://www.globalbrigades .org/?page_id=741.

Chapter 7: The Early Years after College

1. For more information, see www.peacecorps.gov/index.cfm?shell=learn.whyvol.eduben. mastersint.

2. See www.cimmyt.org.

3. ESL stands for "English as a Second Language." See the site at www.eslcafe.com.

4. See www.americorps.gov.

5. Alicia went on one of the international programs offered by the Council of Christian Colleges and Universities. See www.bestsemester.com.

6. Relevant websites are www.accordnetwork.org; http://ccih.org; www.interaction.org; and www.devdir.org.

7. Learn more about these programs at www.usaid.gov/careers/dli.html for the DLI and www.pmf.opm.gov for the PMF.

8. Yes, these are strong statements, but they identify the dangers and temptations some of us fall victim to, though to different degrees. It is also true that many Christians work faithfully in secular organizations and many development workers in completely Christian contexts keep learning from their secular colleagues.

9. See www2.ed.gov/programs/iegpsflasf/index.html.

10. Jacqueline Novogratz, *The Blue Sweater: Bridging the Gap between Rich and Poor in an Interconnected World* (New York: Rodale Books, 2010). Learn about the Acumen Fund at www.acumenfund.org.

11. See www.reliefweb.int.

12. In English, Children of the World—Human Rights.

Chapter 8: Into the Future

1. Bryant L. Myers, *Walking with the Poor: Principles and Practices of Transformational Development* (New York: Orbis, 1999), 165.

2. C. S. Lewis, *The Lion, the Witch and the Wardrobe* (New York: Harper Collins, 1950), 78–80.

Chapter 9: Resources for the Road

1. These guidelines are drawn from fundraising tips from International Justice Mission, Partners Worldwide, and WorldTeach.

Index